AF683985

Analysis Techniques for non-Experimental Data:
An Introduction

Analysis Techniques for non-Experimental Data: An Introduction

C.C.J.H. Bijleveld

S.G.A. van de Weijer

S. Ruiter

V.R. van der Geest

eleven

international publishing

Published, sold and distributed by Eleven International Publishing
P.O. Box 85576
2508 CG The Hague
The Netherlands
Tel.: +31 70 33 070 33
Fax: +31 70 33 070 30
e-mail: sales@elevenpub.nl
www.elevenpub.com

Sold and distributed in USA and Canada
International Specialized Book Services
920 NE 58th Avenue, Suite 300
Portland, OR 97213-3786, USA
Tel: 1-800-944-6190 (toll-free)
Fax: +1-503-280-8832
orders@isbs.com
www.isbs.com

Eleven International Publishing is an imprint of Boom uitgevers Den Haag.

ISBN 978-94-6236-835-4

Printed in The Netherlands

Preface

Scientists search for the causes of the phenomena they study. Once we know the causes of disease, of happiness, of business success, we can try to impact those causes and thus intervene in the occurrence of disease, promote happiness and further business success. Research to determine the causes of phenomena must ideally be conducted in a certain standard 'experimental' setting. If we follow the prescriptions for such a standard experimental setting we will be able to determine causality, using common analytic methods such as t-tests or analysis of variance to assess the impact of a certain factor X on an outcome Y.

In some situations it turns out to be impossible to conduct research according to this gold experimental standard. It may be impossible practically, or ethically abject, or even undesirable. To give some examples: it is impossible to design such an experimental setting to investigate whether marriage makes people happy, legal chances may have been introduced across an entire country so that we cannot compare the outcome in one part of the country that is governed by the new law against the outcome in another part that is not governed by the law. Judges tend to mete out punishment 'tailored' to the person of the offender so that we cannot assess the effectiveness of punishments as they may be confounded with the characteristics of convicts. In such situations it is impossible to determine the causal impact of the variable we are interested in (marriage, a legal change, punishment) according to the gold standard.

(Partial) solutions exist, however, that enable the researcher to investigate causality as far as possible. These are techniques that in various ways tease out the effect of the causal factor X we are interested in, by controlling for confounding factors, or through other ingenious solutions for the fact that the data are non-experimental. This book gives an overview of these techniques. These methodological tools make it possible to assess – although with less certainty and therefore exercising the necessary caution in our statements – whether we may assume that X causes Y.

This book was written for a 6 ECTS master course 'Advanced Methods' for criminology students. The book starts with a short refresher course of regression analysis, the workhorse of quantitative analysis. Parts of the texts are based on earlier textbooks, such as Bijleveld (2015) and Bijleveld and Commandeur (2017). The book next discusses five analysis techniques that make it possible to make causal inference – with the necessary caution: – namely *propensity score matching*, *instrumental variables*, the *regression discontinuity design*, *fixed effects* models and *trajectory analysis*. Even though the examples we employ throughout the book are clearly criminological, the techniques can be applied in many other disciplines such as sociology, psychology, political science, empirical legal research.

Given our cursory introductory discussion of causality and regression models, we assume that readers have some familiarity with causality and regression analysis. The five analysis techniques are discussed relatively briefly and conceptually, with a minimum of formulas – reason this book cannot be regarded as more than an introduction to each of these techniques. At the end of each chapter we list the key publications for each technique that the reader can refer to for more information on statistical issues, and for variations on and special cases of the techniques.

We illustrate each technique with a worked example on a fictitious dataset. This dataset is downloadable from www.analysistechniques.elevenpub.com. For all analyses that we discuss in this book, we give the complete syntax for both SPSS and Stata. This means that readers can replicate the examples that are discussed and use the syntax as a starting point for their own analyses. We note that as new versions of the statistical software packages are published, output may differ marginally from what we show in the book; the results should remain identical. Both Stata and SPSS offer trial versions that can be downloaded and used, generally for 30 days.

We extend our thanks to colleagues who commented upon earlier versions of the chapters in this book: Arjan Blokland, Vere van Koppen, Geert Mesters, Wouter Steenbeek and Frank van Tulder. Peter van der Voort, who died in 2016, helped us in finding literature sources. Jessica Hill translated the original Dutch text into English. Frits Bijleveld solved pernicious Latex issues. Any remaining errors are ours.

Catrien Bijleveld, Steve van de Weijer, Stijn Ruiter, Victor van der Geest

Amsterdam, December 2017

Contents

List of Figures

List of Tables

Chapter 1

Introduction

1.1 Causality

The primary goal of scientific endeavour is to determine cause and effect. Even though scientists carry out a range of different kinds of research, from descriptive to phenomenological, ethnographic to quantitative, the driving force behind all of these is ultimately the same. We want to know what causes the particular phenomenon we are interested in: Doctors want to know which pills beat your headache, psychologists want to know whether cognitive behavioural therapy changes behaviour, demographers want to know why women are postponing motherhood.

According to Lazarsfeld (1959), for us to be able to conclude that there is a causal relationship between variable X and variable Y, three conditions must be met. We can only say that X directly causes Y when all of the following conditions are fulfilled:

(1) *X precedes Y*

(2) *X has been shown empirically to relate to Y*

(3) *there is no other explanation for the relationship between X and Y*

The first condition is logical: We would never expect cause to follow effect! Causes occur before effects materialize. Even though this condition is clear, X and Y occurring simultaneously is however generally accepted too. It is fairly easy to assess whether this condition has been met.

Condition 2 states that X can only cause Y if X and Y are actually found to relate to each other, for example if we find a correlation between X and Y which significantly differs from 0. Figure 1.1 illustrates this relationship.

Figure 1.1: Illustration of a direct causal effect of X on Y

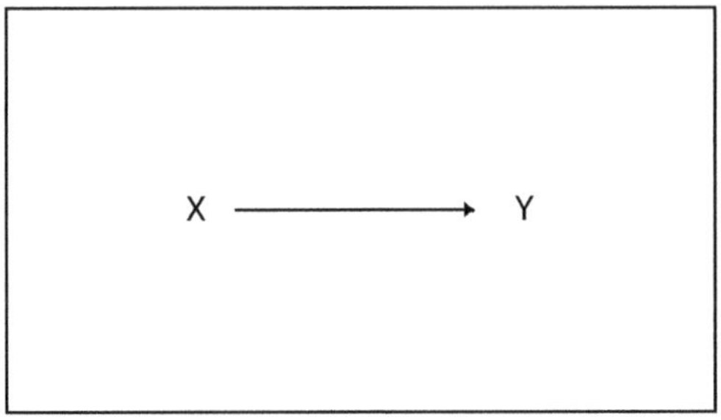

Figure 1.2: Illustration of a spurious relationship between X and Y

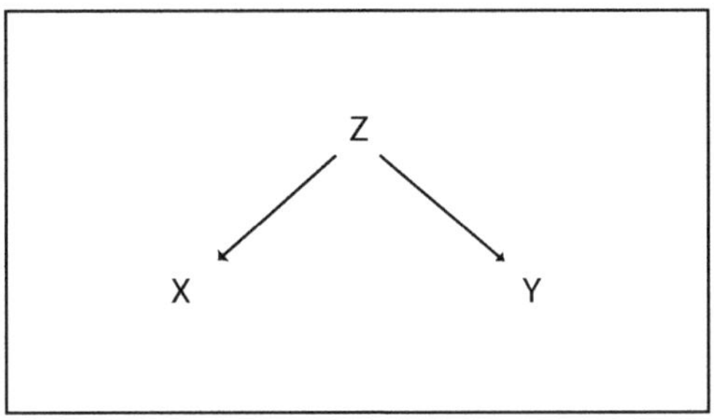

However, ensuring that the third condition has been met is more difficult. According to condition 3 we can only state with confidence that X causes Y when we are sure that there is no other explanation for this relationship. To fulfill condition 3 it is therefore necessary to examine plausible alternative explanations. If we find that a third variable actually explains the relationship between X and Y, we refer to the relationship between X and Y as *spurious*. Such a third variable is usually represented as 'Z', and may be called a 'third variable', but is also referred to as a latent variable, intervening variable, or '*confounding*' variable. Figure 1.2 illustrates a spurious relationship between X and Y, where both are in fact caused by a third variable Z.

We speak of a spurious relationship when we have a third intervening variable Z which determines both X and Y: this variable explains the existence of the association between X and Y. For example, consider the positive association between

Figure 1.3: Illustration of an indirect relationship between *X* and *Y*

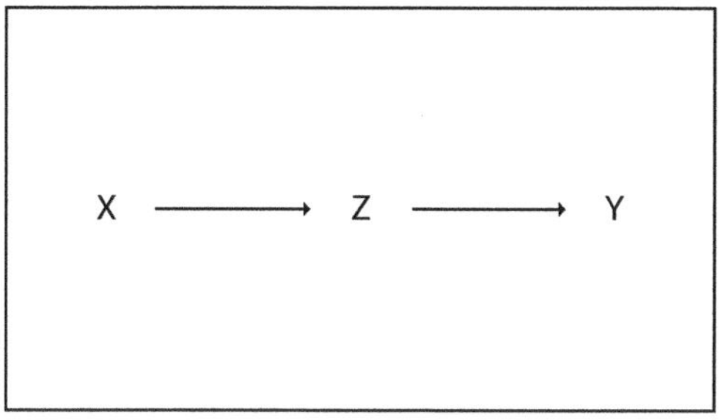

being in hospital and dying. Clearly, being in hospital does not cause you to die. It is an illness or accident that causes persons to be admitted to hospital and that same affliction may be the cause of death. So both of these outcomes (hospital stay and death) are caused by whatever illness a person is suffering from. In order to detect a spurious relationship we need to calculate the relationship between our cause *X* and effect *Y*, whilst controlling for any possible effect of *Z*. We might for example calculate the partial correlation coefficient $r_{XY.Z}$ (see any statistics textbook, for instance Hinkle et al., 2003), in this case the correlation between hospital stay and death, controlling for illness. If an association between *X* and *Y* is indeed spurious, the positive (or negative) relationship between *X* and *Y* will disappear when controlling for *Z*: $r_{XY.Z}$ will then be 0.

This is but one example of a spurious relationship, and other kinds of spurious relationships exist. One such example occurs within an indirect relationship, whereby *X* determines *Z* and consequently *Z* determines *Y*. In this case *X* is the cause of *Z* and *Z* then causes *Y*, but the relationship between *X* and *Y* only exists because of *Z*. If we were to control for *Z* the relationship between *X* and *Y* would disappear. For example, in the past researchers thought that drinking alcohol whilst skiing reduced the risk of breaking a leg. In this case conditions 1 and 2 were met: People drank first and then went skiing, and those who drank more alcohol were less likely to break their legs. However, the number of drinks consumed whilst skiing actually determines the number of hours spent on the piste, and it is this 'exposure' which also determines the chance of breaking a leg or not. When the number of hours spent skiing is taken into account, the negative relationship between drinking alcohol and breaking legs disappears. This kind of spurious, indirect relationship can be summarized as in Figure 1.3.

Figure 1.4: Illustration of multiple causality

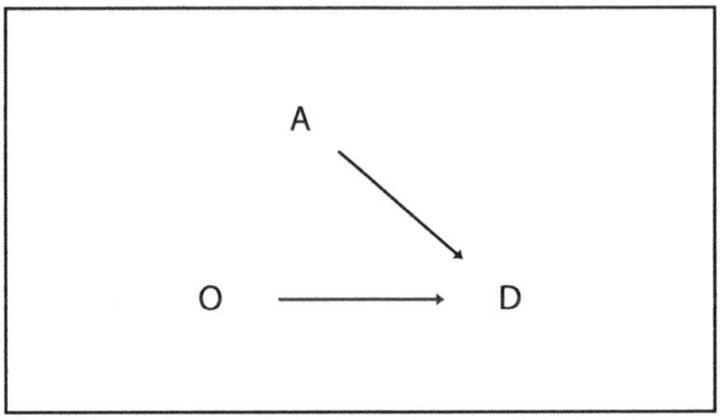

Besides cases of indirect causality (X causes Z, Z then causes Y) or spurious relationships (Z causes both X and Y), other factors can also play a role. It is possible that the effect we are interested in has several causes. See Figure 1.4. For example, growing up in a single parent family (O) increases the risk of delinquency (D), and poverty (A) also increases the risk of delinquency; see Figure 1.4. We refer to this as *multiple causality.*

Cause and effect relationships can also be bi-directional or reciprocal, i.e. first X causes Y, then Y in turn influences X. This can be referred to as a *reciprocal causal relationship, simultaneous causality*, or a *bi-directional relationship.* For example, take the relationship between depression and unemployment. Depression at time t_1 may cause unemployment at t_2. Unemployment is then likely to cause further depression at t_3 and so on. Many examples of this kind of relationships can be found in economics: When demand X is high the price Y increases, only for the increased price Y to lead demand X to fall. See Figure 1.5 for an illustration.

A further, at first sight perhaps slightly puzzling possibility is that the relationship between two variables is suppressed by a third variable. We refer to such a third variable as a *suppressor variable.* In this case the correlation coefficient r_{XY} will be 0 or very small. However, when Z is controlled for, $r_{XY.Z}$ will now increase instead of decrease. When we have a suppressor variable, the problem is not that we think we have a relationship which then disappears when controlling for a third variable as is usually the case for confounding variables, but that the relationship only becomes apparent when controlling for the distorting effect of a third variable.

Berk and de Leeuw (1999) examined the relationship between an inmate's classification score (i.e. the degree to which they were anticipated by prison staff to be prone to misconduct) and their number of conduct violations. At first there appeared to be no relationship between these. However, this lack of relationship was

Figure 1.5: Illustration of a reciprocal causal relationship

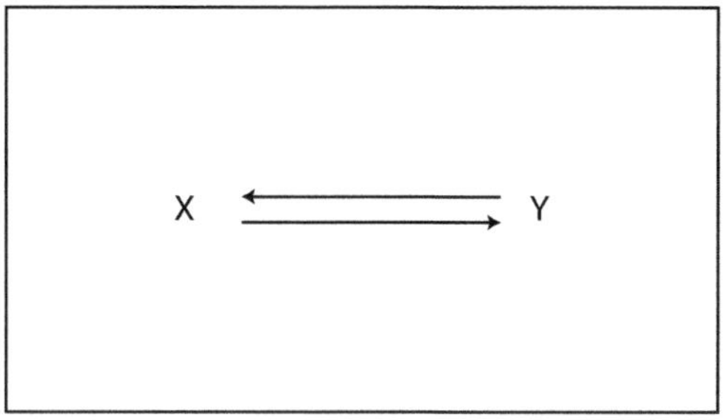

Figure 1.6: Illustration of a suppressor variable

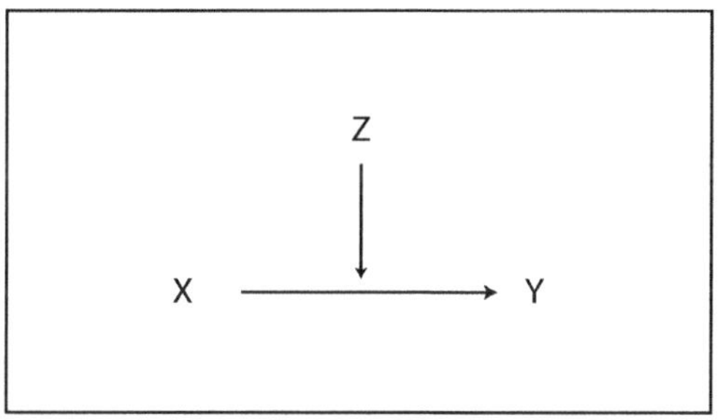

explained by the fact that inmates who were judged to be at risk of misconduct had been placed in high security wards, in which there was much less 'room' for misconduct. This placement thus suppressed the relationship between classification score and number of conduct violations. Figure 1.6 illustrates this situation.

The above examples, with the exception of simultaneous causality, all involve a third factor that interferes with the relationship between X and Y. When the relationship between X and Y changes after controlling for an underlying variable Z, this is referred to as a spurious relationship. As we have outlined, it is possible to find or test for the existence of a spurious relationship. For example, we know that the relationship between X and Y is not causal if their association disappears when we control for a third factor. However, the reverse is untrue: the problem with spurious relationships is that just because we have not been able to identify any confounders, this does not mean that the relationship between X and Y is not spurious.

It would of course be impossible to control for every possible distorting factor Z: we have only a limited number of factors at our disposal in our dataset and even if all of these cannot 'explain away' the association between X and Y, this does not mean that out there in the world there is not in fact another variable – unmeasured by us – that does explain away the association. Therefore, when deciding whether or not we can take the relationship between X and Y as indicative of a causal association, we need to carefully consider and take into account all possible distorting factors. This is the only way in which we can come to a plausible conclusion as to whether the relationship between X and Y truly is causal. However, statements about causality in non-experimental research necessarily remain hypothetical.

Summarizing, we can test a number of different variables to see whether they explain the relationship between X and Y. If the relationship between X and Y holds each time after controlling for a potential confounding variable Z, we can conclude that none of those Z provides an alternative explanation for the relationship between X and Y. As stated earlier, however, this does not mean that further variables do not exist which might explain the relationship. Once we have controlled for all the variables measured in order to rule out the possibility of a spurious relationship, we may conclude that there is no *overt bias*. However, in order to be sure that there is no alternative explanation for the relationship we have found, we would have to control for *all* possible variables in the universe. This is of course impossible. We can never therefore prove that there is no *hidden bias*. In conclusion, in drawing conclusions about causality, we can safeguard against possible distorting effects of variables that we have measured, but we cannot control for possible distorting effects of variables that we have not measured, that is, for unobserved variables.

1.2 Investigating causality: the classic experiment

The majority of scientists agree that if we want to determine whether a variable or an intervention W has an effect on variable Y, the only way to achieve this with certainty is to carry out the classic experiment , also referred to as a pretest posttest control group design. But what do we mean by a classic experiment?

In a classic experiment we examine two groups. These groups could be people, apes, police departments, neighbourhoods, single cell organisms, viruses, companies, etc. For example, imagine we want to know whether a certain pill (W) helps treat headaches (Y). In a classic experiment respondents would be randomly assigned to two groups: the *experimental group* (E) group and the *control group*

(C). The experimental group and the control group are referred to as the *conditions* of the experiment. It is important that these groups are formed at random. One important consequence of the fact that these groups are formed at random is that if there are differences in background characteristics between the groups, these are chance differences.

In the example just given, the researchers interested in the effect of pill W on headache Y now first measure the extent of respondents' headaches in both groups. Next they administer the pill W to the experimental group, but not to the control group. Finally the researchers again measure the extent of respondents' headaches. We can represent this experiment setup as follows:

$$\begin{array}{lcl} E_1 & \ldots\ W\ \ldots & E_2 \\ C_1 & \ldots\ldots\ldots\ldots & C_2 \end{array}$$

where W is the intervention, E_1 are the headache measurements for the experimental group before being given the pill, E_2 the headache measurements for the experimental group after taking the pill, and C_1 and C_2 the corresponding measurements in the control group. Note that W in this case indicates the independent variable, rather than X, which we would normally use as the symbol for an independent variable. An intervention describes a special type of independent variable, hence it gets a special symbol.

The classic experiment, whereby respondents are randomly allocated to either the group that gets the pill (or 'intervention') or the group that does not, followed by a comparison of pre- and posttest measurements, is an incredibly powerful research tool. The reason for this is that any pre-existing differences between the control and experimental groups are purely due to chance (therefore, one would expect E_1 to be approximately equal to C_1). The only systematic difference between the groups is the intervention. Therefore, if the two groups' posttest headache measurements ($E_2 - C_2$) are different there is only one explanation for this: the pill. It cannot be the case that the E-respondents are more ambitious, or more eager to get rid of their headaches, and that this difference in fact explains why they also differ in their posttest headache scores. The groups differ systematically on one and only one aspect: the intervention. Therefor the intervention is the only explanation for any differences in scores between the E- and C-group: all other explanations have been ruled out by the randomization.

For this reason the classic experiment is the gold standard for determining causality. By randomly assigning respondents into either the experimental or the control group the researcher is able to eliminate the possibility that a third variable is responsible for the difference between the groups. Any differences between the groups are coincidental rather than systematic. Consequently, when carrying out a classic experiment condition 3 (section 1.1) is always fulfilled. The only explanation for a difference between the experimental E and control C groups on their posttest measurements is the intervention W. This is also phrased by saying that the factor has been 'isolated'.

So far we have introduced the idea of comparing the posttest measurements of our two groups. However there is more to the classic experiment than just posttest measurements. We also measure our groups pre-test, before they receive the intervention. Using these measurements we can calculate change or improvement in our groups. Change is possible in both the experimental group ($E_2 - E_1$) and the control group ($C_2 - C_1$). Just as we compared the posttest scores of the experimental and control groups, we can also compare the change we see in the experimental group with that of the control group. Because respondents were randomly assigned to groups, the control group is, as it were, 'the experimental group-without-the-intervention'. Therefore, any change we see in the control group ($C_2 - C_1$) can be seen as change that we would have seen in the experimental group had they not undergone the intervention. The results of the control group are basically those we would have found for the experimental group in the hypothetical situation that the intervention had not been administered.

If we take away the change found in the control group ($C_2 - C_1$) from the change found in the experimental group ($E_2 - E_1$) we are left with the net effect of the intervention:

$$\text{net effect } W = (E_2 - E_1) - (C_2 - C_1).$$

But why is it necessary to compare change scores, why would we expect a change in the control group if they are not administered any intervention? Does such a thing as 'a gross effect' exist? Yes, it often does. Imagine that we are researching the effectivity of a fear of flying training course. One group of fearful flyers receives the training. Before the course begins, fear of flying is measured using a questionnaire. On average our E- and C-respondents scored 80. Over the next few weeks our E-respondents attend the training sessions. All is going well. However, after a couple of weeks there is a plane crash involving a well-known airline company. Our E-respondents are once again back to square one – terrified of flying. A few weeks later the training course finishes and respondents take the fear of flying questionnaire again. This time the average score is 82. The gross effect of the course is negative, i.e. respondents are now more afraid of flying following the course than before the course. We might therefore conclude on the basis of these results that the training course did not work and in fact generated a negative impact. However, in this case any positive progress our fearful flyers made as a result of the course was likely cancelled out by the extreme negative, and incidental, effect of the plane crash. This negative effect nullified any positive effects of the training.

By including a control group in the study we can detect whether this is the case, and control for it. We have randomly allocated respondents to the experimental and control group. Their pretest scores on the fear of flying questionnaire were equal. The experimental group has followed the training course, whilst the control group has not. Suppose that we found that the average posttest score for the control group was 90, then we can now calculate the net effect of the intervention thus:

$$\text{net effect therapy} = (82 - 80) - (90 - 80) = 2 - 10 = -8,$$

Here we see not a negative effect, but a net beneficial effect of -8: respondents who received the therapy scored on average 8 points lower than those who did not. Without a control group we could not have drawn any conclusions as to the effect of the therapy. Of course, because we randomly assigned our respondents into either the experimental or the control group we can know for sure that the net effect is entirely due to the therapy.

All this seems to suggest that as long as we ensure that we randomly assign our respondents to experimental and control groups, we will carry out the best test of causality possible. However this is not necessarily always true. Suppose that we randomly assign patients into two groups, experimental and control. The experimental group gets the intervention, a daily headache pill, the control group does not. Can we know for sure that the improvement in headache symptoms we see for the experimental group and not for the control group is entirely due to the innovative pharmaceutical composition of the pill?

Much research has shown that patients feel better simply as a result of being seen by a doctor or receiving attention for their problem. This is called the *placebo effect*. As only the experimental group have been treated, only they, and not the control group, can experience a placebo effect. Because the control group were untreated we cannot definitively say what part of the effect of treatment in the experimental group, i.e. the decrease in headache symptoms, is due to the pill or due to a placebo effect. The solution to this problem is to administer to the control group some kind of pill too, only they will receive a 'fake' pill, without active ingredients. This type of study design is referred to as '*placebo controlled*'.

By administering to both groups some kind of 'treatment', if a placebo effect occurs it will occur in both groups. We can now remove any placebo effect when calculating our net effect:

$$\begin{aligned}\text{net effect pill} = {} & \text{effect pill}_{\text{experimental group}} + \text{placebo effect}_{\text{experimental group}} \\ & - \text{placebo effect}_{\text{control group}}.\end{aligned}$$

So are we finally there? Is this design using randomly assigned experimental and control groups, taking pre- and posttest measurements, and not letting the groups know who is receiving the treatment, a watertight method for testing the causal effect of an intervention? Not quite. There is one more issue to consider. Research has shown that the people who administer interventions unconsciously give off signals, picked up by respondents, indicating which experimental condition they are in. In order to ensure this does not affect findings, many experiments are set up so that not only respondents are unaware of which group they are in but research staff are also unaware. We call this a *double blind* experiment.

Experiments that are designed in this fashion, that is: randomized, placebo controlled and double blind, have strong internal validity. By that we mean to say that, if we find an association between X and Y, and X occurs before Y, the existence of any alternative explanations for the association has been ruled out, and we may conclude that X causes Y. That conclusions is then said to have internal validity.

Zaalberg and colleagues (2009) examined whether taking fish oil would decrease aggressive behavior in Dutch prisoners. A double blind, randomized, placebo controlled trial was carried out to test the effect of fish oil supplements on aggressive incidents in around 200 men from eight prisons in the Netherlands. The prisons chosen to take part were those in which a relatively large number of aggressive incidents occurred. Incidents examined were aggressive behaviour by inmates recorded by prison staff. The reason for choosing prisons with a higher number of incidents was that it would be easier to detect an effect in these locations. Prison staff from the selected prisons, whose participation and support for the project was essential, attended an information evening about the project.

Staff enthusiasm for the project was high. Inmates were randomly assigned to the fish oil group and the placebo group. Neither the inmates nor the prison staff knew which group inmates were in. The experiment was therefore double blind.

Of course there are situations in which such desirable design features cannot be implemented. Someone who gets placed into juvenile detention knows that they are there. Someone undergoing cognitive behavior therapy knows that they are receiving the treatment. Obviously in situations like these, it is not possible to carry out blind or double blind experiments. It is also hard to envisage a control group, of juvenile delinquents, or depressed patients, who do not receive any treatment or intervention at all. In such cases, what can be done is to measure the effect on a control group of a realistic alternative situation. For example, a new treatment given to the experimental group could be compared to the standard or old treatment given to the control group. This is referred to the comparison group receiving *treatment-as-usual*, or TAU for short.

Then, in some situations it does not make sense to take a pretest measure. For example, if we are interested in relapse rates following treatment for violent delinquency, all respondents have been convicted for a violent crime, and thus they all score the same on pretest measurement of 'conviction for violent crime' and no pretest of relapse would make sense. The design of this study would therefore be:

$$\begin{array}{ccc} W & \dots & E_{\text{post}} \\ & \dots & C_{\text{post}} \end{array}$$

and the net effect of an intervention would be:

$$\text{net effect } W = (E_{\text{post}} - C_{\text{post}}).$$

Having a pretest measurement is, all in all, not crucial to the success of an experimental design. Randomly assigning the experimental and control groups, and ensuring that other possible distortions are avoided, is crucial. Only then can we assume that the control and experimental group do not differ systematically, and subsequently compare the results of the experimental group with those of the control group to draw our conclusions. The classic experiment is often referred to as the *randomized controlled trial* or 'RCT' for short. This term applies to designs both with and without pretests.

RCTs are judged to be the most reliable research design when testing for causality and the gold standard for research into cause and effect. Using this design, researchers control every decision made: They randomly assign respondents to the experimental and control groups, they provide the intervention, and they decide on the outcome measurement. Because of the random assignment, the control group can be seen as the experimental group without the intervention. We know that any differences between the experimental and control groups are due to chance. If the experimental group had not undergone the intervention their posttest scores would have been the same as those of the control group.

The control group can, as we said, be regarded as the '*counterfactual*'. But what exactly do we mean by this? Consider the following thought experiment, whereby we only measure the experimental group. Suppose we would be able to measure their scores having undergone the intervention, and at the same time as having not undergone the intervention. If we were able to do this then we would know what their outcome would have been with and without the intervention, and assess the effect of the intervention. Of course this is impossible. We cannot know what their outcomes would have been without the intervention because they *have* had the intervention. Whilst we can use their pretest scores as a benchmark, and compare them to their posttest scores, this does not give us the net effect. If we only use $(E_2 - E_1)$ as our measure of effect, there is a risk that what we are actually measuring is a placebo effect, as described above, or take along any other confounding period, testing or maturation effects. For example, a primary school pupil who tries to learn a new method for calculating will see improvements in their calculating skills regardless of whether they use this method, simply due to their cognitive development over time. We cannot determine how much of this improvement is due to the new method and how much to cognitive development. By employing a pretest posttest design with just an experimental group we will only ever know a gross effect: the effect of an intervention with other effects inseparably glued onto it.

This can only be solved by including a control group in the study design. This group must be formed in such a way that their scores are those that the experimental group would have had had they not received the intervention. They are, as it were, the experimental group without the intervention. We are able to treat the control group as such because the two groups are chosen purely by chance. Random assignment is therefore the key to and the strength of the classic experimental design. For more on experimental designs see the seminal book on the subject by Cook and Campbell (1979).

1.3 Why an experiment is not always possible

We argued that the *randomized controlled trial* (RCT), or classic experiment, is the gold standard. However, this standard is not always achievable. Imagine we want to examine whether a new teaching method helps primary school children with their mathematics. We want to test this new method in a number of different classes. We want to have a control group, to which we can compare our experimental group. Ideally we would assign the children randomly into an experimental class and a control class. Then we would know for sure that any differences between the experimental and control children, before the new method was introduced, were purely due to chance. We could then conclude that any differences we measured in their mathematics following the intervention were entirely due to the new teaching method, as that is the only factor they differ in systematically, and thus the only explanation available for posttest differences. Unfortunately, in this situation this design is not realistic. Primary school children are already assigned into classes and teachers would not take kindly to researchers coming in and re-arranging everyone. We therefore have to make do with the classes, and teachers, as they are. Therefore, we can only introduce this new teaching method in preexisting classes in our primary school. Classes in another primary school (or the same primary school if there are multiple classes per age group) may form the control group.

Whilst this may not sound too serious, we have had to relinquish one of the key features of a classic experiment, namely random assignment to groups. We no longer know whether any differences between students in our experimental and control groups are purely due to chance. As any teacher will tell you, no two classes are alike. Furthermore Mr Jones is an expert in keeping the naughty boys under control. Miss White is the nicest teacher in the school. And everybody knows that the head teacher at Highview school has just returned from 6 months sick leave due to stress. There are, therefore, likely to be differences between the experimental and control groups that we as researchers cannot control. Moreover these differences may be confounded with the effect of the teaching method.

When we have an experimental and control group, but these are not, or not entirely randomly assigned by the researcher, this is referred to as a *quasi-experiment* or a quasi-experimental design. The researcher is able to decide who is and who is not administered the intervention, but any conclusions concerning cause and effect are necessarily less watertight: condition 3 above is not met. The researcher assumes that the experimental and control groups are comparable, and that any differences between them are therefore due to the intervention. But this assumption can never be entirely proven.

In practice the researcher often has even less control. In a quasi-experiment, the researcher is still able to decide who does and who does not receive the intervention and the researcher is also able to implement the intervention him- or herself. However, in reality many interventions are carried out by people other than researchers, e.g. fines for driving through a red light, behavioral therapy, labour market reintegration projects, parenting courses, prison sentences. All these interventions are decided upon and carried out by organizations for whom the primary goal is not to research cause and effect. Whilst we assume these interventions do have an effect, measuring exactly what that effect is, is then even more complicated. It is no longer a question of the researcher finding comparable groups to which s/he can assign an intervention. The interventions themselves are being carried out by organizations, or chosen by participants themselves, over which the researchers have no say. In the best case scenario, the researcher can observe changes in those who underwent the intervention and compare them to changes in those who did not undergo the intervention. The researcher is now reduced to a passive observer, neither exerting control over randomization nor administration of the intervention. This type of study is referred to as an *observational study*.

The criminologist Sherman and his colleagues (2007) rank ordered all possible research designs based on the strength of the evidence they can provide for causality. The resulting scale is called the Maryland Scientific Methods Scale (MSMS). On this scale the classic experiment scores 5. It is the most powerful research design possible. A quasi-experimental design where the respondents in both groups are or have been made as comparable as possible, scores 4. A regular quasi-experimental design where this is not the case scores 3. Lower scores are given to designs where only changes in pretest and posttest scores within the experimental group are examined, or when the experimental group is compared to a control group which we know differs from the experimental group. The lowest score is reserved for a design where only the posttest score for the experimental group is examined. For more information visit http://www.gsr.gov.uk/professional_guidance/rea_toolkit/how_to_do_an_rea/how_appraising_studies.asp.

In many disciplines, research designs without a control group, i.e. with a Maryland scale score of less than 3, are judged unfit for causal inference. This is not to say that these studies are useless or should be disqualified. It does mean that these studies are not able to provide enough conclusive evidence to determine the success or otherwise of an intervention. Does that mean that all designs that score below 3 on the MSMS should be discarded? Employing such strict rules may be futile: in many situations designs with MSMS values over 3 may simply not be feasible. For example, in some countries compulsory wearing of cycle helmets has been introduced nationwide, and for certain patients requiring treatment it is unethical or literally impossible to find comparable control patients.

In the above examples an explicit planned intervention, such as law prescribing the wearing of a helmet or a sought treatment for an illness, is studied. These interventions are 'chosen' (by the state or a patient) in the the hope that they will have an effect or achieve a certain goal. However, as scientists we may also be interested in the effect of events or circumstances which are not implemented with a certain beneficial aim. For example, we might want to examine the effect of divorce or of parental incarceration on a child's well-being. We might want to examine the extent to which being the victim of child sexual abuse negatively affects that victim's life course. We might want to examine whether marriage reduces people's criminal offending, or the extent to which military service increases chances of later employment. In all these examples it is either not possible or not ethical to randomly assign people to one condition or the other. In cases such as these all we can do is observe the outcomes, and compare those who have received the 'intervention' with those who have not.

Occasionally researchers are given a helping hand by a bureaucratic intervention or a naturally occurring circumstance. For example, in the Netherlands until recently all men were conscripted into military service. As the population grew in the post-war years and the army had sufficient manpower the Dutch government decided that none of the men born in the year 1959 would be conscripted. The decision to exempt the 1959 birth cohort was entirely incidental, a random decision. The government could equally have chosen men born in 1960 or 1958. As researchers we can make use of this random assignment to examine the effect of military service on outcomes like employment chances or marriage. We have no reason to believe that men born in 1959 systematically differ from men born in 1958 or 1960. Therefore if military service does increase chances of later employment we would expect fewer men born in 1959 to find work than men found in 1958 and 1960. Such a chance-setting is referred to as a *natural experiment.*

Bruinsma and Luykx (2003) used a natural experiment to research the effect of a fireworks disaster in Enschede, the Netherlands, on crime patterns. In May 2000, a fireworks factory exploded in broad daylight. An entire neighbourhood was destroyed. As one can imagine, the removal of this neighbourhood, the houses, residents and all their activities, severely disrupted the social structure of the city. Crime rates were therefore likely to also have been affected, so researchers thought. Would crime increase as a result of this accident, due to looting, or would crime decrease, with criminals showing solidarity with the affected residents? The researchers set out a number of hypotheses concerning how the disappearance of this neighbourhood might affect crime in Enschede. Strangely enough they found absolutely no difference in crime rates before and after the firework disaster. Similar research has been carried out in the USA following blackouts, which often resulted in widespread looting. These kinds of natural experiments do not happen very often.

In many situations carrying out an experiment raises ethical issues. When the destructiveness of HIV and AIDS first came to light in the West it was judged unethical to carry out experimental research on the drugs used to treat it: in the early years, the victims of this disease did not survive for long. It was therefore judged unethical, to assign patients to a control group and either withhold medicine from them or treat them with 'old' medicine denying them access to the newest innovations. A similar argument is often used in relation to the 'treatment' of criminals. If we divide offenders into two groups, one of whom gets a brand new promising intervention, the other of whom gets nothing or the old intervention that was not judged to work very well, it is likely that the control group will miss out on the chance of improvement. It is then also considered unethical to deprive the offenders of the any new, possibly beneficial intervention.

A similar problem arose when the Physicians' Health Study, a randomized, double blind study in the USA which began in 1982, was halted, much earlier than planned, in 1989 (Steering Committee of the Physician's Health Study Research Group, 1989). This study had been designed to assess whether a low dose of aspirin (325mg once every two days) would prevent heart attacks. It quickly became apparent that, in a large group of male doctors, taking this low dose of aspirin decreased the risk of a heart attack by 44 percent. In the light of such a strong effect it became unethical to deny the control group access to the opportunity to halve their risk of a heart attack. Whilst the intention was to examine the effects of the intervention for a much longer time period, the study was terminated. Another problem with this study besides the ethical issue raised, was that some of the doctors had peeled open the capsules they were taking, and were thus able (as they knew how aspirin tasted) to find out whether they were in the experimental or control condition. The researchers had failed to ensure the control pills tasted the same as the aspirin and therefore to rule out the placebo effect.

We can add another problem to this list of practical and ethical issues. A critique sometimes levelled at the classic experiment is that once we remove it from the sterile clinical setting of a laboratory or hospital, random assignment no longer works. The issue here is *non-response* or *non-compliance*. Say I want to test the effectiveness of food vouchers or parenting classes. I give one group of households the vouchers or access to the classes, and another group gets nothing. It is likely that some of the households that have received food vouchers forget to or cannot be bothered to come and collect them. Also, some of the households that should have received the parenting classes do not turn up to them, because they find them too difficult, they think they do not need them, or their children have gone to live elsewhere.

It should be obvious that those households that withdraw from the study, or choose not to participate, are not the same as those who do take part: it is likely that they are less motivated. In other words, whilst we did our best to randomize assignment to our experimental and control groups, the groups are, due to attrition, no longer comparable. The households left in the experimental group are only those who are motivated to take part. If in our results we find a difference between the experimental group and the control group can we conclude that this is due to the intervention, the vouchers or parenting classes? Or is it (also) due to differences in motivation?

Attrition seriously complicates experiments that stretch over multiple repeated measurements over time. Attrition may virtually wreck longitudinal studies as dropout accumulates. If we lose 10% of respondents every year (a very optimistic rate of attrition!), after 3 years we will have only $.90^3 = 73\%$ of respondents left, and after 5 years only $.90^5 = 59\%$.

When dealing with interventions that take place outside of a controlled laboratory situation or that are more complicated to administer than those in the medical world – where sometimes a glass of water and a pill are all it takes – often a great deal of complications arise. Many of these issues are practical.

> A complication in the fish oil experiment soon became apparent. The researchers had great difficulty in securing the necessary amount of real and placebo supplements. The project was delayed by months, and the researchers were worried that the enthusiasm of the prison staff for the project would wane.
> Once the capsules had been delivered a second complication arose. A pallet of supplements was stolen from one of the prisons. A new order and delivery had to be made.
> Finally the experiment was ready to start. Enthusiasm had waned. However, more surprising was that the number of incidents in the chosen prison locations had already dramatically decreased. It was unclear why. The only explanation the researchers could come up with was that the prison staff, following the information evening about the benefits of fish oil for heart and vascular disease as well as aggression, had begun to take fish oil supplements themselves. This resulted in a decrease in aggressive incidents as of course these incidents arise through interactions between staff and inmates.

Complications are generally more serious for, and more crucial to the success of behavioural interventions. A behavioural intervention can sometimes last several months or even years. Administering such an intervention usually involves a number of different staff members providing the training. The make-up of training groups can change, with for instance inmates transferred from one prison to another. Interventions generally involve a series of sessions. Sometimes a client might miss a session, due to sickness for example. The first thing to check with a behavioural intervention is therefore whether all the sessions have taken place, and whether guidelines were followed. This means that, compared to relatively clean-cut pharmacological experiments, we are not dealing with just one 'pill', but a set of many different 'pills' that vary according to the group composition they were administered in, the extent to which the trainer followed protocol, type and number of missed sessions, etc.

For such more naturalistic experiments, it is important to check whether and why attrition occurs. When a client stops attending the training sessions for a behavioural intervention, because they no longer want to take part or are not able to keep them up, this clearly creates a problem. By not completing the training session they have not taken the entire intervention or 'pill'. This means they can no longer be counted in the experimental group. However, we cannot simply remove them from the experimental group. It is highly likely that those who drop out are those who are most impulsive or least enthusiastic about changing their behaviour. By removing the drop outs from the group, those who would have probably had the worst results, we are only left with the 'good guys', those who would probably have had the best results.

The fish oil researchers concluded on the basis of their results that for this sample of male inmates aged 18 to 25 years, the group who took the fish oil were involved in significantly fewer aggressive incidents than the group who took the placebo. The experimental group saw a 34% reduction in the incident rate, compared to a 14% increase in the control group. The researchers had asked some of the inmates before the study started to guess which group they were in. They asked the same question once the study had finished. When asked before the study started, the men were not able to accurately guess which group they were in. However, after the study had been completed three quarters guessed correctly, a statistically greater amount than could guess correctly by chance. So how did these men know which group they were in when it was a double blind experiment? More importantly did the prison staff, responsible for recording the incidents and thus the dependent variable, know? All in all, it was clear that the experiment that had been designed as a double blind experiment, had somehow evolved in a less than double blind one.

One way some researchers deal with drop outs is to instead re-allocate them to the control group. This is generally regarded as bad practice. By putting the 'failures' in the reference group one is practically guaranteeing the training will have a positive effect: those unwilling or less motivated are not only creamed off from the experimental group leaving a positive selection, but they are added to the controls, further adding to the contrast.

It is hard to give a satisfactory solution for dealing with drop outs. Due to a lack of suitable alternative, the drop outs are usually kept in the experimental group, and their relapse rates counted along with the rest of the group. They are often also analysed separately, to check whether it would have been possible to predict beforehand which respondents would drop out, as well as to examine whether their outcomes differ. The most important reason for keeping the drop outs in the experimental group is to see whether one behavioural intervention has higher drop out rates than another, an essential factor to consider in evaluating an intervention. A behavioural intervention which is able to keep everyone on board is preferable to one that may get higher scores, but which also has a higher drop out rate. It is therefore important that interventions are examined in their entirety.

Whilst we have so far held up the classic experiment as being the pinnacle of research design, and the quasi-experiment and observational studies as being less than perfect, it should now be obvious that a perfectly designed classic experiment can be affected by serious practical complications. Regardless of such practical issues, some scientists believe that the classic experiment is in fact fundamentally inferior to observational studies. The critics have two objections to the classic experiment.

Firstly, they argue that classic experimental studies are expensive and cost the taxpayer too much. Governments and organizations collect huge amounts of data these days, and using these existing data to answer research questions would save a lot of money. Also, an issue often raised is that classic experiments take a long time to carry out, too long to be of use to policy makers who need empirical evidence quickly and cannot wait the years it takes from proposal to final report to judge the effectiveness of an intervention. Imagine that we wanted to test the effectiveness of a custodial sentence. If we were carrying out an experimental study we would have to assign everyone who was eligible for a custodial sentence to either a custodial sentence or another intervention, such as community service or behavioural therapy. Even if this experiment received judicial support, it would take a long time to set up and carry out. To start with, custodial sentences last a certain time span. Then following release we would have to observe our experimental and control group for a reasonable period of time, for instance 2 years, in order to determine the recidivism risk of both groups. On top of this in order to have enough statistical power to ensure we could find an effect, we might need to add to our experimental and control groups over a period of several years. All in all the initial results of such a study would only be available after a period of a number of years at the earliest. This may obviously be too long for policy makers and politicians to wait to make a decision.

A second objection often raised is that an experiment introduces an artificial element to the real-life phenomena we are interested in. The very fact that people know they are being observed and are taking part in research can influence their behaviour in a whole range of ways. One could argue that by including a control group the effect of 'being researched' is factored out. However if, for example, the laboratory is only able to carry out the research because of the intervention, or the intervention only begins once a pretest measurement has taken place, this artificial element remains, and may complicate the interpretation of effects. In such cases the *external validity* of the research is called into question.

There is therefore a clear trade-off. The classical experiment is superior in terms of internal validity: because we have through the randomization ruled out any alternative explanations for the effects we find, we can be sure that any differences between experimental and control groups can be attributed to the intervention W only. The classical experiment often scores much lower on external validity however. Classical experiments have therefore as their plus side strong internal validity, but generally because of their laboratory settings low external validity. We are for controlled experiments less sure whether we would find the same results if the intervention would be administered in the real, non-research world, in the 'wild' so to say. The reverse applies to observational studies. These are generally strong on external validity, but internal validity is compromised.

Advocates of observational studies argue that these are superior to experiments *if* the problems that arise when respondents cannot be randomly assigned can be solved. Nevertheless, less than classic experimental designs inherently complicate causal inference. In the next section we outline the problems we run into when random assignment to experimental and control groups cannot take place.

1.4 Methodological problems in non-experimental studies

We now discuss the problems facing a nonrandomized experiment. We will first discuss the assumptions that may be violated, and then show both in more mathematical format as well as more intuitively what goes wrong if we want to estimate the effect of an intervention from nonexperimental data.

It is often the case when working with preexisting groups that the experimental and the control group cannot be presumed comparable. In these cases there is a fundamental assumption which we cannot make, usually referred to in the literature as the *Stable Unit Treatment Value Assumption*, or SUTVA for short (Rubin, 1986). This assumption is that:

> *The Y_{iw} value of respondent i receiving intervention w will be the same no matter what mechanism is used to assign the intervention to the respondent and no matter what interventions the other respondents receive.*

Loosely translated the first part of this assumption implies that the fact that someone receives an intervention has no relation to their (pretest) Y score, and the second part that respondent i's Y score has no relation to the Y scores of the other respondents. The last part of the assumption implies that the experimental group's intervention must not interfere in any way with the control group. For example, if management training is given in a company it is vital that the control group does not have any exposure to the training, e.g. during coffee breaks or by the water cooler. This last past of SUTVA is essential in order to maintain the 'purity' of the intervention, but does not per se have anything to do with random assignment. Respondents can be selected into experimental and control groups purely on the basis of chance, but if they then interact with each other, the effect of the intervention may be watered down. We are then no longer able to judge its effectiveness, and in most cases this will be underestimated. As an example think of different plots of land, of which some are and some are not, treated with fertilizer. As the experimental and control plots of land have been randomly chosen and are close and adjacent, they may be assumed comparable. However, once rain falls on the land, some of the fertilizer from the experimental plots may wash down to the control plots, stimulating growth on these. We will now underestimate the effect of the fertilizer as the control plots would have shown less growth had the contamination not taken place.

The first part of the SUTVA assumption states that the units or respondents who get the intervention do not differ from those who do not. In other words there is no reason to suspect the controls to score differently from the experimental units. This first part directly relates to random assignment, and is obviously more difficult to achieve when we are dealing with preexisting groups. In the literature this part of the SUTVA assumption is often referred to as the *(strongly) ignorable treatment assignment assumption*, or SITA for short. This assumption specifies that a respondent's (pretest) Y score has nothing to do with whether they are assigned to one group (experimental) or the other (control). We can state this formally as:

> *The assignment of respondents to experimental and control groups is, controlling for covariates $X_1, X_2, \ldots$, independent of their scores on the outcome variable Y.*

This assumption is found in the literature referred to as the *non-confounded* assumption, *selection on observed variables* or *selection on observables* assumption, the *conditional independence* assumption, or the *exogeneity* assumption. We will always refer to this assumption as the exogeneity assumption.

When the exogeneity assumption is not fulfilled, we say that there is *endogeneity bias*. The etymology of these terms goes back to the Greek exo (εξο), meaning external or from outside, and endo (ενδο), meaning internal or from within.

When respondents have been randomly assigned to the experimental and control groups we know for sure that there is no systematic link between group membership and scores on the dependent variable Y, or scores on any other variables. We can be certain that we have fulfilled the exogeneity assumption. But how can we ensure this when we are working with preexisting groups?

We could firstly examine whether the groups differ from each other by testing one by one all possible variables to ensure they are uncorrelated with group membership. If none of them correlate there is no relationship between group membership and the dependent variable or any of the covariates. However, there may be other, unobserved variables that do relate to group membership. Examining these is not possible as we have not measured them. As previously mentioned it would be impossible to examine all the variables which may exist in the universe. So whilst we are able to state that our groups do not differ on any of our observed variables (*overt bias*), we cannot be sure that the groups do not differ on any unobserved variables (*hidden bias*). We simply cannot test for this.

At this point we need to be more clear about the terminology we are using. So far we have repeatedly referred to *overt bias* and *hidden bias* when discussing situations whereby the experimental and control group can differ on observed and unobserved variables. Whilst these terms sound catchy, and many other authors also use them, they are technically speaking not correct.

If the experimental and control groups differed on certain characteristics, whether these are observed or not, this would result in biased *estimators* (e.g. the regression coefficient β) to determine the treatment effect. The β could, for example, be overestimated (see Figure 1.7 referring to entry into the labour market later in this chapter). This bias arises due to differences between the experimental and control groups. These differences can either represent *observed heterogeneity* or *unobserved heterogeneity*. The *heterogeneity* is the result of not using random assignment and it is this heterogeneity that leads to biased estimators. Observed and unobserved heterogeneity can therefore be the cause of bias; it is only for short that we refer to these situations as situations of *overt* and *hidden bias*.

When working with non-randomised groups we can never be certain that the measured effect of our intervention is an accurate assessment of the true effect: we do not know whether our β is unbiased. We can correct for the distorting effect of any observed variables, overt bias. However, we cannot guarantee that there is no hidden bias. As a result it is impossible to say whether differences between our experimental and control group are the result of our intervention or whether they are (partly) due to preexisting unobserved differences between the groups.

In a hidden bias situation, where for example group membership and scores on the dependent variable Y positively correlate with a third unobserved, or *confounding*, variable, Z, the effect of the intervention will generally be overestimated. For example, take Y to be the dependent variable, W to be the intervention (coded 0 for no intervention and 1 for intervention received) and $X_1, X_2, X_3, \ldots$ to be a number of measured covariates. We estimate the effect of the intervention W using a multiple regression model thus:

$$Y_i = a + \gamma W_i + b_1 X_{1i} + b_2 X_{2i} + b_3 X_{3i} + \cdots + e_i,$$

whereby γ is the net effect of the intervention. In a regression model the coefficient of each predictor indicates the contribution of that independent variable to predicting γ, whilst holding constant the effect of other variables in the model (see chapter 2). We are able to determine the effect of the intervention W on the outcome Y, whilst controlling for the effect of the predictor variables, X, included in the model.

However, imagine there was a third, unobserved variable Z, which correlates with both Y and W. For example, motivation (Z) might determine participation in an intervention (W) as well as success in the labour market (Y). Because Z has not been measured it cannot be included in the model. As a result in our estimation of the regression model the effect of the intervention (W) in fact also includes the effect of motivation.

Below we demonstrate in formula what happens if our dependent variable Y is not only determined by W but also by an unobserved variable Z (1.1):

$$Y_i = \gamma W_i + \beta Z_i + e_i. \tag{1.1}$$

When scores on the dependent variable Y are not only determined by W but also by Z the above model (1.1) is necessary. However, if we regress Y onto W *without* including the effect of Z the result is a *biased* estimate of the effect γ of the intervention W. We can demonstrate this using an equation estimating the regression coefficient β_1 for a model with two predictor variables (for ease of interpretation all variables are standardized so that mean is 0 and standard deviation is 1):

$$\hat{\beta}_1 = \frac{r_{YX_1} - r_{YX_2} r_{X_1X_2}}{1 - r^2_{X_1X_2}},$$

and if we extend this to include our predictor variable W and our second variable Z the estimation of γ would be as follows (1.2):

$$\hat{\gamma} = \frac{r_{YW} - r_{YZ} r_{WZ}}{1 - r^2_{WZ}}. \tag{1.2}$$

However, in reality we incorrectly only include W in the model, and therefore estimate the effect of γ using only one variable (1.3):

$$\hat{\gamma} = r_{YW}. \tag{1.3}$$

Figure 1.7: Example of overestimate caused by differences in motivation

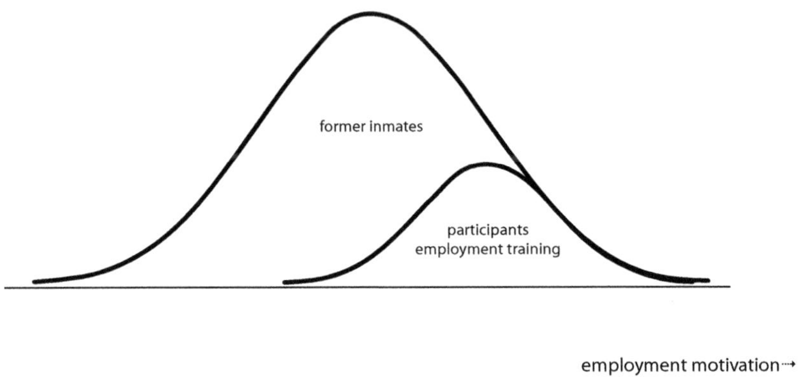

If we compare (1.2) and (1.3) it is obvious that not including Z in the model results in a biased estimation of γ. The correct estimation of γ in (1.2) includes other terms alongside r_{YW}. The only situation in which (1.2) would be equal to (1.3) is when $r_{WZ} = 0$ (i.e. when Y and Z are related but the intervention W and Z are not related). In this exceptional case despite incorrectly identifying the model we would still end up with a correct estimation of γ, as (1.2) would be equal to (1.3). If we fail to include one or more confounders Z we end up incorrectly estimating the effect γ of W.

Figure 1.7 illustrates more intuitively how such *endogeneity bias* distorts our conclusions. This is a fictional but not unrealistic example. A group of former inmates is offered a place on a work training course. Not all the inmates want to take part. As the figure clearly illustrates, those that do want to take part are more motivated. Following the training course we would expect those who took part to be more likely to find work, to be unemployed for a shorter periods, etc. The question remains, however, how much of this difference is due to the training course and how much is due to their preexisting differences in motivation. This example shows how *selection bias* can lead us to overestimate the effect of an intervention.

The opposite effect is also possible. *Selection bias* can also lead to the underestimation of the effect of an intervention. For example, a group of violent juvenile offenders are screened for the seriousness of their crimes. Those for whom the chance of relapse is considered high are sentenced by the judge to attend an aggression control training course. The majority of the offenders are considered to be at too low risk of relapse to warrant intervention and do not need to follow the course. See Figure 1.8.

Following treatment we examine the relapse rates for both groups and find that both groups have committed roughly the same amount of violent crimes, their relapse rates do not differ. These findings might lead to the conclusion that the training course has not helped. This would however be incorrect. The training course worked exactly as it was intended: It reduced the rate of relapse to acceptable levels. The high risk group which followed the training, is now behaving in the same way as the low risk group, which did not need the training. See Figure 1.8.

In the examples shown in Figure 1.7 and Figure 1.8 we are aware of the distortions. If this were the selection bias, and if we had observed (measured) this bias, we would be able to control for it. Our intervention effect would then be accurately estimated as we would be able to control for the third, confounding variable Z. However, in most situations in the real world we do not know what Z is. Because Z is unknown, and because even if by chance we were to have observed a Z, there would still be countless other possible confounding variables. Therefore, whenever we have to work with data from an observational study, we can never be sure whether we have estimated the effect of the intervention correctly.

We can sum up the problem thus: When random assignment is not used, the crucial exogeneity assumption cannot be met. Those who receive the intervention and those who do not receive the intervention may differ in important characteristics relating to the dependent variable. Put another way, the control group is not the experimental group without the intervention: the control group cannot serve as the *counterfactual*. Consequently, we cannot accurately estimate the effect of the intervention. If random assignment had been possible this fundamental problem would not exist. However, in many cases we cannot, or we do not always want to carry out a classic experimental design down to every last detail.

1.5 About this book

In this book we outline a number of techniques used to solve the problems which arise from the lack of a suitable control group. Basically these techniques are intended to increase a research study's score on the Maryland scale (see section 1.3) from 3 to 4. What we generally aim for is a quasi-experimental study whereby the experimental and control groups are as similar to each other as possible.

Some of the techniques we outline achieve this by using observational or quasi-experimental data in such as way as to create a comparable control group. These

Figure 1.8: Example of underestimate caused by differences in risk

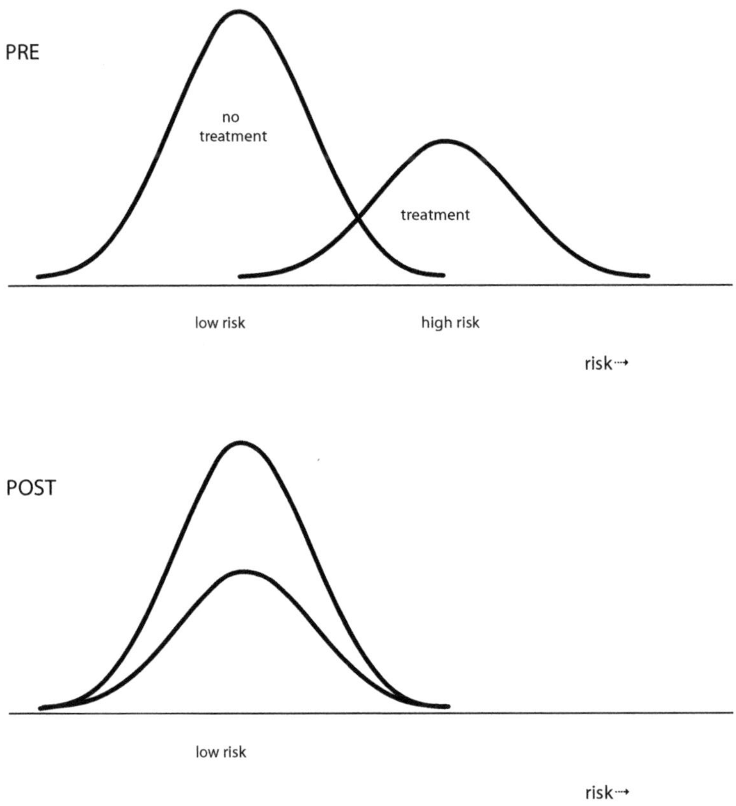

techniques, called *propensity score matching*, are described in chapter 3. Another technique attempts to address the problem of endogeneity bias by using *instrumental variables* to filter out any bias. This technique is described in chapter 4.

Following this, in chapter 5 we describe a technique introduced in 1960 which, until recently, has been surprisingly seldom used. This technique, the *'regression discontinuity design'*, whilst it has its disadvantages, is extremely inventive. It is generally considered to be the next best thing to a controlled experiment.

In chapter 6 and chapter 7 two techniques are outlined which both control for the effect of selection bias by using repeated measurements. In chapter 6 *'fixed effects'* models are described. By using repeated measurements we can compare the scores of our research subjects after having received the intervention with their own scores previous to the intervention. For example, we can examine whether people commit fewer offences during the period when they are married compared to the period when they are not married. The basis of these models is that we do not have to compare non married with married people, whereby selection bias would distort our findings, but that every person is compared to him- or herself, when not married and when married. In this way every research subject becomes their own control group or counterfactual.

The final technique, *trajectory* models, is described in chapter 7. This technique, rather than taking each research subject as their own control, examines the effect of independent variables within subgroups that share a common developmental growth curve. The assumption is that these subgroups are homogenous and so selection bias is not an issue when looking at the effects within each subgroup. As a result the effect of independent variable X (or intervention W) on the dependent variable Y can be accurately determined. Effects are assessed separately for each homogenous subgroup.

The book ends with an overview in which the limitations of these ingenious, but ultimately not perfect, techniques are stressed. We also briefly outline a number of techniques not covered in the book, which may, under certain circumstances, provide a nice solution to the endogeneity bias problem.

1.5.1 The dataset

Throughout this book we illustrate the various techniques using an example dataset. This dataset is based on real data (Hendriks, 2006; Bijleveld et al., 2010). However, whilst the variables we have constructed resemble those in the cited research and the relationships between them are similar to those in the real dataset, the data itself is fictitious.

The dataset provides details of 500 fictional juvenile male sex offenders, with an average conviction age of 14 years. In all cases the boys have committed at least one hands-on offence, i.e. a sex offence involving physical contact between victim and offender. Sex offenders who committed only offences such as indecent exposure are therefore not included. Also, all offenders played an active role in the offence. Some were very young when the offence took place, the youngest was in fact 9 years old, and were therefore not prosecuted. These offenders were nevertheless included in the dataset. Some offenders were 18 years or older, and therefore no longer classified as juvenile. They were still included in the dataset, however, as offenders with delayed development can still be judged and sentenced according to juvenile law.

All offenders (all individuals in the dataset were either convicted or had confessed to an offence, and we are therefore able to refer to them as offenders) underwent personality examinations. These involve a trained psychologist and/or psychiatrist examining the juvenile sex offender, and getting them to complete a number of standardized measurements, giving insight into their personality characteristics. A risk assessment instrument, J-SOAP, was also administered for each young offender. There are three categories of offender: offenders who victimise a child, group offenders who victimise a peer, and solo offenders who victimise a peer. We refer to these as child abusers, group offenders, and peer abusers. A child abuser is defined as someone who abused a prepubescent child at least 5 years younger than themselves. In cases involving any other age difference the offender is categorised as a peer abuser. All offenders could be placed in categories. An overview of the background variables is given in Table 3.1.

Follow-up information on the offenders is also available. We know the recidivism rates of the offenders for sex offences. This information is analyzed in chapter 3. Using *propensity score matching* we examine whether sex offenders who received cognitive behavioural treatment are less likely to relapse than sex offenders who did not get such treatment. We also know whether probation conditions were applied, and if so which court had applied them. This information is used in the instrumental variables analyses in chapter 4, where we examine whether probation leads to more or less recidivism. In addition we also know whether and at what age these males have committed any other offences. We use this information together with their risk assessments to illustrate the *regression discontinuity design* in chapter 5. Specifically we examine whether treatment results in less recidivism across all offences ('general recidivism'). We also have a range of information about the offenders as adults. We know at what age they had work and whether they were unemployed for any period of time. We know if they have ever been married or had children. With the help of *fixed effects* panel analysis in chapter 6 we examine whether marriage or parenthood decreases the risk of offending when adult. In the final empirical chapter, chapter 7, we use trajectory analysis to examine the relationship between employment and offending.

1.5.2 SPSS and Stata

The dataset is analysed in the chapters using either Stata or SPSS. Whilst all of the techniques can be carried out using Stata, this is not the case for SPSS. However SPSS is by some considered to be more user friendly, and relatively more students have had training in SPSS. We have decided therefore to use SPSS wherever possible, and on occasion to use both software packages. It should be noted that in Stata, it regularly happens that new updates of procedures generate additional, or less output. However, the core results will always be generated.

An SPSS dataset always has the file extension '.sav' and a Stata dataset has '.dta'. When using SPSS it is possible to simply open the data file in SPSS, the commands will automatically be carried out on this dataset. The same goes for Stata.

Throughout the book we almost always use the SPSS 'syntax', i.e. the commands indicating which calculations need to be carried out, as well as the Stata commands necessary to perform the analyses. The advantage of using syntax is that whilst the menu for carrying out analyses changes from one SPSS version to the next, the syntax remains the same. A second advantage is that the Stata commands and SPSS syntax can both be saved in one document. These instructions or syntax can be preserved, preferably in the same folder as the dataset, the output and the final article or report, and the analyses will then be replicable and can be reconstructed at a later date.

When writing syntax it is highly recommended to insert comments. Particularly with more complicated calculations it can be difficult to reconstruct later the exact steps taken with each command. By providing a commentary alongside the syntax it should be possible at a later date to understand why the analyses were carried out in a certain manner. In SPSS commentary is prefixed by a '*':

```
* Here I am trying to predict recidivism from.
* descriptive details of the women.
* First I recode the income variables.
* because one woman was an outlier.

RECODE INCOME (5=4)(ELSE = COPY) into INCOME_rec.
EXECUTE.
LOGISTIC REGRESSION VARIABLES recidivism_general
    /METHOD=ENTER CHILDREN INCOME_rec ETHNICITY
    EDUCATION MARRIAGE
    /CRITERIA=PIN(.05) POUT(.10) ITERATE(20) CUT(.5).
```

Commentary can also be included by adding the very visible command COMMENT, for example together with blocks of asterisks:

```
COMMENT ********************************************.
COMMENT Here I am trying to predict recidivism from.
COMMENT descriptive details of the women.
COMMENT First I recode the income variables.
```

```
COMMENT because one woman was an outlier.
COMMENT .
COMMENT ********************************************.

RECODE INCOME (5=4)(ELSE = COPY) into INCOME_rec.
EXECUTE.
LOGISTIC REGRESSION VARIABLES recidivism_general
    /METHOD=ENTER CHILDREN INCOME_rec ETHNICITY
    EDUCATION MARRIAGE
    /CRITERIA=PIN(.05) POUT(.10) ITERATE(20) CUT(.5).
COMMENT ********************************************.
```

In Stata commentary can be saved using a '*'. Instructions including commentary would look as follows:

```
* idnumber is the unique code for every respondent
* IQ is a time invariant variable
  reshape i idnumber IQ
* year is time varying
  reshape j year
* delinquency work marriage and children vary between
* persons and over time
  reshape xij delinquency employment marriage children
  reshape long
```

At the end of this book are two appendices containing the entire syntax with commentary for SPSS and Stata respectively. Analyses from all the chapters are included, from propensity score matching to trajectory models. To enhance legibility Stata commands which stretch beyond the width of the page are indented on the following line. When using these commands they must however be continuous, i.e. without pressing 'enter' or using indents.

One final point for attention is the following. Often when analyzing data different computers are used. Syntax commands which indicate which folders should be used do not always work on every computer, as not all computers have the same folder structure. For that reason it is useful to refer to the location of files just once at the top of each syntax file. Then, when using different computers just this one command needs to be changed. For example, if the data is in `C:\Data\`, in SPSS one would include the following command:

```
define !data ()'C:\Data\' !enddefine
```

And from then on the file `VM-JSO.sav` would be read in SPSS as follows:

```
get file=!data+'VM-JSO.sav'
```

Consequently if on a different computer the data are in a different folder only the first line needs to be adjusted. In Stata the same idea can be applied by using the 'global' command as follows:

```
global DATAMAP "C:\Data\"

use "${DATAMAP}VM-JSO.dta", clear
```

1.5.3 Symbols

In this book we try on the one hand to use consistent symbols for the models we describe and on the other hand we also try to use common, but at times different, symbols used for models in the literature. As a consequence we are not able to be entirely internally consistent. It is possible therefore that the reader may find a regression model illustrated using the following symbols:

$$Y_i = a + b_1 X_{1i} + b_2 X_{2i} + b_3 X_{3i} + \cdots + e_i,$$

as well as using the following symbols:

$$Y_i = \gamma + \delta_1 X_{1i} + \delta_2 X_{2i} + \delta_3 X_{3i} + \cdots + \varepsilon_i,$$

or even the following symbols:

$$Y_i = b_0 + b_1 X_{1i} + b_2 X_{2i} + b_3 X_{3i} + \cdots + e_i.$$

As another example, we have used the symbol Z to indicate a confounder, but in chapter 4 we will use the same symbol to indicate an instrumental variable. We hope that these small internal inconsistencies do not take away from the legibility of the text, but rather help other texts to become more accessible.

Chapter 2

Regression Analysis

2.1 Multiple regression

In the coming chapters of this book regression analysis and variants thereof will be repeatedly employed. As stated in the introduction we expect the reader to have some knowledge of and experience with using regression analysis. This chapter is therefore intended to serve as a refresher for regression analysis in general, as well as to provide a review of some of the less well known variants of regression analysis. Most regression methods included in this chapter are explored in more detail in textbooks such as Kleinbaum et al. (2014).

2.1.1 The multiple regression model

In regression analysis a dependent variable Y is predicted by a linear function of a (number of) independent variables X. When we only have one independent variable we refer to this as simple regression. The model is as follows:

$$Y = a + bX.$$

Here Y is the dependent variable we want to predict, X is the independent variable, a is referred to as the intercept and b as the regression coefficient or regression weight. As this is a model, we have no error term or indication of individual variable scores.

Of course, in practice we want to predict every research unit i's score on the dependent variable. We can (almost) never perfectly predict this. In some cases our prediction of a research unit's (i) Y score, indicated by $\hat{Y}_i$, will be too high, in other cases $\hat{Y}_i$ will be too low. The difference between the observed Y_i and the $\hat{Y}_i$ as predicted by our regression model is referred to as *prediction error*:

$$e_i = Y_i - \hat{Y}_i,$$

so therefore the regression equation becomes:

$$Y_i = a + bX_i + e_i.$$

When carrying out a regression analysis, we estimate the unstandardised parameters a and b as follows:

$$\hat{b} = r_{XY}\frac{s_Y}{s_X},$$

where r_{XY} is the Pearson correlation coefficient between X and Y, s_Y the standard deviation of Y and s_X the standard deviation of X, and

$$\hat{a} = \bar{Y} - b\bar{X},$$

where $\bar{Y}$ and $\bar{X}$ represent the means of Y and X respectively. The formulas show that we are computing unstandardised regression coefficients. If for example variable X is measured on a more detailed scale, say centimeters rather than meters, its standard deviation would change correspondingly, and consequently the regression weight b too. This means that both a and b depend on the measurement scales with which X and Y were measured.

The estimation procedure most commonly used in regression is 'least squares' or 'ordinary least squares' (OLS). When we talk about 'OLS' being used to carry out regression what we mean is that the regression weight b and the intercept a are estimated in such a way that the residual sum of squares (or sum of squared prediction errors) is as small as possible: $\sum_{i=1}^{N} e_i^2$ is minimised. Translated into layman's terms: if we estimate the regression coefficients a and b using the given formulas then we know that the amount that Y deviates from $\hat{Y}_i$ is a small as possible: it is not possible to find an a and b with smaller prediction errors.

With multiple regression, several independent variables are included rather than just one. The model for multiple regression is therefore as follows:

$$\hat{Y} = a + b_1X_1 + b_2X_2 + b_3X_3 + \cdots + b_kX_k.$$

We use k different independent variables to predict the dependent variable Y. As an illustration, if we just have two independent variables X_1 and X_2 the standardised regression weights are β_1 and β_2:

$$\beta_1 = \frac{r_{YX_1} - r_{YX_2}r_{X_1X_2}}{1 - r_{X_1X_2}^2},$$

and

$$\beta_2 = \frac{r_{YX_2} - r_{YX_1} r_{X_1X_2}}{1 - r^2_{X_1X_2}},$$

whereby $r_{X_1X_2}$ again refers to the correlation coefficient between the two variables X_1 and X_2. The regression weights are standardised, meaning that they are independent of the scale used. Whether X_1 is measured in centimeters or meters, the regression weight β_1 remains the same. The formulas in case of more independent variables are more complicated.

In multiple regression analysis we want to predict scores on our dependent variable Y using scores from our independent variables $X_1 \ldots X_k$. The regression weights (not for nothing called 'weights') indicate to us which weight belongs to each X variable in the regression equation, or phrased colloquially, how much each X variable contributes to predicting Y.

Having said so, now imagine we have two X predictor variables, X_1 and X_2, which are practically identical. The correlation between X_1 and X_2 is therefore very high, they are as said extremely alike. Suppose that I had started out predicting Y from X_1. Would my prediction improve much if I added X_2 to the model? The answer is 'no': prediction would hardly improve as X_2 – being so similar to X_1 – does not add new information with which I could improve my prediction. What X_2 tells us about Y, was already largely contained in X_1.

In the context of multiple regression this phenomenon, presence in the model of predictors that are much alike, is referred to as 'multicollinearity'. One unfortunate consequence of multicollinearity is that we are using model that is too complicated. We are predicting Y using variables that are practically identical, where we would have achieved almost the same prediction outcome using just one variable. We are therefore using a too complicated model, overloaded with variables that each bring about the same information. A second unfortunate consequence is that by including such 'overlapping' variables in the regression equation the regression weights for each independent variable will be attenuated. This happens because each regression weight takes into account the contribution of the other variables in the equation in predicting Y. The regression weight β_k namely gives the contribution of X_k *given the other predictors* in the model. The β_ks tell us what each variable X_k contributes to predicting Y given the other variables that are in the model. So, if we add to a model that already contains X_1 a second almost identical variable X_2, then in principle X_2's regression weight could be almost zero: X_2 adds little, given X_1. What the regression model computations lead to, is an 'evening out' of the regression weights: the regression weights of X_1 and X_2 will be similar and each about half of X_1's weight had X_2 not been added to the model.

The regression weights by themselves therefore do not inform us to what extent a single variable could predict Y: they can only be interpreted in the context of the remainder of the model. Statements about the regression outcomes must therefore always follow the mantra of: *'Given variables A and B, the contribution of C to predicting Y is ....'* Especially if we have a number of variables that overlap, multicollinearity can cause each separate X variable to have a very small or even insignificant regression weight despite the fact that our regression is able to predict Y scores very well. Consequently multicollinearity, particularly if we have many X variables, causes problems with interpretation: regression weights of variables that correlate strongly with Y may not only become very small, it is even possible to encounter a situation where a variable positively correlates with the dependent variable but has a negative regression weight.

It is therefore generally advisable to only use variables in the equation which have a unique contribution to the prediction of Y, those which are genuinely complementary. This may seem easy to establish, by simply running a correlation matrix on the desired predictors before choosing your model. If the results of this indicate that a number of predictors correlate strongly with each other it is advisable to choose just one of these.

Unfortunately reality can be slightly more complicated. For instance one predictor X_3 may be a linear combination of two other predictors X_1 and X_2. In this case X_3 does not add anything to the prediction of Y over and above the information contained in X_1 and X_2. X_3 is after all made up of X_1 and X_2. See for instance Kleinbaum et al. (2014), chapter 14, for more on multicollinearity.

Up to now we discussed unstandardised and standardised regression weights. As mentioned, standardised weights are independent of the scales used. A consequence of this is that we can easily compare the relative importance of independent variables in the prediction of Y. For example if $\beta_1 = .7$ and $\beta_2 = .5$ we can safely say that in this model (given all the other variables...) X_1 plays a bigger role in predicting Y than X_2. Standardised regression weights would therefore seem to be handy because they immediately reveal the relative importance of a variable in predicting Y. However, a disadvantage is that they cannot be translated directly into the 'scale' used for the independent variable: if $\beta_1 = .7$, we can describe this by saying that a score on X_1 that is one standard deviation higher, adds .7 standard deviations to Y. While true, it is not something all readers can immediately envisage.

Unstandardised variables do allow us to do this. For example, imagine that the unstandardised regression weight b_k for the independent variable 'number of offences convicted for' is 1.5, and that we want to use this variable to predict custodial sentence length Y in months. We can use the unstandardised regression weight to state that, given the other variables in the model, every additional offence a defendant is convicted for adds one and a half months to his or her sentence length.

2.1.2 Model fit

In cases of multiple independent variables the regression equation is as follows:

$$Y_i = a + b_1X_{1i} + b_2X_{2i} + b_3X_{3i} + \cdots + b_kX_{ki} + e_i,$$

Just like was the case with simple regression, as the absolute values of the error terms e_i increase in absolute value, our ability to make accurate predictions has decreased, and as they decrease, our ability to accurately predict Y using a number of from the X variables has increased. This accuracy is often expressed in one measure, the *multiple correlation coefficient*. This multiple correlation coefficient indicates how well our prediction is working.

The multiple correlation coefficient is constructed from nothing other than the Pearson product-moment correlation coefficient between the actual Y_i and the $\hat{Y}_i$, predicted from $X_1, X_2, \ldots$:

$$r_{Y\hat{Y}},$$

and referred to as 'R'. Clearly, the more similar Y and $\hat{Y}$ are, the better the prediction, and the higher the correlation between Y and $\hat{Y}$, R=$r_{Y\hat{Y}}$ will be. Instead of this R, in practice the squared value, R^2, is used as a measure of the quality of the prediction, and is referred to as the multiple correlation coefficient. The R^2 indicates how much of the variation in Y is predicted by the model. The R^2 is therefore a '*goodness of fit*' measure.

It is difficult to say what an acceptable or customary value is for R^2. Values around .80 are considered high for the social sciences, and are rare in reality. Depending on the discipline or dependent value predicted, values of .10 or less are also reported. Much obviously depends on how predictable Y is: if Y is a phenomenon largely generated by chance events, then values of R around .05 may already be acceptable.

Many researchers prefer to use not only the R^2, but also generally report the so-called *adjusted* R^2 or $R^2_{adjusted}$. This adjusted measure of model fit is preferred because it corrects the multiple correlation coefficient measure for the number of predictors included in the model. The rationale behind this is that if we include numerous X variables the model can only fit better. For that reason, the *adjusted* R^2 corrects R^2 with a penalty for incorporating many predictors. Phrased differently, this measure corrects for the fact that if we would use random X_k variables we would still always find that some variation in Y was explained. The formula to calculate *adjusted* R^2 is:

$$adjusted\,R^2 = 1 - (1 - R^2) \times \frac{N-1}{N-k-1},$$

where k is the number of predictors and N the size of the sample. What this measure clearly does is 'punish' modellers for including too many predictors given the sample size: as k increases, R^2 decreases. If the number of predictors k is very large for the sample size N, the downsizing can be quite large.

2.1.3 Choosing predictors

In practice, researchers like to use a set of predictors when they conduct a multiple regression analysis: they may want to use all variables that have been forwarded as predictors in theories, or they may want to test one particular issue such as the extent to which admission criteria predict student outcomes. Two types of considerations need to be dealt with when deciding what predictors to incorporate. A first rule is to include variables which we know are theoretically of interest: haphazardly including just some predictors is a *black box* approach and will not contribute to theory nor advance our understanding of the causal mechanisms underlying our prediction. We must therefore choose predictors that we believe may play a role, based on a certain theory or based on contrasting theories that we want to compare, or based on their face validity.

A next point in deciding what (and how many) predictors to include is quality of prediction. Obviously we want to predict Y as accurately as possible. We want the fit (R^2 or *adjusted* R^2) of our model to be high. In general, adding variables to the model can only improve its fit as measured by R^2. However, there are good reasons for not including too many variables. To begin with we want to build parsimonious models. We prefer to end up with a simple, parsimonious regression model rather than a complicated one.

Furthermore, there is also in a technical sense a limit to the amount of predictors that can be included. It is generally recommended in multivariate regression analysis to have a ratio of respondents to variables of at least 10 to 1. Translated into the practicalities of regression analysis this means that when predicting our dependent variable if we have 100 respondents in the sample, we can include a maximum of 10 independent variables in our multiple regression analysis. If the ratio is lower than this we would be relying too much on and perhaps even capitalising on chance, our results could be unstable and the findings less informative.

In practice, when running a multiple regression analysis, statistical software generally gives a number of options to help build a parsimonious model. We briefly discuss the options that are provided in often used statistical software packages like SPSS. The two most important options which can be used there are 'BACKWARD' and 'FORWARD'. When using the BACKWARD method the package includes all the predictors in the model, calculates their regression weights, and then one by one removes those variables which are – given the other variables in the model – not significant predictors of Y, beginning with the least significant, followed by the next least significant, and so on, until only significant predictors are left in the model. When using the FORWARD method the opposite happens. The statistical software package, using a separate simple regression for each independent variable, calculates the contribution of each variable to predicting Y. Next a multivariate model is built, beginning with the variable which had the most predictive power, followed by addition of the next best predictor, and continuing until adding new predictors no longer significantly improves the prediction of Y. It is also possible to include all the independent variables in the model, regardless of the extent to which they predict Y, using the option ENTER. If one chooses that option, all entered variables are kept in the prediction, regardless of their predictive strength. See Kleinbaum et al. (2014) for more.

There is a third consideration that needs to be taken into account when deciding on what predictors to incorporate in a regression model. In section 2.1.1 we described problems that may be caused by multicollinearity. By multicollinearity we refer, loosely speaking, to overlap between predictors: multicollinearity makes our model unnecessarily 'heavy', as well as the regression more difficult to interpret. In short, we described how we want models which are 'technically' good, in that they have a few select predictors each with unique predictive power and at the same time provide a best possible prediction.

To prevent multicollinearity complicating the interpretation of our model, we already mentioned that it is useful to calculate a correlation matrix of the predictors and to check whether any of the variables are strongly correlated with each other: if two variables have a sizeable intercorrelation, it is recommended to choose only one of these for inclusion. A second option that many statistical software packages provide is to calculate the so-called 'tolerance' for each predictor. The tolerance for a variable X_k is equal to $1\text{-}R_k^2$, whereby R_k^2 is equal to the multiple correlation coefficient for the prediction of X_k by the other X variables. R_k^2 tells you to what extent X_k can be predicted from the other explanatory variables. In software packages such as SPSS, the procedures FORWARD and BACKWARD do not include X_k as a predictor if the tolerance of X_k is smaller than .10. Basically what this means is that an independent is omitted from the model if 90% of the variance of that variable can be predicted from the other variables in the model. Some researchers use a stricter measure, such as .20. Many statistical software packages also report the *Variance Inflation Factor* (VIF). This is simply the inverse of the tolerance. For this criterion too there are no hard and fast rules for deciding whether a variable has too high a VIF. For some researchers a VIF of higher than 10 (with a tolerance of .10, VIF is $\frac{1}{.1} = 10$) indicates too much multicollinearity, others already conclude so for values higher than 4. There is no universal benchmark for acceptable multicollinearity, whether using tolerance or VIF.

In summary, we want on the one hand to include all theoretically relevant variables, and so it would not be a good idea to leave any theoretically relevant variables out of the equation. At the same time, we also want to make as precise a prediction as possible, and the more variables included the better we may expect our prediction to be. On the other hand, we do not want our prediction to be based on coincidental combinations of characteristics, or worse still pure chance. We also want our model to be as parsimonious as possible. We might find that the theoretically relevant predictors actually correlate strongly with each other, and we therefore end up with a sub-optimal regression model. In this case what is best to do? Give the theory priority or let the statistics lead the way? When carrying out regression analysis all these sometimes contrasting demands need to be weighed up in order to build a model that is both interpretable and has good predictive power.

2.1.4 Tests

For every β we can test whether it significantly differs from 0. Formulas can be found in many statistics textbooks, such as Hinkle et al. (2003), p. 468 ff. Tests of each of the β_k's can be used to determine whether each predictor X_k gives a statistically significant improvement in predicting Y over and above the other variables in the model. Usually, before interpreting the significance of each regression weight, we first carry out an all-inclusive test examining the significance of all the weights together. Only if this 'overall' F-test is significant is it advisable to use the significance of each separate regression weight to draw conclusions.

If a regression weight significantly differs from 0 then we can conclude that the variable to which it relates, given all other variables in the model, adds significantly to the prediction of Y.

Just as we can test whether the regression weight significantly differs from 0, we can also test whether R^2 significantly differs from 0. Here we examine whether the variance in Y that is explained by our set of predictors can be considered as 'real' i.e. not due to coincidence. We can also under certain conditions test whether the explained variance in one regression model is significantly greater than the explained variance in another regression model. For formulas again see any statistics textbook, for instance Hinkle et al. (2003), p. 477 ff. These tests are generated as standard by most statistical software packages.

2.2 Assumptions

Multiple regression analysis makes four key assumptions. Any conclusions from a regression analysis are based on these assumptions being met. Whilst the regression model assumes that all assumptions are fulfilled, as we will see some assumptions are more crucial than others: regression analysis can sometimes withstand the violation of a number of these assumptions.

The assumptions are as follows:

(1) both the predictors X and the dependent variable Y are measured at the interval level;

(2) the X variables have a linear relationship with the Y variable;

(3) the X variables are '*fixed*' and the Y variable is '*random*';

(4) the prediction errors are uncorrelated, normally distributed, and for every combination of X variables have the same variance σ.

Assumption 1 implies that multiple regression analysis assumes that a higher score on a variable indicates that there is 'more of' whatever that variable is measuring. The formulas are calculated considering the variables to be at interval level or higher. Violating this assumption for independent variables is not the end of the world however. Dichotomous variables can be included without this causing any practical problems, similarly ordinal variables can generally be included without any problems, providing the respondents are evenly distributed across categories and categories are not too 'illogical'. Even nominal independent variables can be included, as long as dummy variables are used. Regarding the dependent variable however the requirement of measurement at the interval level is non-negotiable.

Assumption 2 is in the strictest sense of the word not an assumption. The model tries to fit a relationship between Y and a linear combination of the X variables. If the relationship takes a form other than linear, regression analysis results will not be meaningful. The regression model is simply not able to detect other kinds of relationships. If we already know that the relationship has a certain non-linear form, this can be accommodated by applying a non-linear transformation to (one of) the X variable(s). Even so, the assumption remains that the relationship between the non-linear transformation of (one of) the X_j and Y is again linear, as exemplified in this formula:

$$Y = a + b_1X_1^2 + b_2\sqrt{X_2} + b_3X_3.$$

Assumption 3 states that X is fixed, and Y is random. What this means formally is that the categories (or levels) of X are chosen by the researcher. For example this can refer to the categories 'aspirin' or 'new medicine', or the categories 'no treatment for fear of flying' and 'treatment for fear of flying'. In a classic experiment in the strict sense this situation can and does occur. It is obvious that for example for personality variables such as impulsivity or intelligence, categories cannot be 'established' by the researcher. For this assumption then, having 'fixed' X variables is fulfilled only in special, experimental situations. Violating this assumption, however, does not in practice cause problems and when this assumption is not fulfilled results can be interpreted. (Multiple) regression analysis is therefore robust against the violation of this part of the assumption. The part concerning Y implies that observations of Y are, for every possible linear combination of the X variables, drawn *at random*. It is difficult to test whether this is indeed the case. In practice we assume it to be so.

In assumption 4, three demands are made regarding the prediction errors or the error terms. The first part implies that there is no dependence between the measurements, i.e. the quality of the prediction for one respondent should not be related to that of another respondents. Generally, when we use respondents randomly drawn from the population, this part of the assumption is met. The second part is generally met if our dependent variable is an interval variable and our sample size is large enough. A generally held rule of thumb is that a sample size of 100 is satisfactory. The third part of the assumption concerning the error terms is referred to as the homoscedasticity assumption. This must always be formally tested. If this part of the assumption is not met, i.e. if the residuals do not have equal variance and are therefore heteroscedastic, there is always reason to doubt the accuracy of the results. It is advisable when testing for heteroscedasticity of the error terms to also search for outliers, i.e. to examine whether there are any respondents with scores so extreme they might distort the results.

Kleinbaum et al. (2014), in chapter 14 discuss in more detail how these assumptions can be controlled for.

2.3 Regression with a dichotomous dependent variable: logistic regression

As we mentioned above in section 2.2, one of the assumptions of regression analysis is that the dependent and independent variables are measured at interval level.

We also said that if the independent variable is dichotomous this is not a problem: When working with dichotomous independent variables these can be treated as a special kind of *fixed* interval variable. For dependent variables however, as we mentioned, this is a problem.

If the dependent variable Y is dichotomous, i.e. it has only two possible values, for example 0 and 1, a special kind of (multiple) regression analysis is needed, called a *logistic regression analysis*. Situations with a dichotomous dependent variable are very common. For example, passing or failing an exam, getting married or not getting married, being found guilty or not guilty.

Logistic regression analysis is a direct parallel of multiple regression analysis, with the proviso that rather than predicting the score of a continuous dependent variable Y, a function of the odds of scoring '1' on the dichotomous dependent variable is predicted. Whilst the estimation method and the output differ somewhat from multiple regression analysis, the interpretation of the outcome is fairly similar.

With logistic regression we have, as said, a 0/1 outcome measure: for example an individual passes an exam ('1') or does not pass it ('0'). As we said previously, with a dichotomous outcome variable we cannot use normal multiple regression. But why is that so? Why can we not just try to predict if the respondents pass or not using linear regression? There are several reasons for why this is not possible.

Firstly, the additive regression model can give nonsense predictions. We will illustrate the problem with an example. Imagine that we have a dataset where Y, the dependent variable, measures whether a respondent follows ('1') or does not follow ('0') a treatment. To keep it simple we have just one independent variable: X which measures depression on a scale from low to high. In Figure 2.1 the x axis shows the depression score, and the y axis the score on the independent variable Y.

The white circles in Figure 2.1 indicate that there is a relationship between depression and therapy: respondents with a low depression score less often follow the therapy than respondents with a high depression score. When we use OLS to try and fit the best possible straight line through each group of circles on the figure we get the result shown in the top plot in Figure 2.1. As is clear from the figure the prediction on the 0/1 dependent variable for the two respondents with the lowest depression scores is in this case less than 0, and for the two respondents with the highest depression scores this is greater than 1. This is an outcome that does not make sense.

It would be better to try and fit an S-shaped curve that indicates the likelihood of following or not following the therapy. The bend in the S-curve should be situated at the point where the chance 'swaps' over as it were, the point where the chance becomes greater that an individual will follow rather than not follow the therapy. The bottom plot in Figure 2.1 illustrates an S- shaped curve that fits these data nicely in that sense.

Figure 2.1: Example of regression with a dichotomous dependent variable

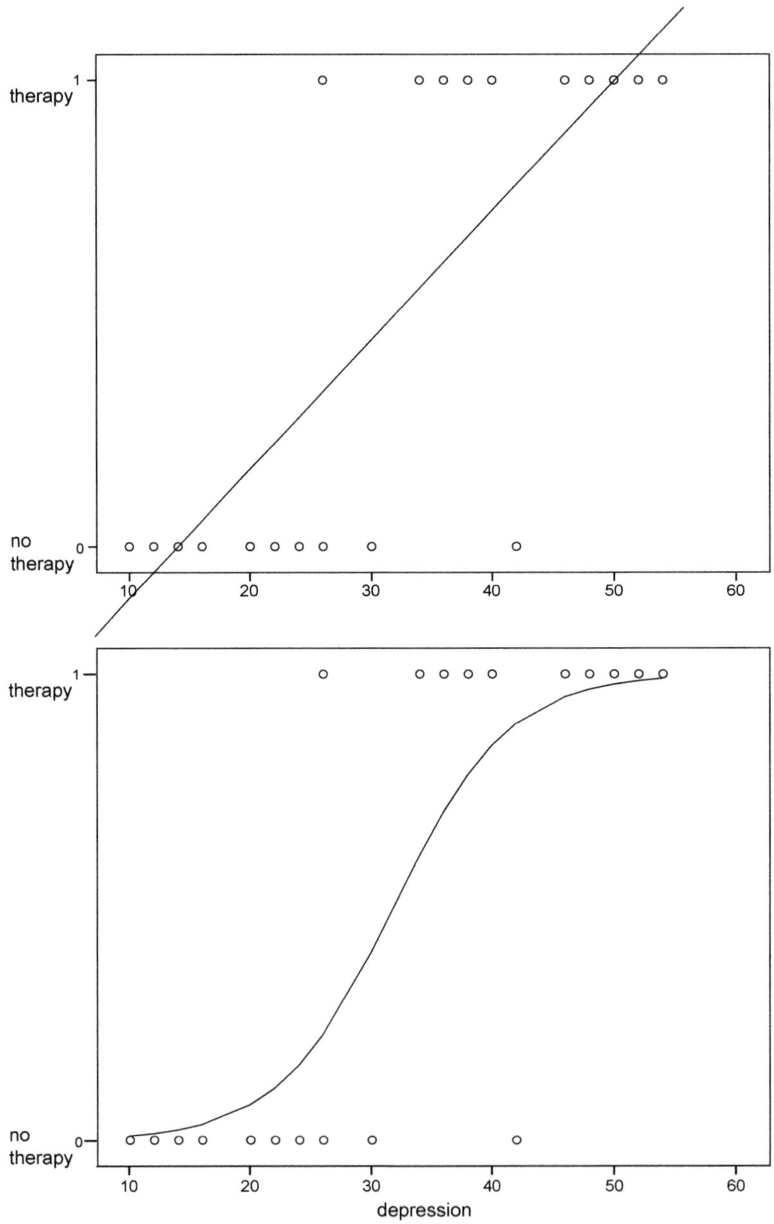

This means that we cannot predict the outcome (either '0' or '1') using a linear regression model. As the reader can easily envisage, we would run into similar problems were we to attempt to predict the chance for '1' (p) using a linear regression model: there would be no way that we can prevent ending up with predicted values above '1' or below '0', outcomes that are again nonsensical as chances are constrained to be in the 0 to 1 interval. However, the phrasing that we just used ('the chance that respondents will follow the therapy rather than not follow the therapy...'), is exactly how the so-called *odds* is phrased, a ratio of chances: $\frac{p}{1-p}$, whereby p is the chance of following and $1-p$ the chance of not following the therapy.

Is it now possible to try and use the same $\frac{p}{1-p}$ to make a prediction using a regression model? Although $\frac{p}{1-p}$ is unconstrained in how large it can be, it is restricted in how small it can be (it cannot be smaller than 0), so we could again end up with predictions that do not make (lower than 0), as the regression model is free in terms of estimating the dependent variable. It could therefore provide a negative estimate of the odds ratio. For logistic regression, this problem is now solved by not predicting $\frac{p}{1-p}$ itself, but its logarithm:

$$ln(\frac{p}{1-p}),$$

which, given that p can range from 0 to 1, ranges from $-\infty$ to ∞, so that $ln(\frac{p}{1-p})$ can be included in an unconstrained regression model as dependent variable. The $ln(\frac{p}{1-p})$ is generally written as '$logit(p)$'. In logistic regression analysis the following equation is used:

$$logit(p) = a + b_1X_{1i} + b_2X_{2i} + b_3X_{3i} + \cdots + b_kX_{ki},$$

where

$$logit(p) = ln(\frac{p}{1-p}).$$

In this regression model we have regression weights and an intercept. So what exactly is the difference between this and the regular regression model used for multiple regression analysis? In a regular multiple regression we assume that the error terms are normally distributed, and that the predictors relate to Y via a linear function (the identity function). In logistic regression we assume that the error terms are binomially distributed and that the predictors relate to the dependent variable via a logit function. There is another subtle difference. You may have noticed that there was no error term included in the regression equation above. The error term is often omitted because strictly speaking p or $logit(p)$ is not actually observed. Where in a regular multiple regression analysis we have an actual observed

Y for every respondent i, here we do not predict an observed dependent variable but a function of the zeros and ones for each of the respondents. There are of course error terms of sorts: after all we classify each respondent in either the category '0' or '1' on the dependent variable, and our prediction will never be perfect.

Now we can try to determine how large the different weights and the intercept are, and to interpret the outcomes. Rather than using the least squares method, regression coefficients in logistic regression are estimated using the *maximum likelihood* method. This estimation method finds the values for a and the b_j $(j = 1, \ldots, k)$ for which the chance of getting the observed data is greatest. In order to estimate the regression coefficients the so-called *likelihood function* is used. This function gives the chance of finding the observed data as a function of the unknown values of the parameters of the regression equation. The best estimates of the parameters are those that generate a maximum value on the likelihood function: after all it is there that the chance is largest for finding the data that we have. We are therefore looking for the maximum value of the likelihood function. In order to find the maximum value of a function normally one sets the derivative to be zero and finds the roots of the resulting equation. When using likelihood functions the maximum value is usually estimated using an iterative algorithm, whereby a number of steps are performed in order to come as closely to the maximum value of the function as possible.

For the regular user this is not really all that relevant. It is sufficient to know that, in contrast with linear regression, the maximum of the likelihood function is found using a number of steps, that with logistic regression slightly different tests are used, and that instead of R^2 another measure of fit is employed.

The alternative measure of fit in logistic regression analysis is based on the *likelihood*, i.e. the chance of observing the data given the values of a, b_1, b_2, and so on. One might think that reporting the likelihood as outcome of the estimation procedure would be useful, but this is not usually done. Researchers actually always work with -2 times the natural logarithm or the log-likelihood, written as '-2LL'. This may seem unnecessarily complicated, but there is a practical reason for doing so. The -2LL follows a χ^2-distribution, with degrees of freedom (df) equal to the number of parameters minus 1. Therefore, if we use the -2LL rather than the likelihood itself, we are able to perform tests using this distribution. We will explain how this is done.

The first test that is generally carried out in most software packages is the so-called 'overall test'. This test examines whether the analysed model fits better than a model including only the intercept (this is comparable to the overall F-test in multiple regression, see section 2.1.4). This test is used to examine whether the prediction using our model is significantly better than the prediction we would get using no variables at all. The log-likelihood of the model including just the intercept is written $log(L_0)$. The log-likelihood of our model, including for example two predictors X_1 and X_2, is written $log(L_1)$. The log of the likelihood is a negative value. Therefore the lower the value of the log, the lower the likelihood. If we then multiple the log-likelihood by -2, the opposite is true: the higher the -2LL, the worse the fit of the model. And so, the lower the -2LL, the better the model fits the data.

Because both of these log-likelihoods have a χ^2-distribution, the difference between the log-likelihoods also has a χ^2-distribution, with degrees of freedom equal to the difference between the degrees of freedom of the two models. We can therefore test whether one model gives a significantly better fit than another model.

Many statistical software packages as well as literature refer to this test as a 'likelihood *ratio* test' rather than a likelihood 'difference' test. The two are in fact equivalent as the difference between two logarithms is equal to the logarithm of their ratio.[1] Using the likelihood ratio test (also called the LR test) we are therefore able to say whether the estimated model fits significantly better than the 'null' model. This is a test comparing the performance of two models, of which one is the 'emptiest' model we can envisage, a model with no predictors. This test does not say how well the model fits in absolute terms (as it cannot answer a question like what percentage of the variability in Y has been predicted by the model).

The appeal of the LR test is however that, as well as examining whether our regression model is better than a null model, we can also examine whether regression model I (for example with predictors X_1, X_2 and X_3) fits significantly better than regression model II (which only includes predictors X_1 and X_2). If the model with X_1, X_2 and X_3 has a significantly better fit than the model with only X_1 and X_2, then we know that adding variable X_3 significantly improves the fit of the model. The likelihood ratio test can only compare so-called *nested* models. Regression models I and II above are seen as special cases of the same model. Model II has one variable fewer than model I, but apart from this they are identical. Model II fits into model I. That is why we say that model II is nested in model I, the larger model is the nest into which the smaller model fits, like a Russian *matryoshka* doll. We discuss statistics for comparing non-nested models in chapter 7.3, in the context of trajectory models

---

[1] For example:

$$^{10}log(10,000) - ^{10}log100 = 4 - 2 = 2,$$

can also be written as:

$$^{10}log(\frac{10,000}{100}) = ^{10}log(100) = 2.$$

The commands for carrying out a logistic regression in SPSS and other statistical software packages look very similar to those of regular multiple regression. With logistic regression we can also build our regression models using for instance the SPSS `BACKWARD`, `FORWARD` and `ENTER` options, i.e. either putting all the predictors in the model and removing the non-significant ones, or beginning with a significant predictor and only adding other significant predictors, or putting all the predictors in at once (see for an overview Field, 2013, Chapter 8). The considerations for choosing predictors are identical to those for multiple regression, except that software packages do not produce a VIF or other such measures. The assumptions made for logistic regression are similar to those for multiple regression, except for the strict assumption of normal distribution (instead the assumption is that the error terms have a binomial distribution) and homoscedasticity of the error terms.

In general it is recommended that when using logistic regression, the ratio of respondents to variables needs to be larger than for multiple regression. One often encountered rule of thumb is that the ratio be 30:1, so 30 times as many respondents as variables used in the logistic regression model. This ratio is however a coarse rule of thumb.

Firstly, without going into detail why, larger sample sizes are needed for logistic regression than for multiple regression because maximum likelihood is used. Furthermore, research has demonstrated that if the sample size is under 500, the odds ratios from logistic regression are overestimated. If the sample is too small, we might therefore end up with an optimistic estimate of our effect sizes. Research has also shown that the significances of the effects are not generally overestimated. Some authors recommend as the rule of thumb that for every independent variable which is included at least 10 '*events*' from the least frequently occurring event in the dependent variable should be available. We illustrate this with an example. Imagine that there are 600 respondents in a dataset, and of those 600 respondents 100 failed their exam and 500 passed. The least frequently occurring event is therefore failing. Using this rule of thumb, for each independent variable we would need to have at least 10 failures. This means that if one were to carry out a logistic regression on this dataset 10 independent X variables could be included (with a total of 100 events there would be 10 events per independent variable). If the number of failures had been 300, then 30 predictors could have been included. The ratio of 30:1 is therefore a rough and possibly (too) generous rule of thumb that can certainly be made more specific.

In order to evaluate the performance of the logistic regression model we generally first examine the so-called *classification table*. This table tells us what percentage of respondents were correctly classified by the model. Respondents are placed by the technique in the '0' category or the '1' category on the dependent variable

Y. This is their estimated Y score. Of course, respondents have also a measured, a real Y score. The tabulation of these observed and estimated Y scores generates the classification table.

How are the scores on the dependent variable estimated by the model? Earlier, we stated that the model does not predict Y itself but a function of the odds of Y, so how then does it arrive at estimated Y scores? We will explain this with a simple example. As said, the logistic regression analysis estimates the model coefficients by optimizing the likelihood function. In doing so it may find that respondents with a high score on depression are more likely to follow treatment than respondents with a low score on depression. For instance, of those with a depression score of 1 only 10% are in therapy, of those with a score of 2 altogether 25% are in therapy, of those with a depression score of 3 exactly 50% are in therapy, and of those with a depression score of 4, the majority, 85% are in therapy. The technique will now assign everyone a so-called '*propensity score*', that is, a score for the chance that that respondent follows therapy. Those with a depression score of 1 receive a propensity score of .10, those with 2 get .25, those with 3 get .50 and those with a score of 4 get a propensity score of .85. Based on the distribution of therapy in the data and these propensity scores, the technique classifies respondents. In this example, the technique will likely estimate that those with score below 3 on the independent variable are not following therapy, and those with score of 3 or higher are following therapy. We can subsequently compare the classification provided by the model with the actual classification of respondents and examine what percent the model has correctly classified. This example reasons from just one independent variable (depression score), but the idea can easily be extended. Every time, the technique assesses what percentage of respondents with a certain profile on the independent variables score '1' on the dependent variable and assigns all respondents that share this profile an identical propensity score. Above a certain cutoff – that depends on the distribution of Y – respondents are assigned a predicted value of '0' or '1'.

Besides the classification table, output generally also provides the 'Nagelkerke R^2', also referred to as pseudo R^2. The Nagelkerke R^2 indicates how much variation of the dependent variable is explained by the model. As in logistic regression it is a function of Y that is predicted and not Y itself, the measure is called 'pseudo', and gives only an indication of model fit. The *Hosmer and Lemeshow-test*, which is by many regarded a better measure of the performance of the model, indicates whether the residuals from the prediction statistically differ from 0. One wants this χ^2-test – contrary to what is usually the case – to be *not* significant: the smaller the error terms the better the prediction, so one wants the test to indicate that the residuals do not differ from zero. It is recommended to examine the residuals for outliers (people with extreme error values). In addition most statistical software packages give the likelihood ratio test (often called 'Model chi-square'), that is roughly χ^2-distributed with degrees of freedom equal to the number of predictors. This test, comparable to the overall F-test in regular linear multiple regression, indicates the extent to which the estimated model differs from the null model, i.e. the model which includes only the intercept and in which all the regression coefficients b are equal to 0.

In order to ascertain the contribution of each predictor variable we generally examine whether the values of the regression coefficients significantly differ from 0, as we would for regular regression analysis. Whereas multiple regression analysis does this using a t-test, logistic regression does this using a *Wald test*, a test which also roughly follows a χ^2 distribution. An alternative for the Wald test is the likelihood ratio test which is used in the `BACKWARD` and `FORWARD` options in SPSS. For smaller sample sizes, however, the Wald test is preferred.

Generally, statistical software packages also report the 'exp(B)' in the output, i.e. the exponentiated regression coefficient. The exp(B) is interpreted just as we would an odds ratio. Imagine we found that the b of a variable indicating 'drug use' is equal to 0.30. The exponential of this is $e^{.30} = 1.35$. This means that, if drug use is coded as '1' and no drug use coded as '0', the 'risk' of the outcome for people who use drugs is increased by 35%. Besides the 'exp(B)' the confidence interval of the odds ratio is generally also given.

If we estimate a logistic regression model with more than one predictor X_j, we often refer to the odds ratio calculated for each variable as the *adjusted odds ratio*, because this odds ratio gives (for a dichotomous variable X_j) the odds for the outcome for being in category '1' as compared to being in category '0', whilst taking into account the other predictors $X_1, X_2, \ldots, X_{j-1}, X_{j+1}, \ldots, X_k$ in the model.

2.4 Regression with a dependent count variable

To answer certain empirical questions, '*count*' data may be encountered. Count data are data which indicate how often something happens, for example the number of goals scored in a football match, the number of divorces per individual, the number of a certain kind of trees in a field, or the number of convictions. Count data are often collected when events are rare.

Count data are whole numbers or integers (the number of times something happens), that can never be smaller than zero. One of the characteristics of count data is that they are skewed, i.e. the tail of the count is long on the right and high on the left (which is limited by zero). Furthermore the number of zeros (the number of times the event does not occur) is mostly large. In many cases researchers with skewed count data just run a regular regression analysis. Either they inspect the distribution

Figure 2.2: Example of the distribution of contacts with the police in the Dutch population

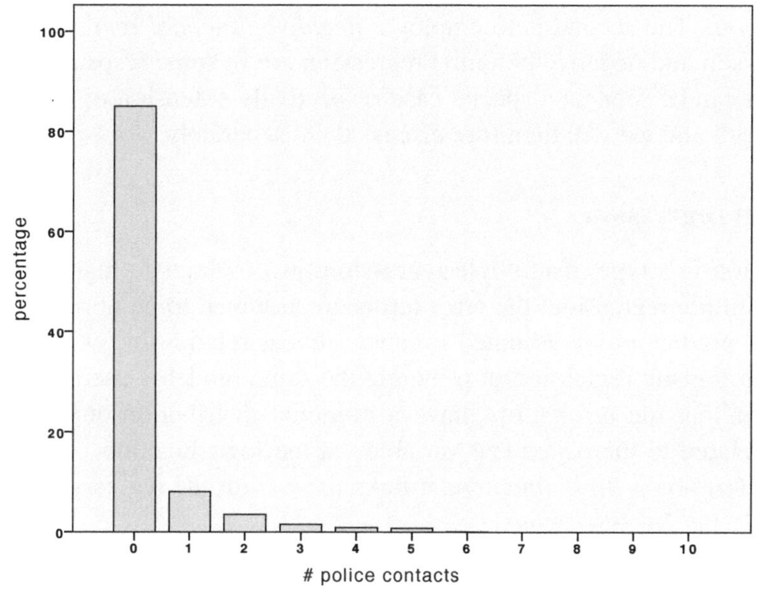

of the error terms and decide that these do not significantly differ from a normal distribution, or they transform the dependent variable, for example by taking the square root of the observations. Count data are however in many cases so skewed that transforming the data does not help. If we were to use the square root (leaving aside fundamental questions as to whether the square root of 0 exists), even after transformation the distribution of the data would remain extremely skewed, see for an example Figure 2.2. This figure illustrates a hypothetical example showing the distribution of the number of times members of the Dutch population come into contact with the police. If we were to take the square root of the observations Y, $\sqrt{Y}$, the right-hand side of the distribution would be pushed towards the left, but the left-hand side would remain heavily skewed.

In cases such as this, transforming the dependent variable is not going to suffice. The dependent variable is so skewed that the normality assumption of the error terms that is central to linear regression analysis will be well and truly violated. Whilst the demand for normality refers to the error terms and not the dependent variable, it is clear that the distribution of the dependent variable has a big influence on the distribution of the error terms. If the error terms are not normally distributed we cannot trust the parameter estimates or tests from regular multiple regression. When we have extremely skewed variables, carrying out a regular linear regression analysis is therefore generally ill-advised.

When we have skewed data there are two solutions. The first is to employ a *Poisson regression.* The second is to employ a *negative binomial regression.* As we will see Poisson and negative binomial regression are in some respects similar as well, as each can be seen as a special case respectively extension of the other. They differ as well and we will therefore discuss them separately.

2.4.1 Poisson regression

Poisson regression is a type of multiple regression, just as logistic regression is. With regular multiple regression, the error terms are assumed to be normally distributed and the predictors are assumed to have a linear relationship with Y. As we discussed, in logistic regression in principle the same model is used, with the proviso however that the error terms have a binomial distribution and that the predictors are related to the dependent variable via the logit function. This logit function – $logit(p)$ – is a *'link' function*: it links the Y with the regression model $a+b_1X_{1i}+b_2X_{2i}+b_3X_{3i}+\cdots+b_kX_{ki}$.

In Poisson regression we assume that the error terms follow a *Poisson distribution,* and that the scores of the predictors X are related to the dependent variable Y via the logarithmic function. Here too we have a model which at its core does not differ from the multiple regression model, but does require two adjustments: a different distribution for the error terms and a specific link function. The model is as follows:

$$ln(Y)=a+b_1X_1+b_2X_2+b_3X_3+\cdots+b_kX_k,$$

with Y the dependent variable, $X_1,X_2,\ldots$ the independent variables and $b_1,b_2,\ldots$ the regression coefficients. The link function is the function $ln(Y)$.

The equation for a Poisson regression is therefore as follows:

$$ln(Y_i)=a+b_1X_{1i}+b_2X_{2i}+b_3X_{3i}+\cdots+b_kX_{ki}+e_i,$$

and the assumption concerning the error terms is that they have a Poisson distribution. Using the link function $ln(Y)$ has as a big advantage that we will not encounter problems with 'nonsensical' Y estimates. If we tried to estimate Y itself we might have a situation whereby the predicted Y score would be -4. This is of course impossible because Y is a count variable – the regression model is *unrestricted,* which means that these kinds of outcomes can happen. This is solved by using $ln(Y)$ and not Y as our dependent variable. Estimates of $ln(Y)$ are still unrestricted but this is no longer a problem because by estimating Y using its exponential function, the Y estimate can never be smaller than 0.

We said that the error terms are now assumed to be Poisson distributed, but what exactly is a Poisson distribution? A Poisson distribution indicates the chance of k events happening in a specified period of time, space, etc. The Poisson distribution is mainly used to describe the distribution of rare events, such as accidents, convictions or epidemics.

Employing a cheerful illustration let us say that we have a field with on average 2 flowers per square meter, and let us assume that the blossoming of the flowers follows a Poisson distribution. As we use the Poisson distribution we can work out what the chance is that we would find 3 blossoming flowers in one square meter of that field. According to the distribution, the chance of finding k blossoming flowers in an interval or unit where on average we find λ blossoming flowers is equal to:

$$p(k|\lambda) = \frac{\lambda^k e^{-\lambda}}{k!},$$

where e is the base of the natural logarithm ($e = 2.718281828...$), k the number of times an event occurs, and λ the expected number of events in the interval. In our example the mean number of blossoming flowers is 2, therefore λ equals 2. The question is what is the chance of finding 3 blossoming flowers, i.e. $k = 3$. We can use the formula above to work this out:

$$p(3|2) = \frac{2^3 \times e^{-2}}{3 \times 2 \times 1} = \frac{8 \times 0.13533}{6} = 0.180447.$$

In the same way we can work out that the chance of finding 0 flowers (equal to 0.135335), of finding 1 flower (equal to 0.270671), of finding 2 flowers (equal to 0.270671), 4 flowers (0.090224), 5 flowers (0.0360894), and so on. See Figure 2.4.

It is clear from this figure that whilst our data are skewed, they are not as skewed as the data in Figure 2.2. This is not surprising, as the mean number of blossoming flowers λ is 2. Indeed, usually as λ increases the data become less skewed. In fact, once $\lambda = 10$ the Poisson distribution is practically the same as a normal distribution. See Figure 2.5 for examples of the distributions related to different λ values ($\lambda = 1, 2, 4$ of 10).

When λ is small (the smallest in the figure is 1) the distribution is very skewed. This is logical: because the mean is small, there must be very many observations clustering to the left of 1, the left-hand side of the tail, i.e. on 0, in order to balance the distribution. As λ increases, the distribution becomes less skewed. The number of times an event occurs, k, is always an integer, i.e. 0, 1, 2, ... The lines joining

The Poisson distribution is named after Siméon-Denis Poisson (1781-1840), a solicitor's son from Pitviers. When he was 15 years old he went to study medicine, but his very first patient from whom he had to let blood died on the spot. He was so disappointed he gave up his studies. Shortly afterwards he happened upon the journal of the École Polytechnique in Fontainebleau. The young Poisson turned out to be an extremely talented mathematician. By the time he was 18 years old he had graduated from the school. He has worked with all the greats of mathematics and formulated a number of still important laws and functions.

In 1835, in completing a work by Moivre, he came up with the 'Law of Large Numbers'. This law describes the pattern of random events with a small chance of occurring, for a large number of observations. Poisson tried with little success to convince juries of the applicability of this law.

Figure 2.3: Siméon-Denis Poisson (1781-1840)

Figure 2.4: Poisson distribution for the chance of finding k = 0, 1, 2, 3, ... blossoming flowers when $\lambda = 2$

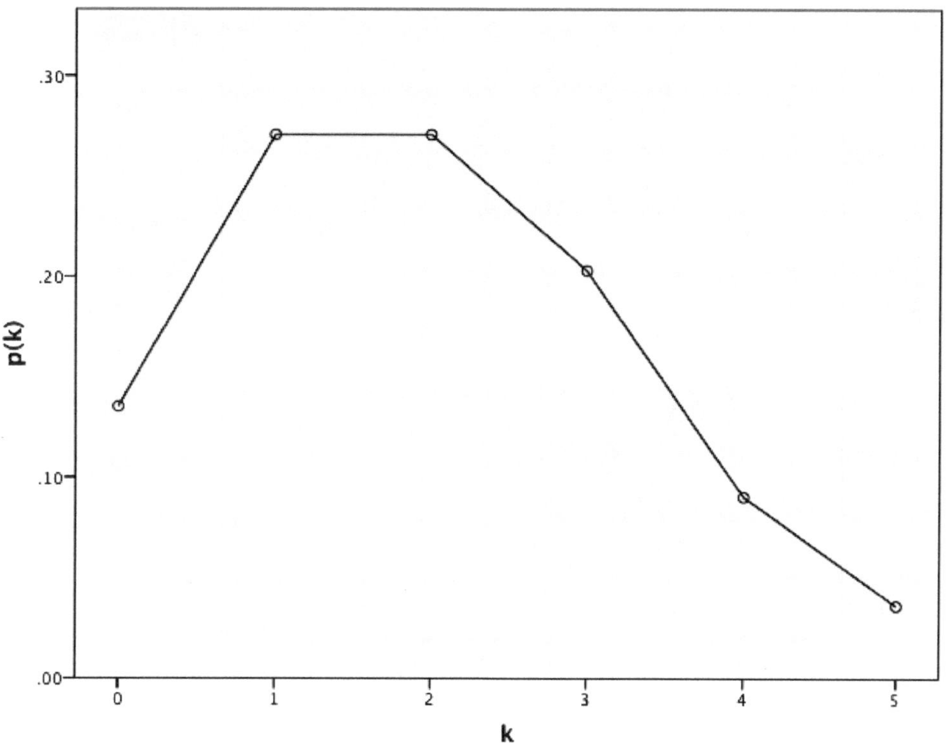

up each discrete value of k in Figure 2.2 are there for easy interpretability and have no meaning.

One of the characteristics of a Poisson distribution is that the mean μ is equal to the variance σ^2. The mean and the variance are thus both equal to λ. In practice, however, the variance is often greater than the mean. This is referred to as *overdispersion.* It is also possible for the variance to be smaller than the mean. We refer to this as *underdispersion.* In cases of over- or underdispersion, the distribution is not a Poisson distribution anymore. We then usually switch to using a negative binomial distribution (we will discuss this later in the chapter).

So how do we go about carrying out a regression if the data are Poisson distributed? In SPSS or one of other statistical software packages, we choose the option for Poisson regression (in SPSS this is called `GENLIN`, in SAS `GENMOD` and in Stata simply 'poisson') and specify the model we wish to estimate, naming

Figure 2.5: Poisson distribution with $\lambda = 1, 2, 4$ en 10

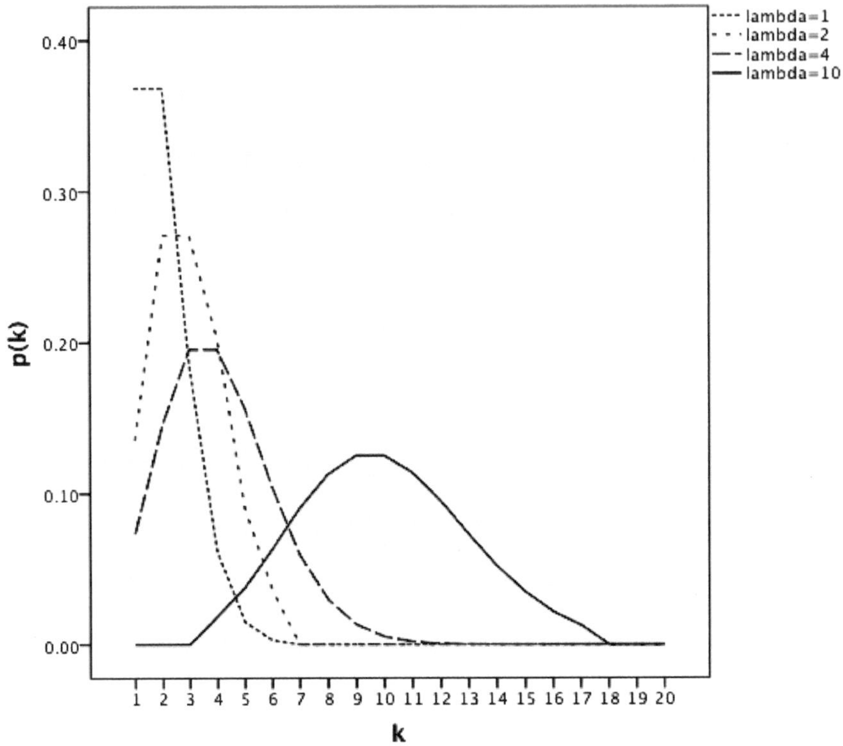

the predictors we aim to use. Again the same considerations regarding choice of predictors as for multiple and logistic regression need to be made: we want to find a model that fits well and is parsimonious.

After estimating our model we can examine the model fit using the *deviance*, which most statistical software packages report. The deviance is -2 times the difference in *log-likelihood* between the chosen model and the *full model* (also referred to as the *saturated model*), i.e. a model with a parameter for each observation. This may seem like a cumbersome new statistic, but remember we said we can compare the deviance of the null model (i.e. how much the fit of the null model deviates from a perfectly fitted model) with the deviance of the model we have just estimated (i.e. how much the fit of our model deviates from a perfectly fitted model). As we discussed earlier when referring to logistic regression, the difference in deviance of the two models has a χ^2 distribution, with degrees of freedom equal to the difference in degrees of freedom between the two models. This means

Many years later, in 1898, Ladislaus von Bortkiewicz, knowing nothing of Poisson's earlier publications, described exactly the same law. He called it the Law of Small Numbers. He applied the law to two datasets, one which described the distribution of the accidental deaths of 14 Prussian soldiers by horse kick between 1875 and 1894, and the other of suicides by German children under the age of 10 over a number of years. He did not only put the law into words, but showed that the distribution practically exactly described the pattern of accidents and suicides. Some people believe that the Poisson distribution should actually be called the 'Bortkiewicz' distribution.

Figure 2.6: Ladislaus von Bortkiewicz (1868-1931)

that we can in this manner also find out whether out model fits better than the null model without variables. Most software packages report the two values and their respective degrees of freedom. If the model we have built has a significantly better deviance than the null model we generally conclude that our model fits the data.

Besides comparing the null model with our estimated model we can again also compare the performance of nested models with different combinations of predictor variables, just as we can do for logistic regression. In this way we can test whether a model including the predictor variables age, addiction problems, and gender better predicts the number of offences post treatment than a model including just age and addiction problems. This is possible because the two models are *nested*. The second model (with just the predictors age and addiction problems) fits 'into' the first model (with predictors age, addiction problems and gender) as the second model is a simpler version of the first. (If we were to test a model predicting number of offences using addiction problems and ADHD this would not be nested in either the first or second model.) The difference in deviance for the two models just described has a χ^2 distribution with 1 degree of freedom (adding the gender variable means that there is one degree of freedom difference between the first and second model).

In order to determine whether the model meets the assumptions and can be interpreted safely, we examine the error terms. Most statistical software packages have an option to save the error terms. A first thing to do is to look for outliers, people with extreme error terms. Next it is advisable to check whether the error terms have a Poisson distribution, as is assumed for this kind of model. One way to test for this is simply to calculate the variance of the error terms. The variance should be equal to λ. It can be that the variance is smaller than λ, in which case we say that there is underdispersion. If we have good reason to believe that this is the case, i.e. our data are not actually Poisson distributed, we should instead use a different kind of regression (but see Berk and MacDonald, 2007), one that is suitable for modelling variables with a different distribution. One such alternative is a negative binomial regression.

If the variance is larger than the mean λ, we have overdispersion. A number of issues can cause overdispersion and we will now zoom in two of these. The first is that the dependent variable simply does not have a Poisson distribution, and therefore neither do the error terms. As we mentioned above, the distribution of the dependent variable has a large influence on the distribution of the error terms. In this case, we should used a different type of regression model. A second, more problematic explanation is, however, that the data are actually Poisson distributed, but that the model is misspecified. We will explain how this can result in error variance that is too high.

One of the consequences of leaving predictors which play an important role in predicting Y out of our regression model, is that the error terms no longer behave as we expect, since our prediction of Y is poor. To envisage this, remember that if we use a linear regression function when the relationship between the dependent variable Y and the predictor variable X is in fact quadratic, we also get error terms which do not have the expected distribution. In this example it is easy to imagine that the error terms' variance would be strangely distributed: for small X values a far too large Y value would be predicted and consequently we would have very high positive error terms, for large X values a far too small Y value would be predicted and consequently we would have very high negative error terms. In the case of a misspecified Poisson regression it is similarly possible that the error term variance, in the same manner, becomes too large. Determining exactly what the cause is of a λ that is higher than expected, and whether it is this second issue that is causing the problem, is not easy.

2.4.2 Negative binomial regression

The negative binomial regression model is very similar to that of the Poisson regression. In fact the model looks exactly the same as that for a Poisson regression model:

$$ln(Y) = a + b_1X_1 + b_2X_2 + b_3X_3 + \cdots + b_kX_k,$$

where Y is the dependent variable, $X_1, X_2, \ldots$ are the independent variables, and $b_1, b_2, \ldots$ are the regression coefficients. The link function is again $ln(Y)$, and here too it has the same advantages as described above for the Poisson model. However, the assumption relating to the error terms is that they follow a *negative binomial* distribution.

The negative binomial distribution is an extension to the Poisson distribution, which applies when the variance of the distribution is not equal to the mean. One could also say that a Poisson distribution is a special kind of negative binomial distribution, namely the case where the mean and the variance are equal.

The outcome of a negative binomial distribution, just as with a Poisson distribution, is a whole number. With a Poisson distribution Y measured the number of rare events happening within a certain interval. With a negative binomial distribution, Y is the number of attempts N necessary to achieve m successes. For example, the number of times needed to roll a dice in order to throw a '6' twice. The phrasing is therefore slightly different for a negative binomial than for a Poisson distribution. Instead of talking about 'successes' in one interval, we talk about the number of attempts necessary to achieve a certain number of successes. This slightly different approach is exactly why it is somewhat trickier to compare the models using formulas (and doing so requires some rather complicated mathematics, which we will not do as that goes beyond the scope of the current publication).

The number of attempts N necessary to achieve m successfully is described thus:

$$p(N|p,m) = \binom{N-1}{m-1} p^m (1-p)^{N-m}$$

where p is the chance of success, m the number of successes (or successful attempts), and N the number of attempts. If we have m successful attempts, and if we reach the mth success at the Nth attempt, it means that N-1 attempts have already been carried out. By the Nth attempt we have achieved the mth successful attempt, meaning that $m-1$ successful attempts have already occurred. This is why the formula is calculated using $N-1$ attempts over $m-1$ successful attempts.

The mean of the distribution is equal to:

$$\frac{m}{p}$$

and the variance is equal to:

$$\frac{(1-p)}{p^2}.$$

We will use another example to illustrate the formula. Say we want to know what the distribution is for the chance of throwing a '6' twice on a dice. The chance of throwing a '6' is $\frac{1}{6}$. Because we want to know how often we need to roll the dice in order to throw a '6' twice, m is equal to 2. So what is then the probability that in 12 throws we will throw two '6's? The formula we need is:

$$p(N|p,m) = p(12|0.166666...,2) = \binom{12-1}{2-1}(\frac{1}{6})^2(1-\frac{1}{6})^{12-2} =$$

$$\binom{11}{1}(\frac{1}{6})^2(\frac{5}{6})^{10} = 11 \times \frac{1}{36} \times (\frac{5}{6})^{10} = \frac{11 \times 0.1615}{36} = 0.0493.$$

Intuitively this chance seems very small. If the chance of throwing one '6' is one in 6, we would after all expect to have to throw a dice roughly 12 times in order to get two times '6'? However, remember this is the probability of throwing exactly 12 times and getting exactly two times a '6'.

The number we just calculated was the chance of exactly getting a certain outcome for a specific number of throws. The negative binomial distribution now gives the chances for all possible N: in this example the chance of throwing a '6'

Figure 2.7: Negative binomial distribution of the chance of N = 2, 3, 4, 5, ... attempts leading to 2 successful attempts, when $p = 0.4$

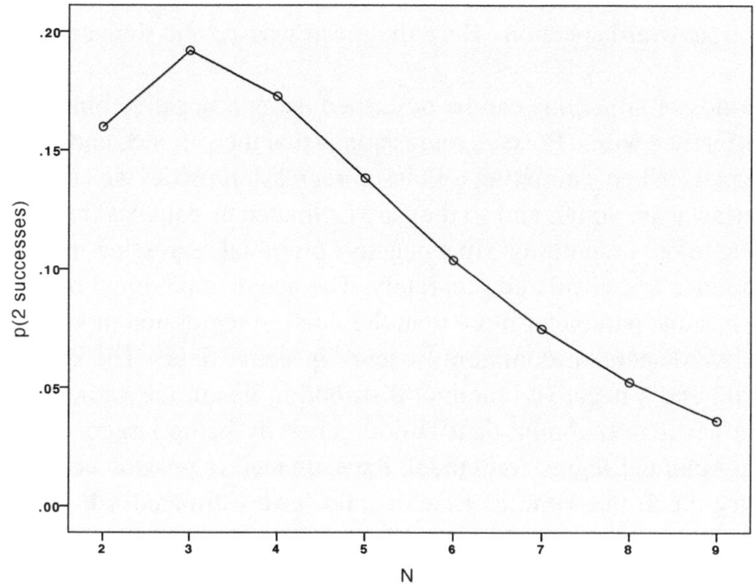

twice when rolling the dice twice, the chance of throwing a '6' twice when rolling the dice three times, the chance of throwing a '6' twice when rolling the dice four times, and so on. From all these chances we can create a distribution function.

Figure 2.7 is an example of the distribution function. The y axis indicates the chance that in N attempts (shown on the x axis) we will have m successful attempts. We changed the example somewhat and describe the number of attempts necessary to achieve two successful attempts, when the chance of this success is 0.4. Notice that the x axis begins at 2, because of course we need to have thrown at least twice to achieve two successful attempts.

In this last example the distribution mean is equal to:

$$\frac{m}{p} = \frac{2}{0.4} = 5$$

and the variance is equal to:

$$\frac{(1-p)}{p^2} = \frac{(1-0.4)}{0.4^2} = 3.75.$$

Here we see that overdispersion is not the case but *underdispersion* is, i.e. the variance is smaller than the mean. We can see this by looking at Figure 2.7: in this plot the chances are not extremely skewed on the right-hand side as we would expect to see for overdispersion. They actually decrease quite steadily. The example that we used earlier (the number of attempts N necessary to throw a '6' twice) does illustrate overdispersion. Here the mean was 12 and the variance 30, much higher.

Both these kinds of situations can be described using a negative binomial regression. The difference with a Poisson regression is that the variance and mean do not need to be equal. When estimating a Poisson regression model we assume we the mean and variance are equal, and so they are estimated as equal as that is what they are according to our assumption. In a negative binomial regression model, the mean and the variance are calculated separately. The negative binomial regression model therefore has one parameter more than the Poisson regression model.

In practice, overdispersion commonly occurs in count data. The difference between a Poisson and a negative binomial distribution lies in the variance, with the variance of a negative binomial distribution generally being larger. If we estimate a negative binomial regression model, the estimated regression coefficients will remain pretty much the same as if we would have estimated a Poisson regression model, as the means of the two distributions do not differ. However, because the variance in the two distributions does differ, the significance levels of a Poisson regression and a negative binomial regression may likely differ. With overdispersion (the variance is greater than is assumed for Poisson distribution) the regression weights are less likely to be significant. A Poisson regression in case of overdispersion would be too quick to conclude that effects are significant. With underdispersion we get the opposite situation. Here a Poisson regression would overestimate the variance and therefore underestimate the significance of the findings, and the conclusions would be too conservative. This shows that the choice between a Poisson and a negative binomial regression is not simply a cosmetic choice. Choosing one or the other can influence whether effects are found to be significant or not. This is of enormous importance in the context of, for example, evaluating interventions.

We can carry out negative binomial regression analysis using different software packages, although the choice is not as extensive as for other regression analyses. There is at the time of writing of this textbook no option to do a negative binomial regression in SPSS. We need to therefore use Stata (command `nbreg`) or SAS (command `GENMOD`, this command specifies that we have a negative binomial distribution). Here too the same considerations concerning choice of predictors as for multiple, logistic and Poisson regression apply. After we have estimated our model we can examine the model fit using the likelihood ratio test. We use this test to ex-

Table 2.1: Regression models with a link function and error term assumptions

regression models	link function	distribution of error terms
multiple regression	identity function	normal
logistic regression	logit function	binomial
Poisson regression	logarithmic function	Poisson
negative binomial regression	logarithmic function	negative binomial

amine if the estimated model describes the data significantly better than a model with only the intercept (the null model). Because the null model is nested inside our estimated model, 2 times the difference in likelihood of the two models (the deviance) again has a χ^2 distribution with degrees of freedom equal to the difference in degrees of freedom of the two models. Most statistical software packages report the two values as well as the respective degrees of freedom. If the extended model has a better fit compared to the null model we can conclude that we a model with good fit.

For negative binomial regression too, as well as comparing the null model, we can compare the performance of different combinations of predictor variables. Again the criterion is that the models are nested. If the models are not nested then other measures of fit can be employed. We discuss these in chapter 7.3 in the context of trajectory models.

In Table 2.1 we outline all of the regression models we have so far discussed.

As Table 2.1 shows, the various regression models actually form a family of regression models, that share the same basic regression model, but differ with respect to the link function employed and the distribution of the error terms. This 'family' of models is referred as generalized linear models, first introduced by Nelder and Wedderburn (1972), and described more extensively in McCullagh and Nelder (1989).

2.4.3 The *zero-inflated* extension to a model

In a number of situations neither a Poisson model nor a negative binomial regression will describe the data well. The most well known of these is a situation where we have too many zeros, so-called *excess zeros*. What do we mean by this? We will use an example to illustrate.

Say we want to predict how many cigarettes people smoke in a day, using a regular sample of the Dutch population. Once we have carried out our survey, if we were to plot the number of smoked cigarettes we would likely to end up with a figure that looks very similar to that in Figure 2.2. Roughly a quarter of the population smokes, and therefore three quarters of the population will answer that they smoke 0 cigarettes per day. Of the smokers there are likely to be some social smokers, who have days where they do not smoke any cigarettes. There will probably also be a large number of people who smoke about one packet a day, on the right-hand side of the plot, and then there will be a few chain smokers who light up every six minutes and manage to fit 160 cigarettes into 16 waking hours of the day.

This sort of data follow neither a Poisson distribution nor a negative binomial distribution. It is therefore inappropriate to carry out either one of these two regressions. A more crucial issue is however that these data likely do not have one but two different distributions, i.e. they relate to two different populations. There is a group of smokers and a group of non-smokers. All the non-smokers score '0' for the question of how many cigarettes they smoke per day. They will always score '0' because they are non-smokers. Consequently the non-smokers have in a sense their own distribution. The smokers on the other hand may score between 0 (a smoker can happen to have a day where no cigarettes are smoked) and 160, and therefore their smoking pattern conforms to a different distribution. The two distributions hardly overlap, and for each of the two categories of respondents the distribution of the other category is completely inappropriate. It would therefore be inadvisable to estimate a model for these two types of respondents together and to try and force their patterns of smoking behaviour into one distribution. We therefore should not analyse this sample in one regression model.

For situations such as these we need to use a *mixture model*. A mixture model assumes that two different processes have generated the data. For each of these two processes a separate (regression) model is estimated. In our example, one regression model would be estimated to predict whether somebody is a smoker or not, and then another separate model would be estimated to predict how many cigarettes somebody smokes. The first part can be done using a logistic regression model (where, as we know, we predict a dichotomous outcome). The second part can be estimated using either the Poisson regression or the negative binomial regression model.

When we use a combination of two models in this way we add the term *'zero-inflated'*, to indicate that we explicitly model the fact that part of the respondents score '0' on the dependent variable and respondents from the other part need not. The Poisson version becomes a *zero-inflated* Poisson regression (or ZIP for short), and the negative binomial version becomes a *zero-inflated* negative binomial regression (or ZINB for short).

Because we are using separate regression models for the 0/1 prediction and the count data this means that we also get separate output for both models. It is possible for example that one variable predicts being a smoker or not being a smoker, but does not predict the number of cigarettes smoked in a day. Other variables may on the other hand predict the number of cigarettes that people smoke.

Procedures for carrying out ZIP and ZINB are available in Stata and SAS. The statistical quality of any estimated model is again judged using the likelihood ratio test. This test is an all-encompassing test which examines both the logistic and the count parts of the regression. The so called *Vuong* test indicates whether a zero-inflated regression model is statistically better than a regular, not zero-inflated, Poisson or negative binomial regression model.

An extremely instructive explanation of all four models (Poisson, negative binomial, ZIP and ZINB), including detailed examples without too many formulas, can be found in Atkind and Gallop (2007). For a very instructive website with explanations regarding the practical application of all kinds of regression models in all kinds of software packages (SPSS, SAS, Stata, as well as Mplus) visit www.ats.ucla.edu/stat/spss/output/.

2.5 Regression models for dependent variables with other distributions

Besides Poisson regression, negative binomial regression, and the two extended versions of these with the zero-inflated addition, there are a number of other different regression models which apply to data with other special characteristics. We will briefly discuss some of these.

As well as logistic regression, probit regression belongs to the same family of regression models for dichotomous outcome variables. *Probit regression* looks very similar to logistic regression, and the outcomes of both are often practically identical. The difference with logistic regression is found in the link function, as in the probit regression this is slightly different. The only difference is found in the tail of the distribution. With probit regression the S-shaped curve which is fitted to the odds is slightly steeper and therefore bends more sharply on the left- and right-hand side of the distribution than in a logistic regression, see Figure 2.1. Differences between logit and probit regression lie in statistical intricacies that we will not go into here.

Tobit regression models are used when the dependent variable is a positive integer. These models are able to accommodate the fact that the Y variable is constrained. They derive their name from their discoverer Tobin whose name combines with probit to arrive at 'tobit'. These regression models are able to deal with the fact that the data are in a sense 'censored': for instance wages cannot be lower than 0 and are generally constrained to be not below the minimum wage. Tobit regression is also encountered as 'censored regression'.

Multinomial regression can be used to predict outcomes on categorical variables that have several categories. Multinomial regression is therefore an extension of logistic regression (and logistic regression is a special case of multinomial regression, namely for cases where the categorical outcome variable only has two categories). Also, many statistical software packages also provide an option to predict *ordinal* categorical outcome variables. This is referred to as *ordinal logistic regression* or *ordinal regression.*

The last regression model we will mention is for data which is *'truncated'* or *capped.* Imagine one wanted to predict age from people's voting behaviour. The dependent variable age is 'capped' at 18 years, people are only allowed to start voting at the age of 18. The dependent variable is therefore abruptly cut off at the bottom. A special kind of truncated data is *zero-truncated* data. *Zero-truncated* data are data whereby it is impossible for a variable to equal '0'. An example is if one would want to predict how many days people stay in hospital using a whole range of different characteristics. Even if the data have a Poisson distribution, it is however impossible to have spent 0 days in hospital (because if that were the case the person would not be in the dataset). A regular regression can however generate as an estimate '0' which would in reality be impossible. A zero-truncated regression model takes this kind of impossibility into account.

Stata and SAS provide the most options for carrying out these kinds of special regression analyses. Scott Long (2007) provides a very readable overview of the most important alternative regression analyses.

2.6 Some more statistics basics

In reviewing the different regression models above we have mostly focussed on issues concerning model specification as well as practical concerns, such as what is the model, why would you choose one technique over another, etc. A regression model, as with other models, is however based on various aspects of statistical theory. In the final sections of this chapter we will provide a brief overview of relevant statistical theory.

All the regression models we have discussed are concerned with estimating regression coefficients. And every now and then we have used the term 'estimate' or 'estimating'. But what do we mean by 'estimate' and by 'estimating'? In statistical books the section on estimating usually discusses finding an estimate (a number) for a certain parameter (a characteristic of the population) based on data from the sample. We nearly always work with samples. A good estimate of the population mean μ using a certain variable is, given a number of conditions relating to how the sample is selected, M, the sample mean. The sample mean is then the 'estimator', and the estimator produces the actual number that we end up with, for example 103.5.

In the same way, in regression analysis we are trying to estimate population values. We assume that the population has a certain regression weight β (a rather confusing symbol to use, as the standardised regression weight is also indicated using 'β'!), and that we estimate this regression weight using the chosen regression model. Here again we assume that our use of the sample weight *b* (again confusing because this symbol is also used for the unstandardised regression weight!) as an estimator for the population regression weight is correct. Basically we are assuming that the sample value *b* is a good estimator for the population value β. Taking into account respective differences, this is also what we do for the population intercept α and the sample intercept *a*. But how do we know that *a* and *b* are good estimators? What exactly is a good estimator? What conditions must an estimator meet to be judged as 'good'?

Statistics is the science of uncertainty. This uncertainty comes from working with samples. We cannot, for a myriad of reasons, research the entire population. Working with samples means working with incomplete information. There are rules and recommendations in statistics which help us to cope with the uncertainty as well as possible. They help us draw the best possible conclusions regarding a population using incomplete information. In the following section we will elaborate on what 'the best possible' is for a number of different criteria related to the estimators in our regression models.

2.6.1 Variance and bias

Take again the simple case of a population mean μ and an estimate of that population mean M, itself often written as $\bar{X}$:

$$\bar{X} = \sum_{i=1}^{N} \frac{X_i}{N}.$$

Our situation, in estimating the population mean, is that we have an unknown population parameter μ, and the sample value $\bar{X}$, that we use to infer something about μ. $\bar{X}$ is therefore an estimator. It is the instrument with which we will infer something about μ. In general we want an estimator to have two properties. We want the estimator to be unbiased and we want it to be accurate. We will explain what this means.

There is a population, with an population mean μ. From this population we can draw different samples. Every sample will be slightly different, which means that the estimate of the population mean will also be slightly different every time. In one case the sample mean might be 103.7, in another it is 103.2, then 103.4, and then again 103.5. This is not a problem, it is merely an inherent fact from working with samples.

A pure or *'unbiased'* estimator is an estimator that will give us an estimate of the population mean that is, on average, exactly the same as the population mean. Formulated differently, if we would draw a very large number of samples from our population, then took the mean of the sample means, we would end up with exactly the population mean. Loosely put, we can accept that our unbiased estimator varies somewhat (we are after all using samples) but we want our estimator to be on average close to (and in fact: equal to) the population mean. This is what we refer to as an *'unbiased'* estimator. We do not want our estimator to be systematically wrong, either systematically too high or too low. It may vary, but averaged over the long run, it should be exactly right. In that case we refer to the estimator as *'unbiased'*.

Next, as well as being unbiased, we would also want our estimator to be as close as possible to the population mean, every time we draw a sample. We can accept that working with samples results in some variance, but we would nevertheless prefer any of this non-systematic variance from the population mean to be as minimal as possible. An estimator which swings backwards and forwards, up and down in large sweeps can, of course, on average still be equal to the population mean. However, in practice we are only going draw one sample. This means that in practice it is a very attractive property of an estimator that each time we draw a sample, the estimate generated for that sample for the population mean is not too far off. Clearly, if we know that estimator A deviates on average less from the population mean than estimator B, then we would always employ A. Estimator A has less variance. It has on average the lowest estimation error. In contrast estimator B is 'noisier'. Figure 2.8 illustrates this issue.

In Figure 2.8 the top left situation is the best. Here we have an unbiased estimator with little noise. The worst situation is bottom right. Here we have an estimator that is systematically incorrect (on average it will give us an estimate of the population mean that is 'off') as well as exhibiting lots of fluctuation. The top left situation is in fact the really desirable one. Essentially the requirement of unbiased and accurate estimators is non-negotiable. We do not want to use biased estimators, as these are useless, and noise also disqualifies an estimator.

That said there is in practice always some leeway when determining in these things. Importantly, it is not clear which of the other two situations (top right and bottom left) shown in Figure 2.8 is preferable. Choosing an unbiased estimator over one with less variance might seem intuitively logical to some, but this is not necessarily always the best choice. All in all, we want unbiased estimators with as little noise as possible. These are clear 'quality criteria' for comparing estimators.

Figure 2.8: Illustration of *bias* and *noise* in estimators

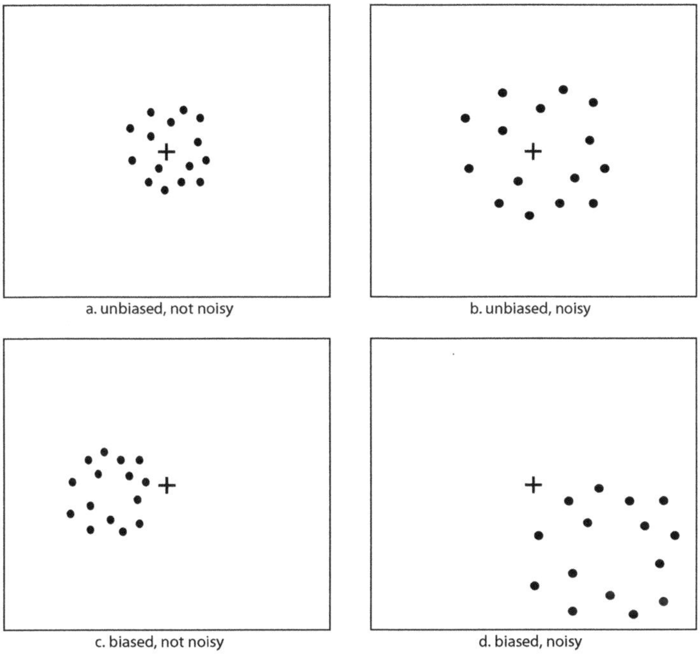

2.6.2 Consistency and efficiency of estimators

There are two more criteria for judging the quality of estimators. These are consistency and efficiency. Readers might at this point be thinking that we are going into far too much detail, considering this book is supposedly practice-orientated with a focus on non-experimental methods. The reason for highlighting these two characteristics as well is, however, that these are often discussed in the literature. For example one may read that 'estimator P is more efficient than estimator Q', or that one is better off using method K because it provides more efficient estimators. We have good reason therefore to briefly outline two further criteria which can play a role in method choice.

We will again refer to a situation where we have an unknown population from which we can draw a large number of samples. For every sample we estimate the population mean by using an estimator. Given that we want an unbiased and accurate estimator, what are these other criteria for choosing an estimator?

The first next criterion is *consistency*. Consistency refers to the following. We would intuitively expect that as the sample size increases, an estimator would produce an estimate which is closer to the unknown population parameter. Simply put, the larger the sample, the more we have seen from the population and the better we expect our estimate to be. A consistent estimator is one that behaves in this way. Put formally, if an estimator is consistent, then the estimate of an infinite sample is closer to the population mean μ the larger the sample studied.

Whilst consistency seems to be very similar to unbiasedness the two are not the same. A biased estimator can be consistent (for example because it provides good estimates from an infinite sample, but not in other situations) and an unbiased estimator can be inconsistent. We will not elaborate further on the theoretical reasons for this in this book.

Another criteria to consider is *efficiency*. Efficiency refers to the variance of an estimator. An estimator which gives estimates that fluctuate more for a given sample size is less efficient than one whose estimates fluctuate less. Alternatively put, if we can choose between two estimators, one of which provides estimates with a smaller range around the population mean than the other, we would choose the former. Mathematically there is then more to efficiency. Efficiency relates to the issue of noise which we discussed earlier. The two are not the same, however. Efficiency refers to the number of measurements that are needed to achieve good estimates. Situations where the same quality can be achieved with a smaller number of measurements are preferable to those where more measurements are required are to be preferred. It is possible to determine how efficient an estimator is, or whether the efficiency reaches a certain minimum level. We will not go into this further.

For more information about the characteristics of estimators and more mathematical detail on what we have discussed here see Lindgren (1985), chapter 5 'Estimation'. Wikipedia also has some fine pages on the topic, see for example en.wikipedia.org/wiki/Estimator, en.wikipedia.org/wiki/Consistent_estimator and en.wikipedia.org/wiki/Efficient_estimator.

Chapter 3

Propensity score matching

In this chapter we discuss *propensity score matching*. Propensity score matching is a method which tries to make two non-comparable research groups as comparable as possible. It does this in a clever way. Propensity score matching is not difficult, but if one would choose to do it 'by hand' it can involve quite a bit of work. We will try to explain this method at a conceptual level as clearly as possible, using many examples, and as few formulas as we can. We end the chapter with a detailed example, which the reader can also work through using SPSS or Stata.

In this chapter we assume that the reader has some prior knowledge of multiple regression and logistic regression analysis. A short overview of these analysis techniques was provided in the previous chapter. Readers requiring more detailed background reading are directed to Field (2013), Chapter 8, and Kleinbaum et al. (2014). Before introducing propensity score matching we first focus on what we mean by *matching*.

3.1 Matching

Over the years, researchers have often tried to come up with ways to fit data from observational studies into experimental and control groups which can then be compared. One of the first methods used for this was *matching*.

The idea behind matching is simple. For every person in the experimental group we try to find someone from the control group with exactly the same background characteristics. This is also referred to as or *variable by variable matching*. Once we have respondents in the experimental and control groups with entirely comparable background profiles, we assume that we can then make valid comparisons between them. There are two problems with this technique though. The first is more fundamental, the second more practical.

The fundamental problem is that even if the experimental and control groups have exactly the same background characteristics as measured by us, we can still not be sure that they do not differ on characteristics we have not measured. This is again the same problem of hidden bias we discussed in section 1.1. We can assure ourselves that the two groups do not differ on all kinds of observed characteristics, but to what extent do unobserved characteristics play a role? If we have failed to or been unable to measure any other relevant characteristics, then no matter how well we match our groups on observed characteristics, the groups will not be truly comparable: they still differ in relevant aspects. We can then still not be sure that any differences between experimental and control groups are attributable to the causal factor we are investigating. The issue of hidden bias is a recurring theme in this book (and as we will see in this chapter propensity score matching is unfortunately also not able to solve it).

The practical problem with matching is that matching people on a number characteristics quickly becomes unwieldy. Say we want to match on gender. Matching on just this characteristic is easy: for every experimental male we need to find a control male and for every experimental female we need to find a control female. Say we now want to introduce matching by age (in intervals). Now we need to find control males and females of the same age interval to match those in the experimental group. Next we add education, with four categories, into the mix. The matching is already becoming a little complicated, but it is probably still possible. But now imagine we want to add nationality and number of previous convictions with three categories (none, 1-2, and $\geq$3). We now need for every experimental Venezuelan female, who is 40 years old, with a high school diploma and 1-2 previous convictions to find a matching control person who is also Venezuelan, female, 40 years old, with a high school diploma and 1-2 previous convictions. It is quite likely we will not be able to find just such a control person in our sample. It is of course necessary to match on as many different characteristics as we can in order to make our experimental and control groups as comparable as possible. But the more characteristics we try to match on, the more likely it is that we will not be able to match people with specific profiles to a suitable control person.

Given the practical problems associated with this sort of matching researchers have come up with less stringent matching procedures. One of these is *marginal matching* or *blocking*. This procedure does not attempt to meet the stricter demand of matching at an individual level. Instead it is sufficient for (subgroups of) the experimental and control groups to have the same average scores on the variables chosen for matching. For example both groups would have the same percentage of males and females, the same age distribution, the same distribution of previous convictions, and so on. Whilst this is evidently easier to achieve, the end result is obviously less controlled. The combinations of characteristics are no longer the same, so we are less certain that any differences between the two groups are attributable only to our causal factor of interest, and not to, for instance, a particular distribution of combinations of background characteristics.

Another approach is to use regression to control for differences between experimental and control groups. The idea is to include in one regression model the treatment variable W alongside all the other variables on which the two groups may differ (those which we would use for matching if it was not so complicated). The result of the regression model would indicate the effect of treatment W *controlling for* the other variables in the model. In itself this solution has its advantages. It manages to avoid the complicated matching procedure. However, simulation studies have demonstrated that, regarding its performance on observed bias, this solution actually performs worse than propensity score matching, the method we focus on in this chapter. For further information on this see Guo and Fraser (2015), chapter 5.

3.1.1 A precursor to propensity score matching: Mahalanobis metric matching

In 1936 Mahalanobis, an Indian scientist, published a method for calculating the so-called multivariate distance. The calculation of this distance is best described as follows. If we take two points on a line, we can calculate the distance between the two points on that one dimension. If we have the coordinates of two points on a flat plain we can, using Pythagoras, also calculate the distance between the two points. If we have two points in space we can also calculate the distance between them. Trying to imagine two points in a four-dimensional space is obviously more difficult, but distances between points exist in four-, five- and higher-dimensional space.

Whilst it is difficult for us to conceive of visually, it is possible to calculate the distance between two points in higher-dimensional space using linear algebra. Using vectors (columns of numbers) and matrices (more than one column of numbers) we can easily calculate the distance between two points in a four, seven or even twenty dimensional space.

Mahalanobis used this principle to calculate a measure of the difference (distance) between two objects for which several characteristics had been measured. Say we have two respondents, and for each of these respondents we have measured several characteristics, e.g. height, IQ, impulsivity, number of previous convictions, etc. Using Mahalanobis's formula it is possible to express how much these two people differ on all these characteristics using just one measurement. Because the difference between respondents is expressed in terms of all the measured vari-

Prasanta Chandra Mahalanobis was born into a progressive, intellectual family in what was previously India, now Bangladesh. After completing his studies in natural sciences in Calcutta, he travelled to England to study further. A missed train lead to a chance meeting, which saw him lodging with a friend studying at King's College Cambridge. Mahalanobis also became a student at this college. He is said to have very much enjoyed punting on the Cam. He worked with Karl Pearson (yes! him of correlation coefficient fame) in London.
After returning to India he established the Indian Statistical Institute in 1932. The institute was a world pioneer in the field of sampling and surveys. Mahalanobis was the first to suggest the use of pilot studies. In 1933 he started the journal Sankhya, to this day a highly prestigious journal.

Figure 3.1: Prasanta Chandra Mahalanobis (1893 – 1972)

ables this is a multivariate distance measure. The distance $d_{i,j}$ between respondent i and respondent j is called the *Mahalanobis distance* and is written as follows:

$$d_{i,j} = (\mathbf{u}-\mathbf{v})'\mathbf{C}^{-1}(\mathbf{u}-\mathbf{v}),$$

where $\mathbf{u}$ is the vector with the variable scores from respondent i, $\mathbf{v}$ the vector with the variable scores from respondent j, and $\mathbf{C}$ a matrix containing the variance and covariance for the variables on which i and j are compared.

Explaining exactly what the formula does is difficult to summarise for readers not used to working with matrix algebra. However, understanding the following two parts of the formula is sufficient. First, $(\mathbf{u}-\mathbf{v})$ is a vector of the differences between i and j on the measured variables. Second, in the formula $\mathbf{C}$ contains all the variance within each variable and covariance between the variables, and adding the '$^{-1}$' power corrects the differences $(\mathbf{u}-\mathbf{v})$ for, amongst other things, variance on the different variables, resulting in their standardisation. In other words, $\mathbf{C}^{-1}$ ensures that the distance measure is independent of scale.

To summarise, the Mahalanobis distance is a scale-invariant multivariate distance measure. Because the distance measure is multivariate it can be used for a more complicated type of matching. How does this work?

Say we have an experimental and control group with 50 respondents in each. The two groups were not determined at random and so we are going to try and match them. We have k variables on which the two groups differ, and which may cause bias. Mahalanobis metric matching works as follows. We take the first respondent from the experimental group. We calculate the multivariate distance between this respondent and each of the control respondents, resulting in 50 multivariate distances. We now take our experimental respondent and match him or her to the control respondent with the smallest multivariate distance, i.e. the control respondent who is 'closest' on the set of k variables. Once these two are matched, they are removed from the dataset, and the next experimental respondent is chosen. Again the Mahalanobis distances are calculated to each of the remaining control respondents, now just 49, and the experimental respondent is matched to the control respondent who looks most like him or her. These two are then removed, and the process continues until every respondent is matched.

If we discount the formula, this process sounds very simple, but it does raise questions. Is it possible to match everyone? What if the experimental and control groups differ greatly on the variables? Do you not reach a point where you would not want to match any further? Or is this procedure only suitable when we have a small experimental group and a large pool of control group respondents from which to match? Should we compute all $\frac{50\times 49}{2}$ distances to start with and start by matching those who are most similar, to be sure that we achieve optimal matching?

As we will see, Mahalanobis matching is akin to the idea of propensity score matching, namely that we try to sum up the similarities between individuals on a large number of characteristics into one single indication of similarity, the distance measure. We will see that Mahalanobis matching not only is the conceptual basis of propensity score matching, but can also provide a solution for situations when propensity score matching is not possible.

3.2 Propensity score matching

In the previous section we described a number of increasingly clever ways of making non-comparable experimental and control groups as comparable as possible. We refer to these two groups as 'experimental' and 'control' even though strictly speaking we have not carried out a classic experiment. We assume that respondents have been placed into two research groups, that one of these groups has undergone an intervention or treatment, that we have information on a range of characteristics on which the groups differ, and that these characteristics may distort our assessment of whether the treatment has worked. We want to get rid of any distortions.

Using the regular matching method we would solve this problem by only including pairs of respondents with the same profile, i.e. matching a respondent from the experimental group with a control group respondent who looks exactly the same. When using blocking or marginal matching we are not as strict. We no longer insist that the profiles are identical at an individual level. It is sufficient for matched groups to have the same average scores. However, as mentioned this approach is risky. Mahalanobis metric matching is a little more inventive. This method converts k differences between respondents in the experimental and control groups into one distance, so that we can compare respondents, and pair them, on the basis on a single criterion. This makes Mahalanobis matching much more practical.

Propensity score matching builds on this idea. Scores on possible confounding variables, those which relate to both outcome and chance of treatment, are transformed into one score, again removing the fussy business of matching variable by variable. With propensity score matching the same idea is followed, but a different method is used to create this score.

Propensity score matching was first proposed by Rosenbaum and Rubin (1983). The method focusses on establishing the effect of an intervention W. One of the fundamental assumptions of propensity score matching is that there is an element of chance involved in the administering of this intervention. We know that respondents were not randomly allocated to the intervention and that there exist differences between experimental and control respondents. The idea is that, nevertheless, some of the respondents receiving the intervention could just as well have not received it, and some of those who did not receive it might just as well have received it – we therefore assume that the allocation of respondents to the two groups was not entirely deterministic. Propensity score matching now searches for those respondents who had equal chances of receiving or not receiving the intervention. It does this as follows.

First, using a range of different respondent characteristics, a logistic regression is estimated to predict whether respondents received or did not receive the intervention. In doing so, logistic regression (see section 2.3) calculates a *propensity score* for each respondent, i.e. a chance that a respondent, given their set of characteristics, or profile, would receive the intervention. Respondents are placed into either class '0' or class '1' depending on whether they fall below or above a certain boundary, the distribution of 0/1 in the sample determines exactly where the boundary lies. In general, after one performs a logistic regression analysis, one compares predicted with actual group membership. A so-called classification table is examined to see who actually received the intervention, whether the model correctly predicted that they would receive the intervention, and vice versa. If the numbers along the diagonal are high the model has worked well, i.e. the model does a good job in predicting who does and who does not receive the intervention.

In propensity score matching, however, we are not actually that interested in the classification table, but more in the propensity scores used to form the table. The reason for this is that people with the same propensity score have an equal chance of undergoing the intervention. These are exactly the people we are after! If we have two people with the same propensity score and one gets the intervention and the other does not, the decision as to who gets the intervention cannot have been dependent on differences between the respondents on any of the confounding variables. These confounding variables were namely included in the logistic regression, and based on this regression there is no difference in chance of receiving the intervention. We know this because they have identical propensity scores and because of these identical scores we know there is no difference in their chance of having received the intervention. Therefore, if we have two respondents with equal propensity scores, and one received the treatment and the other did not, the latter respondent is therefore the *counterfactual* for the experimental respondent. This control person, who did not receive the intervention, has an identical profile to the experimental respondent (which is why the two have identical propensity scores), the only difference is that the control person did not get the treatment. We can therefore conclude that it is pure chance, and not related to any measured characteristics, that the one respondent received the intervention and the other did not.

This, in essence, is propensity score matching. Respondents are matched using one score. This score is a combination of characteristics on which the experimental and control groups can differ. The crucial assumption is that experimental and control respondents with the same score do not systematically differ anymore from each other and that we can therefore make valid conclusions regarding the effect of the intervention.

3.2.1 Choices when matching respondents

This is, of course, far from the end of the story. There are a number of choices to be made in how exactly the propensity score is put to use. And as we will see later, the matching does not remove all of our problems with bias. But let us first look at the practical choices that need to be made for propensity score matching.

The first thing to consider is whether we want respondents in the experimental and control groups to have *exactly* the same propensity scores, or whether we are happy for them just to fall within a certain bandwidth of each other. If the latter is true we will probably be able to match more respondents, but the match will of course be less precise. A lack of precision may increase the risk that we still end up with biased results.

A second consideration is how much of the control group to use. Many research projects have a larger control group than experimental group. In this case if we match every experimental respondent to one control respondent we end up throwing a lot of information away. It might be better to match every experimental respondent to two or more control respondents. This may increase the power of our tests.

A third consideration is whether we can re-use respondents that have been matched already. Imagine that we have two experimental respondents with the same propensity score, but just one control respondent with a matching score. Can we use this control respondent twice, use this respondent as a match for both the first and second experimental respondent? If we do not do this we throw away information in the form of an unmatched experimental respondent.

3.3 Matching methods

In this section we will discuss a number of methods for matching respondents once we have calculated their propensity scores. There are many books, conference papers and articles written covering a range of variations on and hybrids of the methods we cover here. However, we are just going to focus on the most important matching methods. This is not to say that we recommend all of the following methods. On the contrary, we advise against using some of them. It is however important to discuss them so that informed decisions can be made about which methods to choose and which to leave aside.

As previously mentioned, all the methods involve an experimental and control group. For the whole group we have carried out a logistic regression trying to predict who gets the 'treatment' and who does not. The chance of being treated is then saved in a propensity score. This propensity score is used to match experimental with control respondents.

The matching methods fall into two different classes. In the first class a control person is sought for every experimental person ('person-by-person'). There can be two of each, i.e. one control person can be matched to two different experimental persons, or vice versa. The principle however remains the same, respondents are matched to real other respondents. The first three methods we discuss fall into this category. In the second class of matching methods, experimental respondents are not matched to other respondents in the sample, but a hypothetical control respondent is created from all the control respondents' scores and this 'virtual' respondent is then used as a match. The last method we will discuss, *kernel matching*, falls into this second category.

3.3.1 Nearest neighbour matching

Nearest neighbour matching is the crudest method of propensity score matching. Respondents are ordered from low to high on their propensity scores. Next we look for the first experimental respondent on the list. This respondent is then matched to the closest control respondent. Once these two are matched, we remove them, and continue on to the next experimental respondent. They then get matched to the control respondent with the closest possible propensity score. This process is repeated until all the experimental respondents have been matched. This method is also referred to as greedy matching, because for each experimental respondent we take the nearest control respondent, regardless of whether they would be perhaps better matched to another experimental respondent.

It is also possible, for instance if there are many more control than experimental respondents, to match every experimental respondent to not one, but to two or even several control respondents. This method is referred to as *k-nearest neighbour* matching.

In general we do not recommend greedy matching. The reason for this is that it is not strict enough, and therefore does not offer a satisfactory solution to the problem of two incomparable groups. We will use an example to explain why this is. Say we have an experimental group that is bigger than our control group. The two groups differ on their average propensity scores. This is something that

Figure 3.2: Illustrated example of greedy nearest neighbour matching

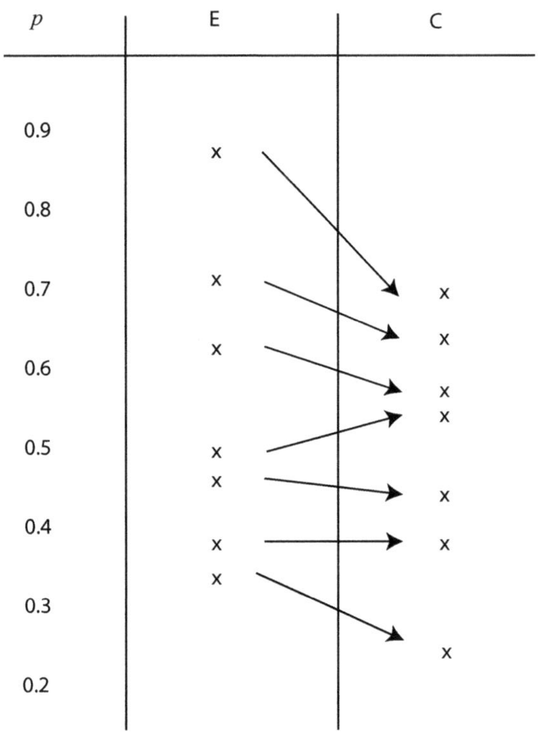

logically happens often, after all it is not for nothing that one group is given the intervention and the other not. There might be an overlap in propensity scores, in which interval of propensity scores respondents from both the experimental and control group have an equal propensity to receive the treatment, but the average propensity score for the experimental group is generally going to be higher than for the control group. See Figure 3.2, for a small scale example of nearest neighbour matching. As the figure illustrates, this method does not guarantee that the experimental group and control group will have comparable propensity scores. This method only requires that the closest control respondent is found for each experimental respondent. That person can still have a score that is a long way off that of the experimental respondent. The differences between the two groups are therefore far from eliminated. All in all, this means that when we employ greedy matching, we can almost be certain that bias will remain and will not be filtered out.

There are variations to nearest neighbour matching. The method as just described was carried out without returning the control respondents back to the pool once they have been matched. This can have disadvantages, for example if there are more experimental than control respondents so that some of the experimental respondents will be left without a match. It is therefore also possible to carry out the same procedure, but to put the matched control respondents back into the pool to be re-matched if possible. The problem then arises, however, that some control respondents are likely to be used twice (or even more often), and consequently one of the central statistical assumptions of independence of observations is violated. Some statistical software modules can control for this. Of course, the same problem can arise when instead of using one control respondent per experimental respondent, two or more control respondents are matched to each experimental respondent.

If control respondents are placed back into the pool for re-matching the problem illustrated in Figure 3.2, namely that the nearest neighbour is not necessarily very near, can be avoided. This is done by only selecting someone as nearest neighbour if their score is within a given distance of the experimental respondent's score. We discuss this method in the following section.

3.3.2 Caliper and radius matching

Caliper and radius matching are different variations of the same method. Caliper matching looks for a control respondent within a given distance, or 'caliper', of each experimental respondent. Radius matching takes all the control respondents that lie within a given distance of each experimental respondent. Radius matching therefore allows for more leeway than caliper matching, and leads to fewer respondents being discarded.

See Figure 3.3 for an illustrated example of caliper matching. As we can see from this figure, the number of respondents included is smaller when using caliper matching than if we had done (greedy) nearest neighbour matching. Now, we lose one experimental respondent with a large propensity score and one control respondent with a low propensity score. When using choosing caliper matching one needs to consider how strict to set the caliper, i.e. how much experimental and control respondents are allowed to differ. If it is set to be very strict, fewer respondents will be included; if the caliper is chosen wider, this results in less loss of respondents – and therefore have greater statistical power. In the latter case of course the risk of retaining bias is again increased.

In the literature it can be read that researchers should provide an argument as to why they have chosen to set a particular caliper, .05 or .01 (or .123?). It is difficult, however, to imagine what such an argument would be substantively based on. Intuitively it can be argued that the caliper should never be so large that the propensity scores of the experimental and control respondents significantly differ. In such a case arguably not enough bias would have been removed. On the other hand, it is fairly unrealistic to require the propensity scores of the experimental and control respondents to be exactly the same, and likely not necessary.

A standard width of caliper used often in the literature is $.25s_p$, with s_p the variance of the propensity scores. Austin (2011) showed using simulation studies that if at least one of the predictors in the logistic regression is an interval variable, the caliper can be best set at around 0.2 of the standard deviation of the propensity score logit. In this case the treatment effect is estimated precisely enough, and the procedure meets a number of other statistical criteria. When all the covariates are dichotomous the choice of where to set the caliper is less influential.

The range on which the propensity scores of the experimental and control respondents overlap is called the *area of common support*. If this area is large respondents can be easily matched. If the overlap is small, fewer respondents are available for matching. How large the area of common support is, is relevant. As we already said, losing respondents means losing power. We will discuss this subject in more detail in section 3.5.2. Caliper matching is illustrated in section 3.8.

When using the caliper method we can choose to either return respondents to the pool or to remove them once they have been matched. It is also possible to use combinations of caliper and nearest neighbour matching. For example, within a given caliper the k control respondents with the closest propensity score could be selected. We would in this case be stipulating that we want a certain number of control respondents per experimental respondent, but that we only want those respondents if their propensity score does not differ too much, i.e. no more than the caliper.

3.3.3 Stratification or interval matching

A variation on these two methods, nearest neighbour and caliper matching, is called *stratification* or *interval matching*. In this method the entire range of propensity scores from the experimental and control respondents is cut into a number of intervals. Mostly quintiles, or five intervals each containing 20% of respondents, are chosen. This choice of grouping is based on research by Cochran (1968) which demonstrated that when using five classes more than 90% of bias can be removed. This research despite its age is often cited. There does not however appear to be much recent corroboration of this rule.

The idea of stratification is that we calculate the treatment outcome in the experimental group as the un-weighted average of the five sub classes. We calculate the outcome for the control group in the same way. The overall effect is then the

Figure 3.3: Illustrated example of caliper matching and the area of common support

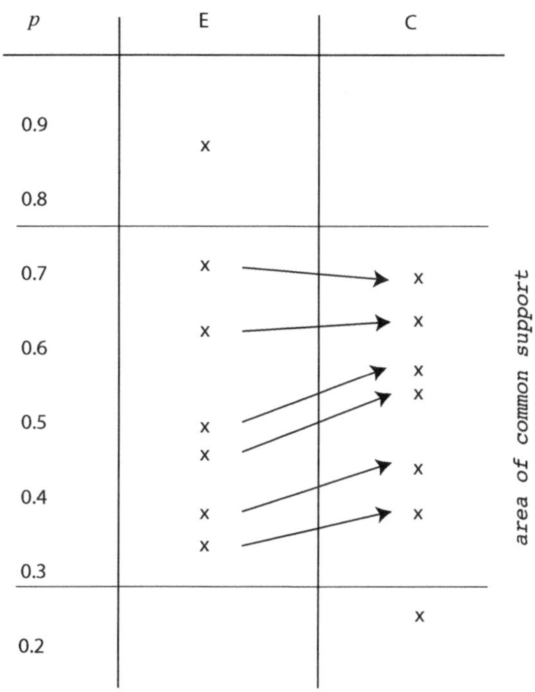

difference between these two effects. By calculating the un-weighted average for the two groups we discount for the fact that we have fewer control respondents with a high propensity score and fewer experimental respondents with a low propensity score.

The idea is that within each stratum any differences between experimental and control respondents are coincidental. Based on their propensity scores we say that their differences on certain characteristics can be attributed to chance. In this way stratification matching is similar to caliper and radius matching. Stratification matching can be seen as a mixture of nearest neighbour matching, caliper and radius matching. In common with radius matching everyone in a given sub-interval is included, like caliper and radius matching a certain range is selected within which

Figure 3.4: Illustrated example of stratification matching

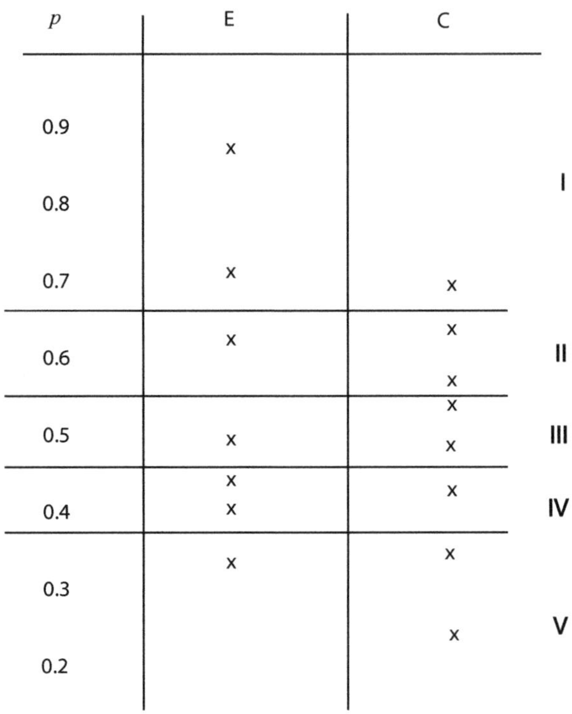

respondents in a subgroup are included, and like nearest neighbour matching all respondents are included. See Figure 3.4.

3.3.4 Kernel matching

In *kernel* matching the idea that for every experimental respondent one or k control respondents needs to be found no longer applies. The first reason for this is that when using one-on-k matching, information gets thrown away. For example, in radius matching we include a control respondent if their propensity score falls within a certain range of the experimental respondent, but we do not consider how far the control respondent's propensity score actually is from that of the experimental respondent. A control respondent whose score is closer to that of the experimental respondent is a better match than one whose score is further away, and should therefore perhaps count for more? A second reason is that, given that with caliper or radius matching respondents who fall outside the caliper are dropped, experimental respondents with a high propensity score and control respondents with a low propensity score often cannot be included. These respondents fall outside the area of common support. This area of common support is of course determined by the logistic regression analysis carried out in the first step. Depending on how one builds the logistic regression model, propensity scores, and therefore the overlap between experimental and control respondents and the area of common support, will differ. So different respondents fall outside the area of common support depending on how logistic regression model is specified, and are consequently also not included in assessing the effect of the intervention. The respondent-by-respondent matching that propensity score matching uses is therefore sensitive to the precise specification of the logistic regression model. This is one of its disadvantages.

Kernel matching methods solve the first and second issue. All respondents are included, and control respondents whose scores are closer to those of the experimental respondents count for more in the calculations. How do kernel matching methods achieve this?

Basically kernel matching involves constructing a virtual control respondent for every experimental respondent. How exactly this is done goes beyond the scope of this book. We will however illustrate the concept with a very simple example. For every experimental respondent i a control respondent is constructed from the weighted scores of all the control respondents, where the weights are equal to a function of the inverse of the difference in propensity score of the experimental and control respondent. Say we have an experimental respondent i with a propensity score of 0.7. We have 3 control respondents, one c_1 with a propensity score of 0.75, another c_2 with 0.60, and a third c_3 with a score of 0.35. In this simple example the score on the dependent variable of the virtual control respondent v_i could be constructed as follows:

$$Y_{v(i)} = (\frac{1}{.05}Y_{c(1)} + \frac{1}{.1}Y_{c(2)} + \frac{1}{.35}Y_{c(3)}),$$

which we would write and normalise thus:

$$\frac{20 \times c_1 + 10 \times c_2 + 2.87 \times c_3}{\frac{1}{.05} + \frac{1}{.10} + \frac{1}{.35}}$$

$$= \frac{20 \times c_1 + 10 \times c_2 + 2.87 \times c_3}{32.87}$$

$$= \frac{20}{32.87} \times c_1 + \frac{10}{32.87} \times c_2 + \frac{2.87}{32.87} \times c_3$$

We see that roughly two thirds of control respondent 1 is used in constructing the virtual control respondent v_i, roughly one third of control respondent 2, and less than a tenth of respondent 3 is used. Respondents count for more, relative to how close their propensity score is to that of the experimental respondent to whom we are matching.

Person v_i does not actually exist, but is a composite of the scores of all the control respondents, who are used to construct a virtual control respondent for experimental respondent i. In practice this process is carried out with slightly more complicated functions. The formula by which the virtual respondent's score is estimated is called a *kernel estimator*, and hence the term kernel matching. This general idea is the starting point of a number of variants: a range of weighting functions are suggested in the literature, each of which weight the distance between the experimental and control respondents in a slightly different way.

The most important weighting functions are the normal or Gaussian kernel, the uniform kernel which gives equal weight to all control respondents within a certain range and therefore looks rather like radius matching, and the Epanechnikov kernel, which does not include control respondents with a propensity score that differs too greatly from the experimental respondents' and therefore resembles caliper matching.

Local linear regression, often shortened to 'lowess', is recommended on top of kernel matching. This additional procedure involves trying to fit the virtual respondents' estimated scores to a certain distribution. The estimated scores are smoothed for this, using regression functions – hence the term local linear regression. Research has demonstrated that this smoothing has certain advantages: the matching procedure performs better (we will not go into the details here). A disadvantage however is that the standard errors of the estimates can not longer be determined. Bootstrap methods are then needed to estimate these (bootstrap methods are an artificial way of estimating population characteristics by repeatedly analysing a sub-sample of the sample). Whilst bootstrap methods are generally accepted, using them in this 'lowess' method is seen by some as a disadvantage.

In the literature, one of the advantages of kernel matching often mentioned is that all of the respondents are included in the matching process and therefore information is not thrown away. However, research has shown that including respondents with extreme scores is not efficient. The propensity scores which fall outside the range of the majority of scores are in the so-called sparse regions (in caliper matching they would fall outside of the area of common support). Simulation studies have shown that matching performs better if propensity scores which fall into these sparse regions are excluded. This is referred to as 'trimming', i.e. the propensity scores which fall outside the range of the majority of the scores are removed and only those regions which are well filled with propensity scores are used. The end result is that, in essence, the area of common support actually does play a role in kernel matching. In that sense, the reputed advantages (using all respondents) of kernel matching do not materialize in reality. A different solution for the unhelpful effects of the sparsely filled regions is to add a special parameter to the local linear regression model. This ensures that the regression model is not too badly affected by the sparse regions. This is referred to as *ridge regression.*

3.3.5 Performance of (different) matching methods

Simulation studies have tested the performance of the various matching methods for different types of data. Some general recommendations can be derived from these.

First, it appears that nearest neighbour matching does not work as well as kernel matching when the sample size is small, and this is especially true if few respondents have undergone the treatment (Frölich, 2004). Thus, for small sample sizes kernel matching may be a first choice.

Second, it is generally recommended for propensity score matching that all the variables that relate to the treatment and the outcome be included in the logistic regression model (Cuong, 2013). In a sense this is not surprising as we are after all trying to to filter out as many possible confounding factors as possible. Incorporating extra variables that relate only to the allocation of treatment does not substantially improve results, however, and can even increase the standard errors, the same study reported. We therefore recommend that, to begin with, all available variables which we expect to relate to receiving treatment and to the dependent variable are included. In addition variables should be included that relate to the outcome measure. One caveat to this recommendation is of course that including a large number of variables is possible only if the sample size is suitably large.

There are few guidelines regarding other aspects of the matching methods. There is not one method which consistently outperforms the others. Simulation studies have generally shown that performance of a method depends on the type of data and the extent to which the data meet the assumptions of a certain matching method. A method which works well for one dataset does not necessarily work well for another. It is true for all methods, however, that invalid results are produced when observed variables are omitted from the models on which the experimental and control groups differ. In addition, as stated in the introduction, all methods are sensitive to hidden bias.

The question is what are we to do with this information. How can we ensure that our results are valid? How do we know whether we have left out relevant observed variables? We will consider these issues in the following section.

3.4 Controlling for robustness and sensitivity analysis

There are three controls the researcher can carry out to determine whether they should trust the results of their propensity score matching.

The first is simple. After matching experimental and control respondents on their propensity scores we assume that the two groups are now comparable. This is referred to as the *balancing property*. What this means is that the two groups should now no longer differ on the variables included in the logistic regression on the basis of which the propensity scores were computed. The first control which we can do is therefore to check whether this is true. We could, for example, carry out a t-test examining the differences between the two groups on all the independent variables included in the logistic regression. While this is intuitively logical, and simple to do, the disadvantage is of course that the results of these tests are dependent on the size of our dataset. With a large dataset significant differences are much more likely to be found. An alternative, particularly if the sample size is large, is to examine the standardised difference between the experimental and control groups' scores:

$$d = \frac{\bar{X}_E - \bar{X}_C}{\sqrt{\frac{s_E^2 + s_C^2}{2}}}$$

The general rule of thumb is that d should not be larger than .1 (see Austin, 2012, although some authors find a difference of .2 acceptable).

The second control is also easy to comprehend. Propensity score matching is sensitive to how the logistic regression model is built, as mentioned in section 3.3.5 The second control for robustness of results is therefore to build several logistic regression models which are slightly different to the first, by, for example, excluding or including predictors, and then to see whether the results hold. The idea is to check that the results are not just coincidental by examining whether they remain the same under slightly different conditions. A third robustness check is to examine whether the results remain more or less the same with a slightly different caliper.

The fourth control was proposed by Rosenbaum (2002). We will outline this method without going into much detail, and describe its workings mainly conceptually. Say we had used propensity score matching to show that being exposed to a certain food colouring significantly affects aggressive behaviour. We know that we have controlled for all overt bias, but we do not know whether the data is distorted by any hidden bias. Using Rosenbaum's sensitivity analysis we will determine how much hidden bias would be needed in the data to render the results non-significant. This works as follows. First, a hypothetical variable 'Γ' is created which proposes different levels of hidden bias. A value of 1 indicates that, given the scores on the observed variables, an experimental respondent indeed has as much chance of receiving an intervention as a control respondent, i.e. there is no hidden bias. If, however, Γ equals 2 an experimental respondent actually has twice as much chance as a control respondent of receiving the intervention even though they have exactly the same scores on the observed variables. Here hidden bias, caused by some unmeasured factor determining whether someone gets the intervention, is clearly evident. The larger Γ is, the larger the hidden bias is.

This sensitivity analysis is now used to examine how large the hidden bias would have to be in order to topple the results. In other words, how big does Γ have to be to render the difference between the experimental and control group no longer significant? Imagine that with a Γ of 1.2 this is already true. This would be a cause for concern, as already with a slight difference in the likelihood to receive treatment for the experimental group, the conclusions would already not be valid anymore. Basically, this shows that the results would not hold if just a small amount of hidden bias were present. In contrast, if the results of the sensitivity analysis indicate that only if an improbably large amount of hidden bias was present, say 6, the difference was no longer significant, we could be much surer of our findings. Given that it is unlikely that such a large amount of hidden bias would still be present, our results appear more robust.

Some software includes procedures for carrying out this sensitivity analysis. Keele (2010) provides a good overview of the possibilities in `R`. The programme `rbounds` can be downloaded for use in Stata.

Rosenbaum's sensitivity analysis has however been criticised as well. Partly because propensity score matching is a relatively new field, it is not always clear what the merits of different procedures are. This is of course cumbersome, but par for the course when using a relatively new method.

3.5 Conditions for propensity score matching

Propensity score matching, all in all, appears to be a relatively straightforward procedure to carry out, without too many complicated statistical processes. There are however certain conditions which need to be considered. We will discuss these in the following section.

3.5.1 Large sample size

In general propensity score matching is considered to work best with large sample sizes. This is intuitively understandable given that with a small sample the solution from the initial logistic regression is less stable, and therefore the findings from the following analysis using the propensity matched respondents are also unstable. The literature does not however give much detail on how large the sample should be, or how many experimental respondents we need.

One possible option for when the sample size is too small for a logistic regression, is to match using Mahalanobis distances, as Mahalanobis metric matching can be carried out with small samples. If there is doubt as to the adequacy of the sample size we recommend carrying out a robustness analysis as described in section 3.4. This will demonstrate whether the results are unstable, and would take away any worries if they turn out to be robust against small alterations in the design.

3.5.2 A sufficiently large area of common support

As previously mentioned, matching only works well if there is sufficient overlap in propensity scores between the experimental and control group. Propensity score matching is therefore best used when allocation of the intervention has indeed been largely coincidental. Formulated the other way round, if we were able to strongly predict who got the intervention and who did not using the logistic regression, we would not have enough overlap in propensity scores of the experimental and control groups.

As a result we are left with the paradoxical situation whereby we want to be able to predict who does and who does not get the intervention as well as possible (in order to remove any bias), whilst at the same time we do not want that prediction to be too good (as then we do not have a large enough area of common support). These two are in a sense communicating vessels: if we lower the quality of the logistic regression and do not predict group membership well, we will be able to match many respondents; if we improve the quality of the prediction we will filter out more bias, but we will basing our conclusion on a smaller part of the sample (and thus have less power as well as generalizability issues). What this all suggests is that propensity score matching is probably best used in situations where receiving or not receiving the intervention is to a reasonable extent due to chance.

3.5.3 Not too many missing values

Up to now we have not mentioned what we do with missing data. Often all respondents have scores for the outcome measure, but some may have missing scores on one or more of the predictors. If respondents with missing values are included in standard software packages, they are generally left out of the model.

This means that also no propensity scores for these respondents will be computed. Consequently, they drop out of the entire analysis.

If the number of missing values is not too large the most pragmatic solution is generally to impute the missing values (this can be done by imputing the mean or median, or by a more sophisticated regression-type procedure such as 'Multiple imputation' in SPSS, see the IBM SPSS website for more details). But if there is a considerable number of missing values the situation may be more difficult. One option is to estimate the logistic regression excluding those variables with missing values. The problem with this is that both the prediction of treatment allocation and the correction for bias become weaker. The following pragmatic solution is perhaps best: carry out the logistic regression with and without the variables with missing values, i.e. with and without the respondents with missing scores, next compare both sets of results to see if they differ. If they are substantively the same, we can be confident that the respondents with missing values do not form a specific subset and that our conclusions apply to the entire sample.

3.5.4 The correct *functional form* of the logistic regression model

In previous sections we have not discussed what the logistic regression model for propensity score matching should look like. Many researchers include the predictors in their original form, as for example with the variable `age`. It is however possible that whilst age is not confounded with the outcome measure, another function of `age` is, for example `age`^{2}, or *ln*(`age`). If either of these two latter situations is true, but we include `age` in its untransformed state in the regression model, the *functional form* of the regression model is incorrect.

It is of course practically impossible to run logistic regressions using all possible combinations of transformed independent variables, and to then compare all the propensity score matching analysis outcomes. In cases where one suspects the functional form is not correctly specified a '*generalized boosted regression*' can be employed. We will not go into detail as to what this is, but just outline the general idea. This technique builds a series of so-called regression trees. In a regression tree the dataset is split into increasingly small groups, or branches, using profiles from categories of the independent variables. We want these small groups to differ as much as possible on the dependent variable. As the tree is created using combinations of categories of the independent variables, it is not dependent on any specific function given to an independent variable. One therefore simply looks for the unique combination of categories which most strongly correlates with a score on the dependent variable.

Generalized boosted regression is a sum of different regression trees. It gives the same analysis results independent of the exact functional form. Another advantage of regression trees is that continuous, nominal and ordinal independent variables can all be included, as the variables are repeatedly subdivided. For more on this topic see McCaffrey et al. (2004).

3.5.5 No remaining unobserved bias

As previously described, propensity score matching can under certain conditions solve the problem of selection on observed variables. If this selection, or bias, is present only in variables included in the dataset, and if we correctly identify these variables, and if we correctly include these in the logistic regression, and if we then have a substantial overlap between the experimental and control groups on their propensity scores, propensity score matching is going to work well.

However, if there are unmeasured characteristics on which the experimental and control groups differ and if these also relate to both the chance of intervention and score on the outcome measure, propensity score matching is not going to solve much. After all, we can only include variables we have measured. Propensity score matching, therefore, only provides a solution to the rather hypothetical situation whereby we have a quasi-experimental design with an experimental and control group, groups are formed through processes which we had no control over, but where group membership correlates with differences between these two groups that we know about and have measured.

3.6 Example: Treatment and sex offending recidivism

In illustrating propensity score matching, we will first discuss how to do this using SPSS, and next how to perform the propensity score matching with Stata. Even though the latest version of SPSS (v22.0) has at the time of writing of this book a function for propensity score matching, not all users have access to this function and it appears to generate some problems for users with particular interfaces who do have access to SPSS v22.0. We will therefore illustrate how to perform propensity score matching as it were ‘by hand’. As the reader will see, Stata has a much simpler procedure where the software does all the matching, making it less cumbersome and less liable to mistakes and unreproducability.

Throughout this book we repeatedly use an example dataset to illustrate the statistical techniques we discuss. This dataset comprises 173 offenders who received treatment for sex offending and 327 who did not. The dataset is fictional and so are all variables. The fictional treatment that we are interested to evaluate here is cognitive behaviour therapy. Such cognitive behaviour therapy is in fact a common type of treatment offered to juvenile sex offenders in order to reduce their risk of

Figure 3.5: Contingency table for the variables `treatment` and `type_offender`

type_offender * treatment Crosstabulation

Count

		treatment		Total
		no	yes	
type_offender	child abuser	116	106	222
	peer abuser	107	46	153
	group offender	104	21	125
Total		327	173	500

re-offending. The example in this chapter focusses on this therapy. The question we want to answer, using propensity score matching, is whether this therapy helps, i.e. is the risk of sex offending recidivism lower amongst those who received the therapy than those who did not receive the therapy?

Straight away an overriding problem emerges: the treatment is not allocated at random. It is highly likely that those offenders judged to be the most at risk, i.e. for whom the risk of recidivism was judged highest, are more often assigned to receive treatment than those for whom the risk of re-offending was judged to be low. If we examine the contingency table of the variables `treatment` and `type_offender` in Figure 3.5, we instantly see that the treatment is indeed unlikely to have been allocated at random. For example child abusers have a much higher chance of being treated (48%) than peer abusers (30%), or group offenders (17%). It appears that child abusers either are judged to be at a greater risk of recidivism than group offenders or have certain characteristics meaning they were judged to be in need of treatment.

In Table 3.1 the dossier variables measured for the juvenile sex offenders are shown.

3.7 Propensity score analyse in SPSS

In this chapter the variable by which we assess whether the treatment was successful is sex offending recidivism, coded as '0' (no recidivism') and '1' (recidivism).

Table 3.1: Dossier variables in SPSS file `VM-JSO.sav`

Variable	category meanings	
age_ offence	9- 18	
ethnicity	1 = Dutch	2 = non Dutch
IQ	1 = extremely low (<85)	4 = high average (106-115)
	2 = low average (85-95)	5 = superior (>115)
	3 = average (95-105)	
neuroticism	1 = low (perc <30)	3 = above average (perc 70-85)
	2 = average (perc 30-70)	4 = high (perc >85)
impulsivity	1 = low (perc <30)	3 = above average (perc 70-85)
	2 = average (perc 30-70)	4 = how (perc >85)
conscience development	1 = very poor	5 = good
	2 = poor	6 = desirable
	3 = deficient	7 = unknown
	4 = satisfactory	
self esteem	1 = very low	3 = normal
	2 = low	4 = positive
psychopathology	1= none	2 = psychopathology
neglect	1 = no	3 = emotional
	2 = pedagogic	4 = both
victim of abuse	1= yes	3 = emotional
	2 = physical	4 = both
sex_abuse	1 = no	3 = yes
	2 = possible	
completed_education	1 = none	5 = VBO/MAVO
	2 = primary school	6 = HAVO
	3 = special education	7 = MBO
	4 = IVBO	
current_education	1 = none	5 = VBO/MAVO
	2 = primary school	6 = HAVO
	3 = special education	7 = MBO
	4 = IVBO	8 = VWO/HBO
special_ education	1 = no	2 = yes
victim_bullying	1 = no	3 = regularly
	2 = occasionally	4 = often
self_bully	1 = no	3 = at school
	2 = home	4 = both
contact_ peers	1 = poor	3 = normal
	2 = some	4 = good
truancy	1 = no	3 = often
	2 = occasionally	
previous_ sexoffence	1 = no	2= yes
type_offender	1 = child abuser	3 = group offender
	2 = peer abuser	
treated	0 = no	1 = yes

Figure 3.6: Contingency table for variables `treatment` and `recidivism_sex`

recidivism_sex * treatment Crosstabulation

			treatment		
			no	yes	Total
recidivism_sex	no	Count	276	146	422
		% within treatment	84,4%	84,4%	84,4%
	yes	Count	51	27	78
		% within treatment	15,6%	15,6%	15,6%
Total		Count	327	173	500
		% within treatment	100,0%	100,0%	100,0%

Let us therefore start by examining whether there is a relationship between sex offending recidivism and treatment, using the following command in SPSS:

```
CROSSTABS
     /TABLES=recidivism_sex BY treatment
     /FORMAT=AVALUE TABLES
     /STATISTICS=RISK
     /CELLS=COUNT COLUMN
     /COUNT ROUND CELL.
```

When we use SPSS to examine this, we get the contingency table shown in Figure 3.6, and the odds ratio results seen in Figure 3.7. In the contingency table we can see that the recidivism rates for both the treated and untreated groups are approximately the same, rounded to 15.6%. The odds ratio is consequently very close to 1 (see Figure 3.7). These results might lead one to conclude that being treated makes no difference for recidivism. But this outcome could also be argued to be actually the 'ideal' outcome, that is the outcome in an ideal world where effective treatment is imposed on those who are in need of it. In that world, the low risk offenders were judged to have an acceptable level of sex re-offending risk, and therefore did not need to be treated. The high risk group however, needed to be treated in order to bring their risk of re-offending down to an acceptable level. The results shown here conform to that ideal scenario. The treated offenders now have a risk level equal to that of the acceptably low risk non-treated offenders.

Figure 3.7: Odds ratio of the variables `treatment` and `recidivism_sex`

Risk Estimate

	Value	95% Confidence Interval	
		Lower	Upper
Odds Ratio for recidivism_sex (no / yes)	1,001	,602	1,663
For cohort treatment = no	1,000	,839	1,192
For cohort treatment = yes	,999	,717	1,393
N of Valid Cases	500		

(The question of whether 15.6% really is an acceptable level of recidivism is a discussion we will not go into here.)

Nonetheless, we still do not know for sure that the 'ideal world' scenario as described above is actually what has happened. It might have happened exactly as described, as would have been intended. It might, however, be the case that the risk of recidivism was always 15.6%, that the juvenile offenders were allocated treatment in rather a haphazard manner, that the treatment did not help, and that this is why we did not find any difference between the groups. The problem is that our results can equally be explained by this second, rather cynical, scenario. We therefore need to examine the data to find out which of these is more likely to be true, and this is why we carry out propensity score matching.

We carry out the necessary analyses step by step to show the reader what happens at each stage.

3.7.1 Step 1: logistic regression

The first step is to estimate a logistic regression. From this logistic regression we get the propensity scores. The dependent variable is of course the variable '`treated`'. Using logistic regression we try to predict who does and who does not receive the treatment, and then for every offender in the treatment group we select an untreated offender with exactly the same chance of receiving treatment. We know what our dependent variable is, but what should we choose to be our independent variables? To begin with, variables which are theoretically expected to play a role should be included, for example characteristics which are in practice actually used to determine whether someone receives treatment (and are therefore likely also associated with the likelihood of recidivism).

Practitioners consider the following set of factors when deciding on allocating treatment: these factors are the variables `contact_peers`, `psychopathology`, `age_offence`, `IQ`, `neuroticism`, `ethnicity`, `type_offender` and `previous_sexoffence`. These variables are thus *a priori* of importance, because they are those used in practice to select offenders for treatment. Next, we look for other theoretically plausible variables which may empirically relate to receiving or not receiving treatment. The variable `impulsivity` is one of these. This has in fact a Pearson correlation with treatment of 0.124 (p=.014), and with recidivism to a sex offence of .161 (p <.001), thereby meeting the criteria set by Cuong (2013). We therefore run the logistic regression using the following command:

```
LOGISTIC REGRESSION VARIABLES treated
     /METHOD=ENTER contact_peer
     psychopathology age_offence IQ
     neuroticism impulsivity ethnicity type_offender
     previous_sexoffence
     /CONTRAST (type_offender)=Indicator (1)
     /SAVE=PRED
     /CRITERIA=PIN(.05) POUT(.10) ITERATE(20) CUT(.5).
```

This syntax indicates that the dependent variable is `treated`, and that we want to predict this variable using `contact_peers`, `psychopathology`, `age_offence`, `IQ`, `neuroticism`, `impulsivity`, `ethnicity`, `type_offender` and `previous_sexoffence`. The variable `type_offender` is given as a categorical variable, with the first category being the reference category, in this case child abusers. The coefficients for the other categories therefore indicate a higher or lower risk in comparison to child abusers.

When we run this syntax the output (not shown) indicates that all 500 cases are included, i.e. there are no variables with missing values. The Nagelkerke R^2 is 0.159. The 'classification table' in the output also shows that the model did a good job of correctly classifying the untreated respondents in particular: of the untreated respondents 86.5% were correctly classified, and of the treated respondents 41.6% were correctly classified, giving an average over the two groups of 71%. It is not surprising that more untreated offenders were classified correctly, given that the untreated respondents are in the majority: there is then more to gain by correctly classifying this group. Figure 3.8 provides the SPSS table for the predictors and their significance levels.

Figure 3.8: Predictors and their significance levels from the logistic regression

Variables in the Equation

		B	S.E.	Wald	df	Sig.	Exp(B)
Step 1[a]	contact_peers	-,140	,155	,823	1	,364	,869
	psychopathology	-,234	,228	1,055	1	,304	,792
	age_offence	,032	,062	,258	1	,611	1,032
	IQ	,293	,105	7,714	1	,005	1,340
	neuroticism	,021	,092	,053	1	,818	1,021
	impulsivity	,194	,093	4,300	1	,038	1,214
	ethnicity	-,496	,231	4,633	1	,031	,609
	type_offender			20,651	2	,000	
	type_offender(1)	-,597	,241	6,112	1	,013	,551
	type_offender(2)	-1,357	,305	19,800	1	,000	,257
	previous_sexoffence	-,225	,321	,491	1	,483	,799
	Constant	-,409	1,223	,112	1	,738	,664

a. Variable(s) entered on step 1: contact_peers, psychopathology, age_offence, IQ, neuroticism, impulsivity, ethnicity, type_offender, previous_sexoffence.

The results show that, in contrast to what practitioners may think, impulsivity, ethnicity, and offender type are the most important predictors of treatment allocation. We had already guessed that offender type was an important predictor in Figure 3.5 above. The significance levels of the respective variables are not actually of great interest to us, and therefore not worth interpreting. What is of importance is the propensity scores. These scores are saved using the subcommand `/SAVE=PRED` in the syntax above. SPSS has labelled these scores `PRE_1`.

Those respondents who received the treatment should arguably have a higher propensity to be treated. Their average propensity score is 0.426, against the average propensity score of the untreated group of 0.304. Figure 3.9 shows a boxplot of the distribution of propensity scores for the treated and untreated groups. Whilst there is a large range of scores in both groups, with very high and very low propensity scores present in each group, the distribution of the scores clearly differs. The black lines in the boxed indicate the median values per group. So whilst there is limited overlap in the higher and lower regions, the area of common support is substantial. It is already obvious from the boxplot, however, that we are not going to find a control respondent with the same, or nearly the same, score for every experimental respondent. Those respondents with the highest and lowest propensity scores are unlikely to be matched.

Figure 3.9: Boxplot of propensity scores for the treated and untreated groups

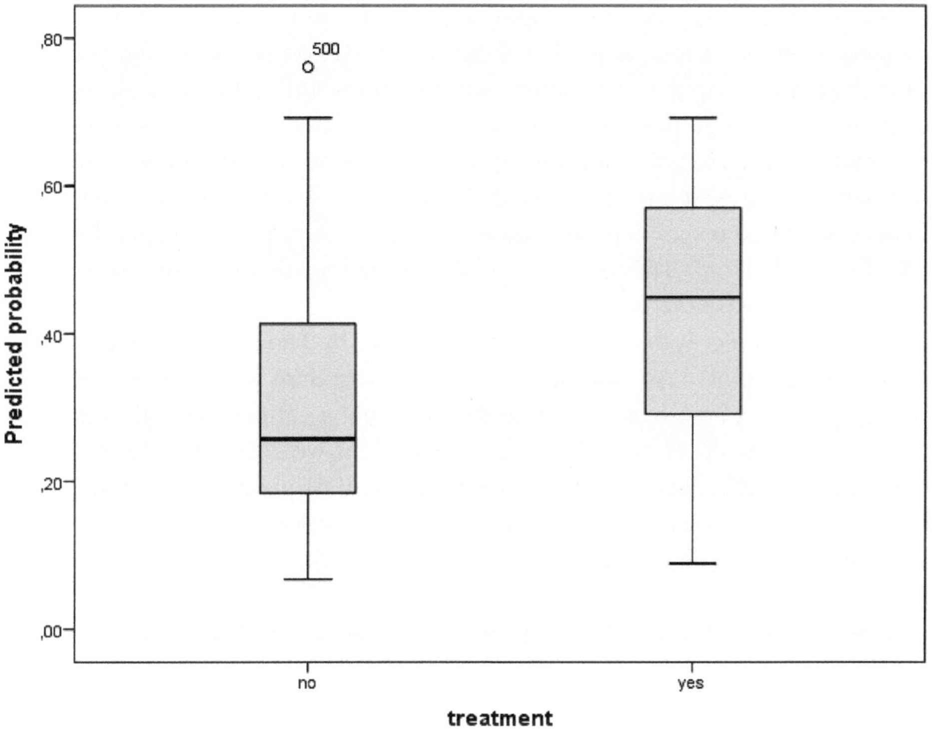

Also, we have more untreated than treated respondents and so we will inevitably end up with a smaller sample size of matched respondents. If we match one treated with one untreated respondent the maximum matched sample we can have is (2 × 173 =) 346 individuals. So whatever else we do we will lose at least 154 individuals from our sample. This is nearly a third of the sample and we are therefore looking at a substantial loss of power.

3.7.2 Step 2: matching

The next step is to match respondents from the treated and untreated groups. We did this manually. For this, we use the propensity score variable (`PRE_1`). We sort the dataset by the propensity scores in this variable, from low to high.

Next we look for untreated respondents to match with every treated respondent. As we saw in Figure 3.9, at the lower end of the range of variable `PRE_1` we will likely find a relatively high number of untreated respondents. It is consequently easy to find a control respondent with the same propensity score for every experimental respondent: there is ample choice. However, we cannot match every untreated respondent to a treated respondent at the lower end of the propensity scores. The higher up the distribution we go, things will get easier. Here we will be able to match large numbers of treated and untreated respondents, we are then in the midst of the area of common support. But, as we travel higher up the range of propensity scores, it will get more difficult again. We will then encounter large numbers of treated respondents but we will have a lack of treated respondents from which to choose from. This is not surprising. The logistic regression was after all better able to classify the untreated respondents..

For our example, we carried out the matching by hand, picking matches who were reasonably close. An automatic matching procedure with a pre-set minimum difference was not employed, and it is therefore not a caliper-method in the strictest sense of the word. For each treated respondent we searched one by one and 'eyeballing the differences' for the closest untreated respondent. Once the process was completed we were left with 250 matched respondents, 125 treated and 125 untreated. Our sample has now been reduced by half: we have lost 50% of our sample.

As we carried out the matching process by hand, it is not necessarily very precise. However, there was no significant difference on average propensity scores of treated and untreated respondents: the t-value was 0.026, with a p-value close to 1. We also examined whether the two matched groups significantly differ on the possible confounders which we had included as predictors in our logistic regression. We ran t-tests or χ^2-tests on the scores of the 250 respondents left in the sample and found that, as we hoped, they did not significantly differ. We are therefore able to state that our hand-matching procedure meets the necessary balancing property.

3.7.3 Step 3: analysis of the matched groups

We now have what we set out to achieve: two groups of juvenile sex offenders, one treated the other not, who have practically the same chance of being treated, as demonstrated by their very similar propensity scores. We have been able to remove the bias in treatment allocation, as far as was possible given our measured variables. Our tests showed that the matched groups do not differ on the independent variables and that therefore the *balancing property* is met.

Now we can repeat the analysis from Figure 3.6, for the 250 respondents matched by their propensity score. For that we had earlier created first a vari-

Figure 3.10: Contingency table for `treated` and `recidivism_sex` for propensity matched respondents only

recidivism_sex * treated Crosstabulation

			treated		Total
			0	1	
recidivism_sex	0	Count	103	115	218
		% within treated	82.4%	92.0%	87.2%
	1	Count	22	10	32
		% within treated	17.6%	8.0%	12.8%
Total		Count	125	125	250
		% within treated	100.0%	100.0%	100.0%

able `CALIPER` that indicates whether a respondent was included in the set of 250 matched respondents (in which case the value was 1) or whether we were unable to match a respondent (the value was then 0). We use the following syntax command to select these respondents:

```
TEMPORARY.
SELECT IF (CALIPER EQ 1).
CROSSTABS
     /TABLES=recidivism_sex BY treated
    /FORMAT=AVALUE TABLES
     /STATISTICS=RISK
    /CELLS=COUNT COLUMN
    /COUNT ROUND CELL.
```

When we input this into SPSS we get the output reported in Figure 3.10, the contingency table, and odds ratios as in Figure 3.11.

We can see that, compared to our unmatched results, recidivism in the untreated group is higher and recidivism in the treated group has been dramatically reduced. The odds ratio is significant, with a confidence interval of 0.184 – 0.900, and at 0.407 it is substantially less than 1. We may conclude therefore that the recidivism risk for treated respondents has been more than halved, as a result of the treatment.

Figure 3.11: Odds ratio for `treated` and `recidivism_sex` for propensity matched respondents only

Risk Estimate

	Value	95% Confidence Interval	
		Lower	Upper
Odds Ratio for recidivism_sex (0 / 1)	.407	.184	.900
For cohort treated= 0	.687	.523	.902
For cohort treated= 1	1.688	.995	2.865
N of Valid Cases	250		

3.8 Propensity score analysis with Stata: caliper matching

In this section we will answer the same research question using Stata. In Stata commands are rather more brief, and the procedure for propensity score matching itself is more compact than that above. It is also automatic, which makes it more precise (and replicable), but which also makes it perhaps less easy to follow.

Stata does not include a propensity score matching procedure as standard. We therefore need to download the procedure `psmatch2`. This can be done using the command `ssc install psmatch2`. The procedure `psmatch2` has many different options relating to propensity score matching: caliper, nearest neighbour, different types of kernel matching, and Mahalanobis matching. There are also options to re-use respondents for matching, to trim the sample, and so on. Here we will carry out an example of propensity score matching from the first class of methods, matching individuals to individuals, followed by a demonstration of the caliper method.

Before starting with this procedure we need to enter several commands into Stata to get the programme ready and clear out any open datasets. First we type

```
clear
```

followed by:

```
clear matrix
```

Next we open our dataset. We indicate where to find the dataset on our computer, in this case it is on the C drive:

```
use "C:\Data\VM-JSO.dta", clear
```

After opening the dataset we can start generating our propensity scores. First we need to convert our categorical variable 'type_offender', which has three categories, into two dummy variables. The information in a nominal variable with *k* categories can be converted into $k - 1$ dummy variables. We do this using the following command:

```
tabulate type_offender, gen(type_offender)
```

We end up with three dichotomous variables, of which we will use the second and third. The results for the second and third variables are contrasted with the first category, the child abusers. (SPSS executed such a procedure automatically after we had indicated that the variable for offender type was a categorical variable). Otherwise, we use exactly the same variables as we did in the SPSS example.

Now we are ready to calculate the propensity scores. We do this using the procedure `pscore`. This procedure is not installed in Stata as standard, and in contrast to `psmatch2` cannot be installed using `ssc install`. One needs to search for `pscore` via `findit pscore`. After entering this command the most recent procedure must be chosen '`Software update for pscore suite`'.

```
pscore treated contact_peers
   psychopathology age_offence
   IQ neuroticism impulsivity ethnicity
   type_offender2 type_offender3 previous
   logit pscore(ps)
```

The two new dummy variables are indicated in this syntax by `type_offender2` and `type_offender3`. Readers may notice that the variable with the long name `previous_sexoffence` has been shortened to '`previous`'. In Stata many commands and instructions can be shortened, and we have done this here. Stata produces the output as shown in Figure 3.12. This output shows exactly the same results as that which SPSS produced earlier, see Figure 3.8.

After the propensity scores have been made we ask Stata to carry out matching using the procedure `psmatch2`. This is a lot simpler than doing it by hand as in SPSS, as Stata does all the matching for us. We can make the caliper wider or stricter with one command.

We first run the caliper matching using a caliper of .05. To do this we use a number of commands. To start we provide Stata with a random number. This is because if two control respondents have the same propensity score, and therefore would both be a good match for an experimental respondent, Stata will choose one

Figure 3.12: Results of the logistic regression from Stata

```
Logistic regression                               Number of obs   =        500
                                                  LR chi2(10)     =      61.40
                                                  Prob > chi2     =     0.0000
Log likelihood = -291.76912                       Pseudo R2       =     0.0952
```

treatment	Coef.	Std. Err.	z	P>|z|	[95% Conf.	Interval]
contact_pe~s	-.1403635	.1547498	-0.91	0.364	-.4436676	.1629405
psychopath~y	-.2337405	.2276115	-1.03	0.304	-.6798508	.2123697
age_offence	.0317235	.0624487	0.51	0.611	-.0906738	.1541207
IQ	.2929346	.1054671	2.78	0.005	.0862228	.4996464
neuroticism	.0211678	.0920392	0.23	0.818	-.1592258	.2015614
impulsivity	.1938368	.0934714	2.07	0.038	.0106363	.3770373
ethnicity	-.4961934	.2305268	-2.15	0.031	-.9480177	-.0443691
type_offen~2	-.5967471	.2413826	-2.47	0.013	-1.069848	-.123646
type_offen~3	-1.356812	.3049242	-4.45	0.000	-1.954453	-.7591721
previous_s~e	-.2247605	.3206814	-0.70	0.483	-.8532845	.4037634
_cons	-.4088381	1.223475	-0.33	0.738	-2.806805	1.989129

of them at random. To guarantee the same results if we were to run the analysis again, we give Stata this random start number which can be used again the next time. Because Stata generates random numbers via a set procedure, providing a random start number ensures that the results from any future analyses will be exactly the same. This '*seed number*' is set using the following commands:

```
set seed 123456789
```

Next we enter the command `psmatch2` to carry out the matching:

```
psmatch2 treated, pscore(ps) cal(.05)
   out(recidivism_sex) noreplace logit
```

This syntax tells Stata that we want propensity score matching to be carried out, that `treated` is the intervention variable, that respondents should be matched on the variable `ps`, which we made earlier using the `pscore` procedure, that we want the caliper to be set to .05, that the dependent variable is `recidivism_sex`, that matching should be done without replacement of respondents, and that a logistic regression should be used to check whether the matched experimental and control groups differ on the dependent variable.

The command provides the results as shown in Figure 3.13. As we can see in this figure Stata produces very compact results. This is the only table of results which is produced. We can see from the table that there is a significant difference on the 'ATT' (the *average treatment effect for the treated*), namely the effect that we are looking for. The difference is -.094, and this difference is significant. The t statistic is -2.21, with a corresponding p-value of less than .05.

Stata generates a second table which is useful to examine, see Figure 3.15. From this table we can see how well the respondents in the experimental and control groups were matched. We can read in the contingency table that 138 of the treated respondents were matched with 138 untreated respondents. In total 35 treated respondents fell outside the area of common support. Using this procedure, no match could be found for 35 respondents when employing a caliper of .05. In total the analysis therefore uses 276 respondents (more than the 250 we had ended up with our hand-made matching in SPSS). In Stata, as said earlier, we can also carry out t-tests and chi-square tests on the remaining respondents to see whether their scores are roughly the same. It will come as no surprise that this is indeed the case here. We can therefore conclude that the balancing property is met after matching.

We can use these results to calculate the odds ratio by hand as follows: Of the treated respondents 10.1449% re-offended, 89.8551% did not re-offend; of the control respondents 19.5652% re-offended and 80.4348% did not. The odds ratio is therefore:

$$\frac{\frac{10.1449}{89.8551}}{\frac{19.5652}{80.4348}} = \frac{(10.1449 * 80.4348)}{(89.8551 * 19.5652)} = 0.464.$$

These results do not differ greatly from those we calculated earlier using SPSS. The confidence interval, which equals (.232, .930), can also be calculated by hand.

We now repeat the same analysis but this time setting the caliper to .01. The commands look pretty much the same:

```
psmatch2 treated, pscore(ps) cal(.01)
   out(recidivism_sex) noreplace logit
```

This time we get the results shown in Figure 3.14. These results are somewhat stronger. The difference between treated and untreated respondents is larger and the t-value is also larger. They are also of course still significant. This illustrates how a more precise matching process in this case filters out more bias.

Figure 3.16 shows the results of the analysis using a caliper of .01. We can see that, as expected, the area of common support is now smaller. The contingency table indicates that now only 130 of the treated respondents could be matched, and

Figure 3.13: Results of caliper (.05) propensity score matching using Stata

Variable	Sample	Treated	Controls	Difference	S.E.	T-stat
recidivism_sex	Unmatched	.156069364	.155963303	.000106061	.034181563	0.00
	ATT	.101449275	.195652174	-.094202899	.042592083	-2.21

Figure 3.14: Results of caliper (.01) propensity score matching using Stata

Variable	Sample	Treated	Controls	Difference	S.E.	T-stat
recidivism_sex	Unmatched	.156069364	.155963303	.000106061	.034181563	0.00
	ATT	.084615385	.184615385	-.1	.042039863	-2.38

Figure 3.15: Overview of caliper (.05) propensity score matching with Stata

psmatch2: Treatment assignment	psmatch2: Common support Off suppo	On suppor	Total
Untreated	0	327	327
Treated	35	138	173
Total	35	465	500

Figure 3.16: Overview of caliper (.01) propensity score matching with Stata

psmatch2: Treatment assignment	psmatch2: Common support Off suppo	On suppor	Total
Untreated	0	327	327
Treated	43	130	173
Total	43	457	500

so the analysis only uses 260 respondents (still more than our rough hand-matching with SPSS). In total 43 treated respondents fell outside the area of common support.

One could argue that the analysis as we have carried it out is very strict and not very efficient. We have nearly twice as many untreated as treated respondents, but for every treated respondent we are selecting just one untreated respondent. We could perhaps make better use of the sample by using kernel matching. We will demonstrate this procedure in section 3.9.

We could perhaps use more of the sample in another way, too. Stata can namely also carry out *k*-nearest neighbour matching using a caliper. Using this method, Stata tries to match two or more untreated respondents to each treated respondent. Whether this would be possible with our dataset is doubtful. The problem is that we have a large number of untreated respondents with a low propensity score, who are not going to work well as controls for the treated respondents, because these generally have much higher propensity scores. This is likely the reason that Stata, if we use nearest neighbour matching with more than one neighbour, always re-uses control respondents. For reasons already briefly touched upon above, we do not recommend replacement of controls. Re-using control respondents from a finite sample causes statistical problems, namely dependency, which translates into wider confidence intervals which can have undesirable effects on the results. In our data (output not shown) re-using control respondents for the matching procedure resulted in some respondents being matched 11 times! Given our dataset and the area of common support we arrived at, this kind of analysis would rely strongly on a small number of respondents who are, in all likelihood, unique. For example, we may have one single untreated respondent who happens to have a high propensity score. The resulting situation is therefore unstable and likely also not very well generalisable. So we only recommend using k-nearest neighbour matching with a caliper when the untreated part of the sample is many times larger than the treated part. We stress that the untreated part should be many times larger as in our case the untreated numbered twice as many as the treated and this was still not large enough.

The different caliper matching analyses we have shown have all produced roughly the same results as when carrying out the procedure by hand in SPSS. To check for robustness, we also ran several slightly different logistic regression models to produce the propensity scores, as recommended. The propensity scores from all these different models looked very similar (results not shown). The correlations between the propensity scores were 0.97 or higher. Besides this though, the results of our propensity score analyses were not always comparable. We would expect that leaving significant predictors out of the model would change the results. This would after all substantially affect our ability to make a good prediction, as less bias would be filtered out. However, also when we left out predictors that were not significant in the multivariate model we still obtained different results. This demonstrates that our findings are not very robust against slightly different specifications of the logistic regression model.

3.9 Propensity score analyse with Stata: kernel matching

The final analysis we demonstrate is propensity score matching using kernel matching. We use the propensity scores we had already made. The instructions for Stata are very simple:

```
psmatch2 treated, pscore(ps) kernel
```

```
    out(recidivism_sex)
    logit kerneltype(epan)
```

This syntax tells Stata that we want to carry out propensity score matching, that `treated` is the intervention variable, that the variable `ps` should be used for matching, that we want to use kernel matching, that the dependent variable is `recidivism_sex`, and that a logistic regression should be used to test whether the matched experimental and control groups differ on the dependent variable. We also indicate that we want to use the Epanechnikov method for the kernel matching. This is the default method, which according to the literature generally performs well.

The output looks the same as that for caliper matching, and therefore we do not display it. Surprisingly enough though, the treatment effect is no longer significant. The t-value is now -0.86. Whilst the results still indicate lower re-offending rates amongst the treated group, using this matching method the effect is no longer significant.

The examples we have provided demonstrate, all in all, that the analysis chosen can have a dramatic effect on the results, and consequently any conclusions drawn. A possible explanation for the differences we found may be that the caliper analysis only used half of the sample. In the Stata analyses only 276 of the 500 respondents were included. For half the sample, those in the middle who fall into the area of common support, we do find a significant effect. But if we use the whole sample as we do with kernel matching, meaning those with an extremely high or low risk of re-offending are also included, the effect is noticeably smaller.

We can examine this by again using kernel matching, but this time asking Stata to ignore those respondents with extreme propensity scores, i.e. those that fall outside the area of common support, in essence 'trimming' the tails of the distribution of propensity scores. Given we used just over half the respondents in the first caliper analysis, 55.2%, we ask Stata to remove 22% of the respondents at the bottom and 22% of respondents at the top of the propensity score range, i.e. we instruct Stata to 'trim' the sample. We do this using the following command:

```
psmatch2 treated, pscore(ps) kernel
    out(recidivism_sex)
    logit kerneltype(epan) trim(22)
```

We now get the output shown in Figure 3.17. Here we can see that 136 of the treated respondents were matched, i.e. included in the analysis, and consequently we know that 136 virtual control respondents were constructed. We can see from the top table that the data on the unmatched part of the sample remain the same as the results above. The difference in recidivism rates between the treated and their matches is now smaller, and the one-sided t-test values indicate that the difference between treated and virtual untreated respondents is now significant.

We can now confidently state that consistent advantageous treatment effects are found for the part of the sample for whom treatment allocation in a sense 'hangs in the balance'. For respondents who do not have such high propensity scores that treatment is inevitable or such low propensity scores that treatment is superfluous, the treatment appears the desired effect in that it lowers recidivism risk.

3.10 Software

As should by now be obvious, Stata offers the most options for carrying out propensity score matching analysis. The necessary procedures can be easily downloaded and added to the standard package. The procedures provide many different options, for example even the error terms can be corrected for the replacement of matched respondents. For those who are used to working with SPSS, Stata will take a little getting used to. It is certainly worth the effort though, as in versions of SPSS lower than v22.0, certain steps can only be carried out manually, increasing the risk of mistakes and miscalculations. There are in the meantime however 'plugins' available for SPSS, and propensity score matching can be done in SPSS using these. It will always be the preferred option for some researchers. See Thoemnes (2011) for instructions on using these plugins. The statistics programme `R` provides a number of choices for carrying out the more advanced options of propensity score matching.

3.11 Extensions

In many real life situations we do not have two groups who have and have not received an intervention. Rather, many different variations of a treatment or intervention are offered. For example, drug addicts may have three rehab methods to choose from. None of these methods are *a priori* preferred, it is not obvious that one works better than the other. If several, qualitatively different types of treatment need to be evaluated, propensity score matching can be used as well. The procedure is, however, a little more complicated. The logistic regression becomes a multinomial regression, but the principles remain the same. We will not describe the procedure further in this book. We refer to Imbens (2000) for an explanation of such multiple propensity score matching, and to Wang et al. (2001) and Spreeuwenberg et al. (2010) for examples using this procedure in research into the effectiveness of different combinations of psychotherapy medicines. Propensity score matching can also be used in a situation where different treatment doses are

Figure 3.17: Results of kernel matching with 22% trimming in Stata

Variable	Sample	Treated	Controls	Difference	S.E.	T-stat
recidivism_sex	Unmatched	.156069364	.155963303	.000106061	.034181563	0.00
	ATT	.095588235	.157316305	-.06172807	.034243776	-1.80

Note: S.E. does not take into account that the propensity score is estimated.

psmatch2: Treatment assignment	psmatch2: Common support Off suppo	On suppor	Total
Untreated	0	327	327
Treated	37	136	173
Total	37	463	500

offered. Here it is possible to manually carry out an ordered logistic regression for the treatments, and then to perform propensity score matching.

3.12 Further reading

By far the most comprehensive and accessible book on propensity score matching is by Guo and Fraser (2015). It provides an exhaustive account of more formal philosophical questions, breakdowns of the type of effects one might be looking for, technical aspects, as well as practical applications of the method. There are also a large number of manuals available on the internet for carrying out propensity score matching in Stata or SAS.

Propensity score matching is used in social sciences quite regularly. Within criminology we found several studies employing this method. Gibson et al. (2009) report that gang membership did not significantly affect chances of being a victim of a violent offence after having used propensity score matching as a statistical control, although this was also true for the results before employing propensity score matching. King et al. (2007) use propensity score matching to demonstrate that marriage, controlling for propensity to marry, reduces criminal behaviour in men. This was true even for men for whom the chance of marrying was small. For women they found the same effect, but then only for those women with an average chance of getting married.

In the Netherlands, Wermink et al. (2009) researched differences in risk of recidivism between those who received short prison sentences and those who received community service. They predicted allocation of the different sanctions using a limited number of personal characteristics, criminal history, and type of offence. The results, following propensity score matching, indicated that respondents given community service had significantly lower recidivism rates than matched respondents given a prison sentence. Aarten (2014) compared recidivism rates amongst first offenders who received a custodial sentence and those who received a suspended sentence. After propensity score matching she found that recidivism rates in both groups were comparable.

Chapter 4

Instrumental variables

In the previous chapter we read about how propensity score matching can be used to make two dissimilar research groups as comparable as possible. This method uses a number of observed variables in order to be able to compare the experimental and the control groups. The two groups can however still differ on any unobserved variables. In other words, we can use propensity score matching to control for *overt bias*, but not for *hidden bias*. One method that does enable us to control for the distorting effect of observed and unobserved variables, and therefore overt and hidden bias, is the method of instrumental variables.

4.1 Introduction

Much research has demonstrated the desistance effect of employment in adulthood: whereby employed adults are less likely to commit crime than unemployed adults (see for example Stouthamer-Loeber et al., 2004; Uggen and Kruttschnitt 1998). However, this effect has not been found for adolescents. In fact research has found that the chance of delinquent behaviour is higher in adolescents who work, especially those who work many hours, than adolescents who do not work (Uggen and Wakefield, 2008). This finding is counter-intuitive: Why would employment be related to less criminal behaviour in adults, but not in adolescents? It is possible that the positive relationship between work and delinquency in adolescence is actually caused by a third, unobserved, distorting variable. For example, a lack of enthusiasm for school could be a confounding variable. Adolescents who are not interested in school are more likely to be working, and are also more likely to be delinquent as they are less exposed to the prosocial influence of school. Apel and colleagues (2008), examining the relationship between work and criminality in adolescence, controlled for possible distorting variables by using an instrumental variable, namely the law regarding adolescent working hours in different states. As we will see later in this chapter, by using instrumental variables they were able to demonstrate that work actually also reduced the chance of delinquency for adolescents.[1]

In this chapter we discuss the instrumental variables method. Instrumental variables were first used in the book *The Tariff on Animal and Vegetable Oils*, by Philip Green Wright (1928). In this book Wright researched the relationship between supply and demand of linseed. In doing so he discovered a problem of simultaneous causality. In the book's appendix he solves this problem by using *curve shifters*. These curve shifters are now referred to as instrumental variables. Wright's econometric discovery was however not picked up on, and it was only in the 1940s that the instrumental variables method was rediscovered and developed further. Since then the method has been widely used in econometrics. More recently the method has been increasingly used in medical and criminological research. Instrumental variables can be used to prevent three causes of endogeneity bias. First, instrumental variables can be used when a third variables distorts the relationship between the intervention W and the dependent variable Y, as in the example above on the effect of work on adolescent delinquency. Whether this distorting variable is observed or unobserved is not important, as the instrumental variable method is able to solve problems of hidden bias, as well as overt bias. Second, instrumental variables can be used in cases of simultaneous causality between W and Y: W causes Y but Y also causes W. Finally instrumental variables are also a solution to the problem of measurement error in W which is correlated with Y scores.

In this chapter we will outline what instrumental variables are and how they can be used to prevent the three causes of endogeneity bias described above. Following this we will demonstrate how the method can be employed in practice using a detailed example concerning the treatment of juvenile sex offenders. Finally we provide instructions of how to carry out the method in SPSS and Stata.

As we will see in this chapter the use and interpretation of instrumental variables are relatively simple. Anyone who can perform and interpret a simple or ordinary least squares (OLS) regression will be able to carry out the instrumental variables method. Where this method is difficult, is in the search for and choice of a theoretically relevant and strong instrumental variable which meets all the necessary conditions.

---

[1] In chapter 6 we discuss how the research design of Apel et al. is actually a combination of instrumental variables method and fixed effects models. For didactic reasons in this chapter we will only focus on the part of this research pertaining to instrumental variables.

The instrumental variables method was first employed in the work of Philip Green Wright (1928). Wright was born in 1861 and gained his Masters degree from Harvard University in 1887. In 1892 he was made professor at Lombard College, where he taught economics, mathematics, astronomy, and fiscal history. P.G. Wright married his cousin Elizabeth Quincy Sewall Wright and together they had three sons: the famous geneticist Sewall Green Wright, the well-known aviation engineer Theodore Paul Wright, and the influential political scientist Quincy Wright.

In 1928 P.G. Wright's book The Tariff on Animal and Vegetable Oils was published, including the appendix where instrumental variables were for the first time employed. The first 285 pages of this book contained a very detailed description of animal and vegetable oils. Then, out of nowhere Appendix B appears, a clear and comprehensible explanation of the problem of simultaneous causality, including a solution to this problem, instrumental variables. The difference in style between Appendix B and the rest of the book did not go unnoticed. Many researchers cast doubt as to whether P.G. Wright even wrote the appendix and whether he can therefore be rightly viewed as the inventor of instrumental variables (Stock and Trebbi, 2003).

Figure 4.1: Philip Green Wright (1861-1934)

4.2 Instrumental variables

In the following section we will demonstrate what instrumental variables are and which conditions they need to fulfill in order to solve issues of endogeneity. Next we will lay out the three causes of endogeneity bias for which instrumental variables provide a solution. We conclude this section with a review of 'weak instruments' and the consequences of using these instruments.

4.2.1 The instrumental variable method

As we described in section 1.4, the endogeneity assumption is not fulfilled when allocation to the experimental or control group is related to, or dependent on, scores on the dependent variable Y. In this case the intervention variable W is partly endogenous. The fact that the intervention variable is only partly endogenous highlights the possibility that there is also an 'exogenous' part of W. This exogenous part of W is therefore not dependent on the score on Y. The trick of the instrumental variable method is to separate the exogenous part of W from the endogenous part of W. Next (part of) the exogenous variation of W is included in the model, and the endogenous variation in W is not. Because the endogenous variation of W is not in the model any endogeneity bias is removed. This probably all sounds rather abstract. We will therefore first address one or two issues more formally, before using a number of examples to illustrate the method.

How do we go about separating the exogenous from endogenous variation in W? We need a third variable, the instrumental variable (Z). This instrumental variable Z must first and foremost be relevant: Z must correlate with the endogenous intervention variable W. Next the influence of Z on W must be exogenous. We will discuss these two conditions concerning instrumental variables in more detail later. Once these conditions are fulfilled we can use the instrumental variable Z to predict scores on W. These predicted W scores are then used to calculate the effect of W on Y. Endogeneity bias is avoided because we are only using the part of W that is predicted by the exogenous variable Z. In this way the predicted W, $\hat{W}$, also becomes exogenous.

An example of an instrumental variables model is the Two Stages Least Squares (shortened to TSLS or 2SLS) procedure whereby two OLS regression equations are employed. First a regression equation is needed to predict W using Z. Below (4.1) is the regression equation for W_i. In this equation δ is the intercept, γ is the influence of the instrumental variable Z_i on the intervention W_i and v_i is the prediction error. Equation (4.2) is the regression equation for $\hat{W}_i$. In this equation the prediction error is not included because $\hat{W}_i$ is the estimated value of W_i. Given that the prediction error refers to the difference between the estimated value ($\hat{W}_i$)

and the observed value (W_i), prediction error v_i should not be included in equation (4.2).

$$W_i = \delta + \gamma Z_i + v_i \tag{4.1}$$

$$\hat{W}_i = \delta + \gamma Z_i \tag{4.2}$$

Once W has been estimated using Z, we can use the estimated values for W, $\hat{W}$, to predict Y. Equation (4.3) gives the regression equation for Y_i. In this equation α is the intercept, β is the influence of the estimated values of the intervention W_i, $\hat{W}_i$, on the dependent variable Y_i and ε_i is the prediction error. The instrumental variable Z is not included in (4.3).

$$Y_i = \alpha + \beta \hat{W}_i + \varepsilon_i \tag{4.3}$$

At first glance this method may seem relatively simple because it is just made up of two separate regression equations. The difficulty is however in finding suitable instruments. There are two conditions which an instrumental variable has to meet. First, the instrumental variable Z must correlate with the intervention variable W. Otherwise equation (4.1) would not make sense. Furthermore, this correlation should be strong; after all we want there to be as much exogenous variation in $\hat{W}$ as possible. If this is not the case then we have a weak instrument. Later in this section we will explain in more detail what a weak instrument is, as well as the problems this can cause. The second condition is that the instrumental variable is exogenous. Respondents' Z scores must not be dependent on their W scores, otherwise equation (4.1) will be distorted. To meet the exogeneity condition, the instrumental variable Z cannot have a direct effect on the dependent variable Y. Furthermore, the instrumental variable Z should not have an indirect effect on the dependent variable Y via any variable other than the intervention variable W. In other words, all of the effect of Z on Y needs to go through W. When these conditions are not met we are back at our original problem: we have *endogeneity bias*. The best way to ensure that Z scores are not dependent on W, is by allocating, *at random* , respondents' scores on the instrumental variable Z. However, this is not usually possible. Because this condition cannot be empirically tested the researcher has to argue for the exogeneity of the instrumental variable on theoretical grounds. In the following sections we will illustrate the use of instrumental variables and these two necessary conditions using several examples.

Figure 4.2: Example of a distorting variable in the relationship between smoking and health

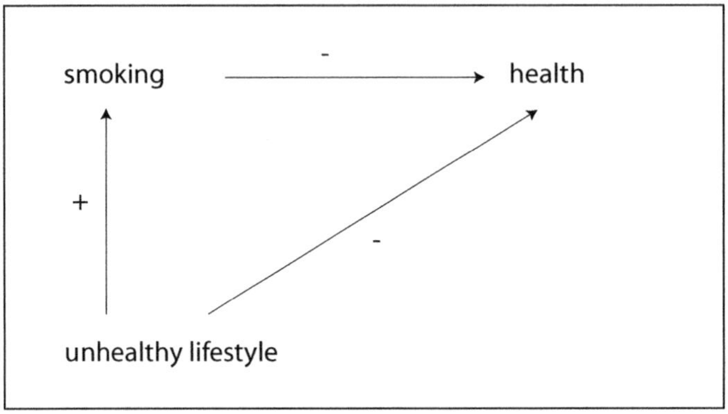

4.2.2 Solution for distorting variables

The classic cause of *endogeneity bias* is when a distorting variable influences both the intervention W and the dependent variable Y. Say we want to research the influence of smoking on health. We expect a negative relationship between smoking and an individual's health. There is however a third variable, an individual's unhealthy lifestyle, which influences both the intervention (smoking) and the dependent variable (health). An unhealthy lifestyle is likely to increase the risk that someone smokes. There is therefore a positive relationship between an unhealthy lifestyle and smoking. On the other hand an unhealthy lifestyle is also likely to adversely affect health. There is a negative relationship between an unhealthy lifestyle and an individual's health. Figure 4.2 illustrates this.

Scores on smoking are related to those on health because of their relationship with unhealthy lifestyle. We refer to this as endogeneity bias. If we were to use an OLS regression analysis to calculate the effect of smoking on health the negative regression coefficient would be over-estimated. As well as the direct negative effect of smoking on health the regression coefficient would also include the indirect negative effect of an unhealthy lifestyle.

When we are unable to control for unhealthy lifestyle, for example because information on this is missing, the instrumental variable method can be used to get round the endogeneity bias problem. An instrumental variable used in previous research predicting smoking habits is the random assignment of an incentive to

Figure 4.3: Instrumental variables model for the relationship between smoking and health

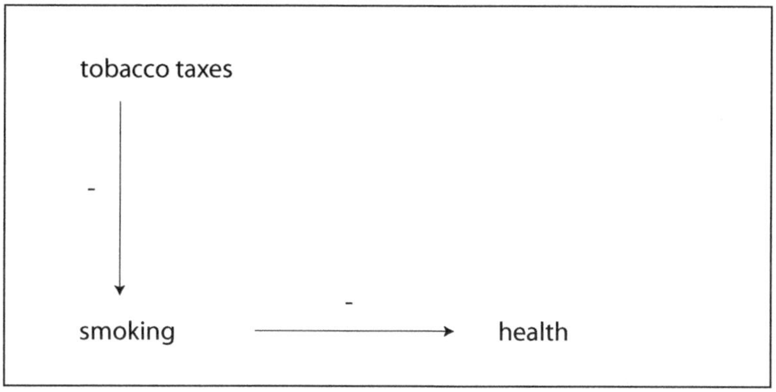

quit smoking (Permutt and Hebel, 1989). Such an incentive can influence whether people decide to stop or reduce their smoking habits. Often however, it is not possible to allocate respondents' scores on the instrumental variable. When this is not possible, we could for example use the level of tobacco tax in different countries as an instrumental variable, if we were carrying out an international study. Higher taxes on tobacco negatively correlate with smoking habits, people smoke less when the price of cigarettes increases. If we can empirically demonstrate that the level of tobacco tax (Z) and smoking habits (W) are correlated, the instrumental variable can be deemed relevant and the first condition is met. We could also argue that this instrumental variable is exogenous and that consequently the second condition is also met. Taxes are established by the government in different countries and are therefore not dependent on an individual's smoking habits, i.e. whether an individual smokes or not has no influence on whether the government decides to increases taxes on tobacco. Moreover tobacco taxes (Z) have no direct influence on an individual's health (Y). That tobacco tax influences health via other variables is also unlikely because it is only a tax on tobacco not other unhealthy behaviours. As both conditions for instrumental variables are met, we can use tobacco tax levels as instrumental variable to establish the true effect of smoking on health. The instrumental variables model is shown in Figure 4.3.

We can test this instrumental variables model using an international study examining smoking habits and health. By comparing the smoking habits of people living in countries with differing levels of tobacco taxes the exogenous variation in smoking habits can be estimated. Next this estimated smoking habit can be used to calculate the influence of smoking on individuals' health. The regression equations are as follows:

$$\text{Smoking}_i = \delta + \gamma\,\text{Tax level} + v_i \tag{4.4}$$

$$\text{Estimated smoking}_i = \delta + \gamma\,\text{Tax level} \tag{4.5}$$

$$\text{Health}_i = \alpha + \beta\ \text{Estimated smoking}_i + \varepsilon_i \tag{4.6}$$

In this model unhealthy lifestyle no longer has any influence on the estimated score for smoking habits. Consequently the indirect negative effect via unhealthy lifestyle on an individual's health is no longer included in the regression coefficient. This coefficient in the instrumental variables model is therefore no longer overestimated, and so provides a better picture of the causal effect of smoking on health.

Within criminology there are many examples of research where unobserved, distorting variables have influenced certain relationships, and thereby caused endogeneity bias. As we mentioned in the introduction, in criminological research a positive relationship between work and criminal behaviour in adolescence has often been found. We would expect a negative relationship, given that the theory and research on work and criminality in adulthood has found that employment results in less criminal behaviour. Possibly a third, distorting variable plays a role here: a lack of interest in school. Lack of interest in school has a positive relationship with both having work and criminal behaviour. As well as the direct effect of work on criminality, an indirect, positive 'effect' of work on criminality is present via lack of interest in school. This model is illustrated in Figure 4.5.

In earlier research on the link between work and criminal behaviour in adolescence the indirect positive effect of lack of interest in school (as well as other possible confounding variables) was apparently as strong or stronger than the direct negative effect, and as a result either no effect or a positive effect of work on criminality has been found. With the help of instrumental variables the endogeneity bias in this model can be corrected for and a better estimation of the true effect of work on criminal behaviour can be made. Apel and colleagues (2008) used the laws relating to working hours for adolescents in the United States as an instrumental variable in their research. In America there is a strict national law regarding the number of hours adolescents up to the age of 16 years are allowed work. Once adolescents are older than 16 this national law no longer applies. For 16 and 17 year olds the working hours law regarding the amount of hours youth can work differs per state. Some states have no limit on the number of hours 16 and

If P.G. Wright did not write Appendix B in his book *The Tariff on Animal and Vegetable Oils* then who did? Many have suggested that his oldest son Sewall Green Wright was the real writer of this piece. By 1928 he had after all become an important statistician in the field of genetics. Furthermore earlier that decade he had developed path analysis (Wright, 1921, 1923), which was also included in Appendix B. S.G. Wright's interest in economy was not great however. His main interest was evolutionary biology, and he actually developed the inbreeding coefficient. This interest in inbreeding is notable given that this parents were first cousins.

In 1988 Sewall Wright died aged 98 years. No one had ever asked him if it was him or his father who had written Appendix B and was therefore the discoverer of instrumental variables. Stock and Trebbi (2003) used stylometry to work out who was the true author. This analysis technique examines a text's literary fingerprints, which can then be used to determine the writer's identity. The analysis clearly pointed to P.G. Wright as the author. Whether instrumental variables really was his idea or whether he had just written it up will remain a mystery. A bigger mystery however, is why the method was hidden for so long, and only decades later was put to use again.

Figure 4.4: Sewall Green Wright (1889-1988)

Figure 4.5: Example of a distorting variable in the relationship between work and juvenile crime

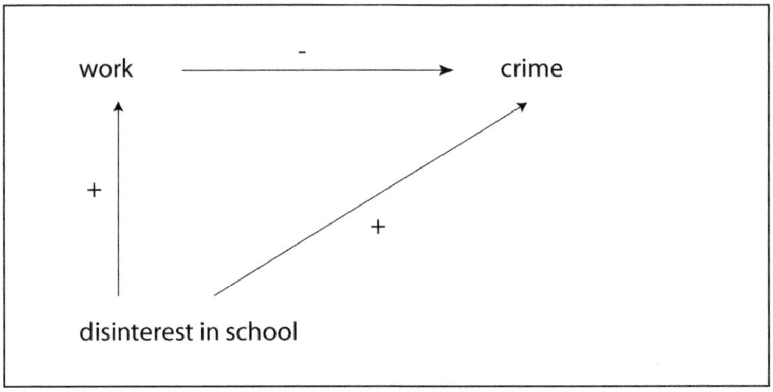

17 year olds may work, some states have a limit of 40 hours, other again set a maximum of 20 hours. This instrumental variable meets both the necessary conditions. The first condition is met because a relationship between the law and the number of hours adolescents work exists: the stricter the law in a state, the fewer hours adolescents in the state work. The second condition is also met, because the law regarding working hours in a state is of course not dependent on whether an individual works or not. Furthermore, it is very unlikely that a states employment law will directly influence an individual's criminal behaviour. In addition an indirect influence via another variable besides working or not working is also improbable as the law specifically applies to working hours. The instrumental variables model is illustrated in Figure 4.6.

Endogeneity bias is removed from this model because criminal behaviour is only predicted by the part of 'work' that can be predicted by the exogenous variable 'working hours law'. Lack of interest in school therefore has no influence on the estimated score for work, and so the indirect positive effect of work on criminal behaviour through lack of enthusiasm for school no longer affects the regression coefficient. The coefficient of the instrumental variables model now demonstrates a negative effect of work on criminal behaviour, an effect which better reflects the true influence of work on criminality (Apel et al., 2008).

When the endogeneity bias is caused by one or more distorting variables, whether these variables are observed or not observed is not important for the instrumental variables method. The influence of these distorting variables is not

Figure 4.6: Instrumental variables model for the relationship between work and juvenile crime

included in the instrumental variables model because only the exogenous variation of the intervention W is used. For this reason the distorting variable does not have to be observed (or measured). The advantage of using the instrumental variables method is therefore that it can be employed whenever there are theoretical grounds for expecting a distorting effect from a third variable, but the distorting effect cannot be tested, because, for example, no information on this variable is available. In this way instrumental variables also provide a solution for when hidden bias is anticipated to be a problem.

4.2.3 Solution for simultaneous causality

Simultaneous causality between the intervention W and dependent variable Y occurs when W does not only cause Y, but Y also causes W. The classic example of simultaneous causality is the relationship between the price of a product and supply of that product. Say we want to research the effect of demand for sprouts on the price of sprouts. In the Dutch city of Moerdijk in 2011 a chemical factory caught fire. As a result all the sprout growers in the surrounding area were not allowed to sell their sprouts for fear of damaging the population's health. This situation would lead to a sprout shortage, which in turn would cause the price of sprouts to increase. Scarce products are after all more expensive. On the other hand, if there was an over-supply of sprouts the price for consumers would decrease as a

Figure 4.7: Example of simultaneous causality in the relationship between supply and price of sprouts

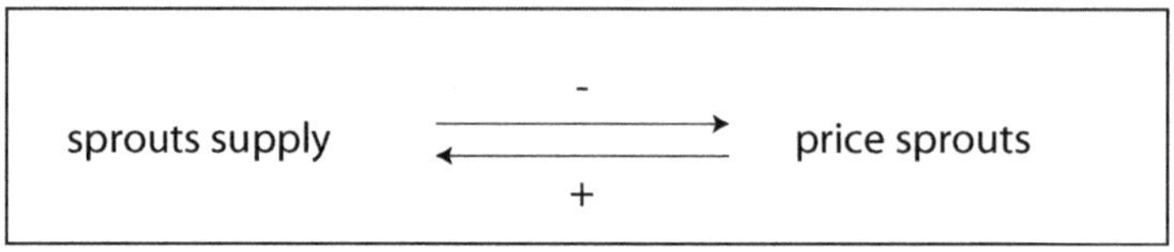

consequence of increased competition. The price of sprouts can however also influence their supply. When the price of sprouts is high, supply of sprouts will also increase, as the sprout farmers will of course earn more money from selling them. So the supply of sprouts has a negative influence on the price of sprouts, but at the same time the price of sprouts has a positive influence on the supply of sprouts, as illustrated in Figure 4.7.

Due to this simultaneous causality, the supply of sprouts (W) is dependent on the price of sprouts (Y) and we therefore have endogeneity bias. If we were to calculate the effect of supply of sprouts on the price of sprouts using an OLS regression the negative coefficient would be under-estimated. Besides the negative relationship between supply and price the positive effect of price on supply would also be included in the regression coefficient, resulting in this under-estimation. The instrumental variables method can be used to control for simultaneous causality between W (supply of sprouts) and Y (price of sprouts), and we would come closer to estimating the true effect of supply of sprouts on their price.

So we need to search for a variable Z which correlates with W and only correlates with Y via W. In this example we therefore need to find a variable which correlates with supply of sprouts and only influences the price of sprouts via the supply. One possible instrumental variable is the number of hours of sun. It is highly likely that this correlates with the supply of sprouts, as sprouts need sun to grow (relevance). Furthermore, the number of sun hours cannot be influenced by people. It is therefore not dependent on the supply of sprouts, nor does it have any direct effect on the price of sprouts (exogeneity). The instrumental variables model is shown in Figure 4.8.

In this model the supply of sprouts is estimated on the basis of the number of sun hours in a period. The price of sprouts no longer has any influence on the estimated supply of sprouts, because this is estimated on the basis of the exogenous variable 'sun hours'. In this way simultaneous causality is avoided and endogeneity

Figure 4.8: Instrumental variables model for the relationship between supply and price of sprouts

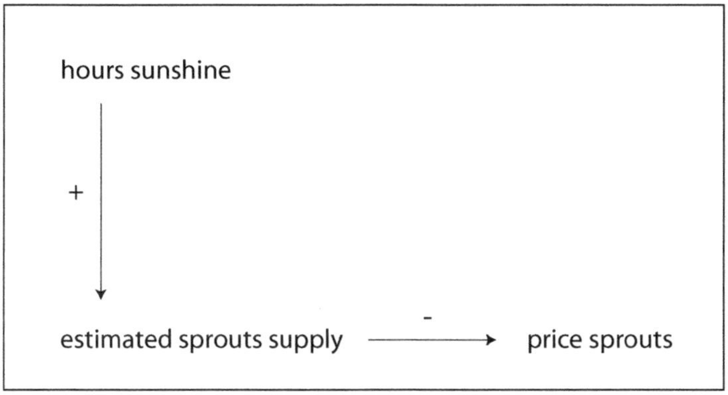

is eliminated. The coefficient indicating the influence of the supply of sprouts on the price of sprouts is no longer under-estimated in this model, and consequently a better estimation of the true effect of supply on price will be given.

In criminology simultaneous causality problems also occur, for example when we want to investigate the influence of crime prevention on crime. More crime prevention, for example more police officers, would be expected to reduce the number of crimes. The opposite could also be true though, higher crime rates could result in more crime prevention, and so we have simultaneous causality. Another example of simultaneous causality within criminology is found in Mehlum and colleagues' research (2006) on the effect of poverty on crime in 19th century Germany. At this time more than 80 percent of people's income was spent on food, and so the price of rye was used as an indicator of poverty. Researchers demonstrated that property crime rates increased as the price of rye increased. People had to pay more for their food and consequently, having no money left to buy other items, they stole the things they needed. In this example a positive relationship between the price of rye and property crime is found. The opposite was however also true: there was a positive relationship between property crime and the price of rye. Historical sources show that in times of social tension stocks of grain and rye were looted. This kind of property crime therefore led to an increase in the price of rye, because as we have already seen lower supply leads to higher prices. Here again we have

Figure 4.9: Example of simultaneous causality in the relationship between the price of rye and property crime

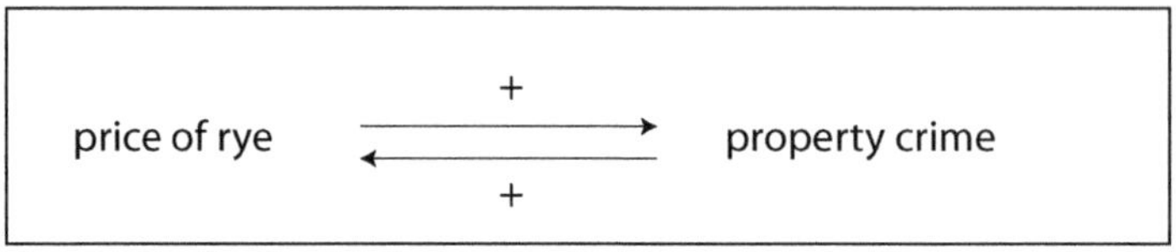

simultaneous causality with a positive influence of W on Y as well as a positive effect of Y on W, as illustrated in Figure 4.9.

In contrast to the sprouts example the OLS regression coefficients here would be over-estimated, as there is a positive effect in both directions. An increasing rye price leads to more property crime, but property crime also increases the price of rye. Because the regression coefficient takes into account both simultaneous effects this coefficient will be larger than the true effect of X on Y. Using instrumental variables in this case would lead to a lower coefficient which would better indicate the actual influence of rye prices on property crime. The instrumental variable that Mehlum and colleagues (2006) used in their research was the amount of rainfall in a period. This instrumental variable meets the relevance condition because rainfall results in a better rye harvest and therefore a lower price. In other words, there is a correlation between the instrumental variable (rainfall) and the intervention variable (price of rye). Whether the other condition is met is less obvious. Whilst a natural occurrence such as rainfall cannot in any way be dependent on the price of rye, rainfall could have both a direct influence on property crime and an indirect influence via factors other than the price of rye. Potential victims of crime are more likely to shelter inside if it is raining, whereby criminals could increase their theft of things outside. At the same time burglars are less likely to be breaking into houses if people are at home, as the chance of being caught is higher. Rainfall may also have an influence on people's mood, with the result that they are more likely to commit a crime. On the other hand criminals are also less likely to go out and about in the rain, preferring to shelter inside. Mehlum and colleagues (2006) also realised this possible direct effect of rainfall on crime, but were able to avoid this problem by using rainfall in the previous year as their instrumental variable. Rainfall in the previous year was a better predictor of for the price of rye than rainfall in the same year, and moreover it met the exogeneity condition. Rainfall in one year does not have a direct influence on property crime in the following year.

Figure 4.10: Instrumental variables model for the relationship between the price of rye and property crime

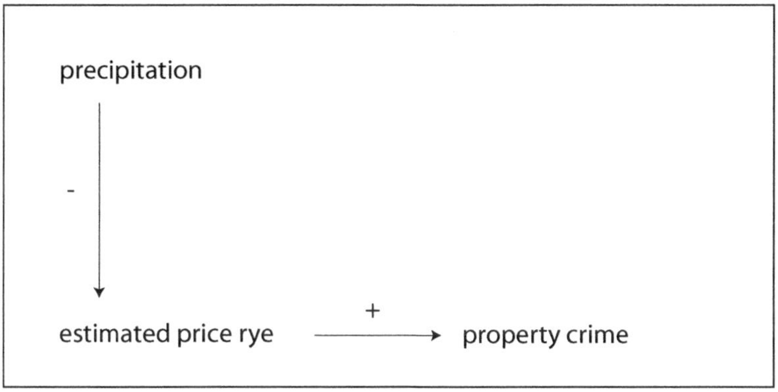

As both conditions are met the variable rainfall is a suitable instrument to control for the simultaneous causality between the price of rye (as poverty indicator) and property crime. The instrumental variables model is illustrated in Figure 4.10.

There is no longer simultaneous causality in this instrumental variables model, because property crime has no influence on the estimated price of rye, as this is estimated from the exogenous variable 'rainfall'. In this way endogeneity bias is avoided and the effect of the price of rye on property crime in the instrumental variables model is determined in a suitable manner. Mehlum and colleagues' (2006) analyses demonstrated that the coefficient using the instrumental variables method was indeed smaller than the OLS regression coefficient.

4.2.4 Solution for measurement error in the intervention variable

Lastly, instrumental variables can be used as a solution for measurement error in the intervention variable. Measurement error in the intervention variable can lead to endogeneity bias when the measurement error is dependent on the scores on the dependent variable. Say we want to research the intergenerational transmission of cultural participation. In other words, we are investigating whether people take part in cultural activities more often if their parents also did this. The use of retrospective data, whereby a respondent provides information on their cultural participation as well as that of their parents, can result in endogeneity bias through measurement errors in the intervention variable (cultural participation by the par-

Figure 4.11: Example of endogeneity bias caused by measurement errors in the relationship between parental and children's cultural participation

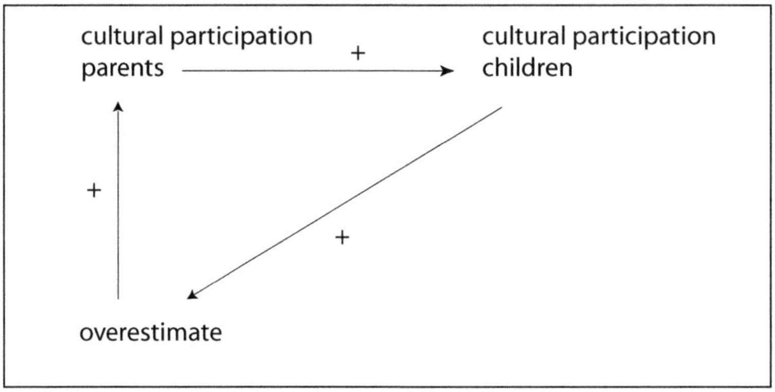

ents). Research by De Vries and De Graaf (2008) demonstrated that when people have a higher level of cultural participation they over-estimate their parents' level of cultural participation. These children actually report a higher level of cultural participation by their parents than their parents report themselves. In this case the measurement error, and therefore the score on the intervention variable (parental cultural participation) is dependent on the score on the dependent variable (children's cultural participation) and we have endogeneity bias. This model is illustrated in Figure 4.11.

If we were to carry out a standard OLS regression analysis the transmission of cultural participation would be over-estimated, because the fact that culturally active children over-estimate the cultural activities of their parents would not be taken into account. The instrumental variables model can here again provide a solution. One possible instrumental variable we could use is the price of theatre tickets during the parents' youth, i.e. before their children were born. This is likely to have influenced parents' cultural participation, as people would have gone to the theatre more often at times when prices were lower. This variable would therefore meet the relevance condition. The exogeneity condition is also met, as the price of a theatre ticket is not dependent on the cultural participation of an individual. Moreover, we use the price of a theatre ticket during the parents' youth before they had children and the price of a theatre ticket at that time has no direct influence on the cultural participation of the children as they had not yet been born. The instrumental variables model is illustrated in Figure 4.12.

Figure 4.12: Instrumental variables model for the relationship between cultural participation of parents and children

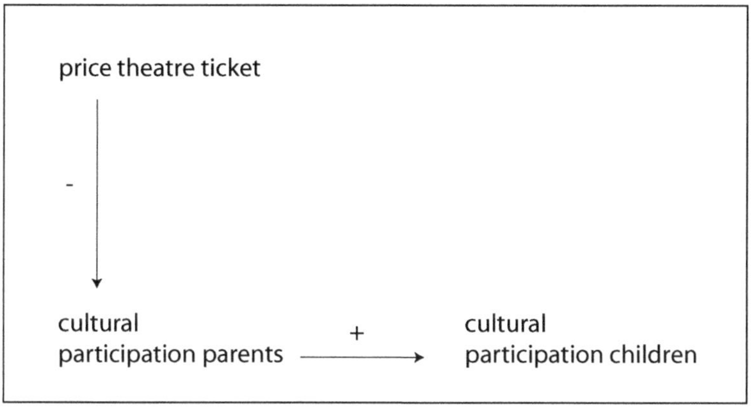

In the model in Figure 4.12 measurement error is unlikely to still be included in the independent variable because the cultural participation of parents is predicted on the basis of theatre price tickets. If there is still some measurement error in the instrumental variable then this is not dependent on the degree of cultural participation of the children. In this way endogeneity bias caused by measurement error in the intervention variable is avoided, and this model provides a more accurate picture of the influence of the cultural participation of parents on that of their children.

Within criminology another example of measurement error is the under-estimation of criminality in the official police crime figures. An example of research in which this under-estimation led to endogeneity bias was carried out by Tita and colleagues (2006) looking at the influence of criminality on house prices. You would expect the price of houses to be lower in areas where crime rates are higher. The results of the OLS regression analysis did not however show this. No effect of criminality on house prices was found, and in low income neighbourhoods a positive effect between violent crime and house prices was found. In these neighbourhoods the price of houses actually increased as levels of violence increased. Tita and colleagues (2006) argued that this surprising result could have been due to measurement error in the intervention variable (violent crime) being dependent on the dependent variable score (house prices). They proposed that (violent) crime

Figure 4.13: Endogeneity bias in the relationship between violent crime and house prices

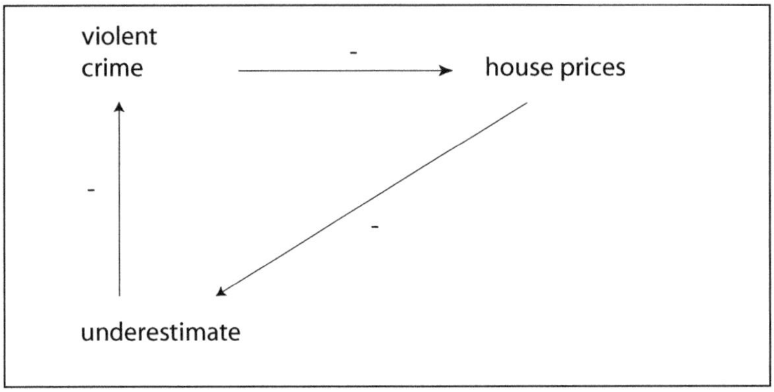

was most highly under-estimated in those neighbourhoods where average incomes were low, and was less under-estimated in those neighbourhoods where average incomes were high. Because house prices were also high in the latter neighbourhoods this results in endogeneity bias. This model is illustrated in Figure 4.13.

In this model the large under-estimation of the measure of violent crime in neighbourhoods with low house prices causes the negative effect of crime on house prices to disappear or even become positive. Using instrumental variables the endogeneity bias that results from measurement error in the crime variable could be avoided, leading to a truer estimation of the actual effect of crime on house prices. Tita and colleagues (2006) chose to use the number of murders in a neighbourhood as instrumental variable. They argued that murder is a crime which is nearly always registered, and therefore is not vulnerable to measurement error. This instrumental variable does meet the condition of relevance because the number of murders in a neighbourhood is likely to correlate with the number of other violent crimes. However, whether it also meets the condition of exogeneity is doubtful. Whether the number of murders in a neighbourhood is not dependent on the amount of violent crime in a neighbourhood is questionable. It seems obvious that more violent crime in a neighbourhood would result in more murders in a neighbourhood, for example revenge murders or criminal liquidations. There is therefore simultaneous causality between the number of murders in a neighbourhood and the number of other violent crimes in a neighbourhood. It is also very likely that the number of murders in a neighbourhood would have a direct influence on house prices. A neighbour-

Figure 4.14: Instrumental variables model for the relationship between violent crime and house prices

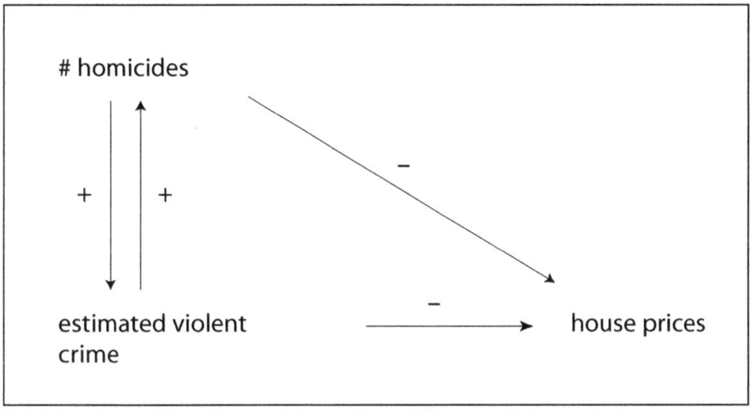

hood where many murders have taken place is not going to be very popular with potential house buyers, and as a result house owners are likely to drop their prices in order to sell their house. So it seems highly likely that this instrumental variable is not exogenous.

This case provides a good example of an unfortunate choice of instrumental variable that does not meet the required conditions. Nevertheless, Tita and colleagues (2006) still found, using their instrumental variables model, that criminality had a negative effect on house prices, especially in neighbourhoods with low incomes. The reason for this becomes obvious if we include the simultaneous causality between the number of murders and other violent crimes and the direct effect of murders on house prices in the model, as illustrated in Figure 4.14.

In this model the instrumental variable ensures that none of the measurement error in the intervention variable is dependent on the dependent variable and causing endogeneity bias. On the other hand the incorrectly chosen instrumental variable results in a violation of the exogeneity assumption in two different ways. First, in the first regression equation there is endogeneity bias caused by the simultaneous causality between number of murders and other violent crime in a neighbourhood. This simultaneous causality results in an over-estimation of violent crime in a neighbourhood. Second, there is again endogeneity bias between violent crime and house prices. This is now not caused by measurement error, but by the fact that the number of murders can be seen as a distorting variable, affecting violent crime and also house prices. In this case the negative effect of violent crime on house prices is over-estimated. It is therefore not surprising that Tita and colleagues (2006) found a negative relationship between crime and house prices. Altogether this case provides a good example of why an instrumental variable needs to meet the exogeneity condition. If this is not the case the use of instrumental variables can cause more problems than it solves.

4.2.5 Weak instruments

In the last example in section 4.2.4 we saw that violation of the exogeneity assumption can cause problems in our model. There is however another problem associated with instrumental variables: weak instruments. These are instrumental variables that are exogenous, but that only correlate weakly or not at all with the intervention variable. These instruments do not meet the first condition and are therefore not relevant. One of the consequences of using weak instruments is that they result in very large standard errors for the estimated intervention variable ($\hat{W}$). The standard error for $\hat{W}$ in the equation explaining Y increases as the instrumental variable Z accounts for less of the variation in W. Because a weak instrument is only able to explain a small amount of the variation in the intervention variable, the standard error for the estimated intervention variable ($\hat{W}$) becomes very large and the estimation less precise.

A second consequence of weak instruments is that they can yield misleading results. Using weak instruments can result in bias, whilst their purpose is specifically to prevent bias. Using a weak instrument can in this way be worse than using no instrument. In both cases we have bias, but in the model with the weak instrument the standard error for the intervention variable $\hat{W}$ is greater.

It is therefore of great importance that the relationship between the instrumental variable Z and the intervention variable W is strong. In the literature the criteria often given is that the F *statistic* from the first regression model (whereby W is estimated using Z) should be at least 10. If this is the case you can be sure that you do not have a weak instrument. In articles which use instrumental variables the value of the F*statistic* as well as the *adjusted* R^2 from the first regression analysis are generally reported, in order to demonstrate that a weak instrument has not been employed.

There is also a limit to how strong an instrumental variable can be. This limit is dependent on the amount of endogeneity bias in the intervention variable W. When the variation in W is largely endogenous, only a small proportion remains exogenous. The exogenous instrumental variable Z can then by definition only explain a small proportion of the variation in W and consequently Z is automatically a weak instrument. When endogeneity bias is (very) substantial the instrumental variables method is thus less suitable because the instrumental variable will often be weak, yielding misleading and less precise results. When the level of endogeneity bias is not too great using the instrumental variables method is suitable because a larger part of the variation in W is exogenous. Therefore the exogenous instrumental variable Z can explain more of the variation in W, yielding unbiased estimates. These estimates however remain less accurate than estimates from an OLS regression, as the standard errors are larger because we are only using just part of the variation in W. This is simply the price we must pay for removing bias using instrumental variables.

4.2.6 What to consider when using instrumental variables

In all the examples we have discussed so far we have looked at the influence of a single intervention variable on the dependent variable. In practice we do not use this kind of simple regression very often. Mostly the influence of several independent variables is measured or several control variables are added to the model. This is also possible using the instrumental variables method. If, as well as the endogenous intervention variable, there are simply other exogenous independent variables in the model then we just need to include these exogenous independent variables in both regression equations. We will illustrate this, using, for simplicity, different symbols for the parameters to those used earlier in equations (4.1) – (4.6).

Say we have included exogenous independent variables X_1 and X_2 in our model. Our regression equation would be as follows:

$$\hat{W}_i = a + bZ_i + c_1X_{1i} + c_2X_{2i} \tag{4.7}$$

$$Y_i = d + f\hat{W}_i + g_1X_{1i} + g_2X_{2i} + e_i \tag{4.8}$$

It is of course also possible that we do not just have one but several endogenous intervention variables. In that case we also need several instrumental variables. You always need to have the same amount of instrumental variables in the model as endogenous intervention variables. When this is not the case this is referred to as an *under-identified model*. When the number of instrumental variables equals the number of endogenous variables we have a *just-identified model*. When the number of instrumental variables exceeds that of endogenous variables, this is referred to as an *over-identified model*, and this is not a problem. Say we have two endogenous intervention variables W_1 and W_2 in a *just-identified model* with instrumental variables Z_1 and Z_2. We use both Z_1 and Z_2 to predict both W_1 and W_2. We therefore end up with three regression equations:

$$\hat{W}_{1i} = a + b_1 Z_{1i} + b_2 Z_{2i} \tag{4.9}$$

$$\hat{W}_{2i} = c + d_1 Z_{1i} + d_2 Z_{2i} \tag{4.10}$$

$$Y_i = f + g_1 \hat{W}_{1i} + g_2 \hat{W}_{2i} + e_i \tag{4.11}$$

Finally, up to now we have been employing a 2SLS procedure with two OLS regression analyses. In the first stage Z is used to predict $\hat{W}$ using an OLS regression analysis. In the second stage $\hat{W}$ is used to predict the effect of Y again using an OLS regression analysis. But what if the intervention variable(s) are dichotomous? If only the dependent variable is dichotomous this is not a problem. We then simply estimate the intervention variable on the basis of the instrumental variables using an OLS regression as before. Next we calculate the influence of the estimated intervention variable on the dependent variable using a non-linear regression analysis. However, when the endogenous intervention variable is dichotomous we cannot simply replace the OLS regression analysis in the first stage with a non-linear regression analysis. Previous research has demonstrated that this can lead to inconsistent estimations (see for example Hausman, 2001). Economist Joshua Angrist (2001; 2006) proposed, however, that in cases with a dichotomous endogenous intervention variable and/or a dichotomous dependent variable the 2SLS procedure can be used. According to him the 2SLS estimates of the causal effect of the intervention are robust against and not sensitive to the non-linearity of the dichotomous variables, as long as there are no or few additional variables in the model. If however a non-linear alternative is preferred we recommend Angrist (2001) and Foster (1997), who review several non-linear alternatives to the 2SLS.

4.3 Example: Probation and general recidivism

Just as in the previous chapter we will illustrate the instrumental variables method using an example. Again, this example is based on the same dataset with 500 fictional juvenile sex offenders. Where in the previous chapter we looked at the influence of treatment on sex offending recidivism, in this chapter we will look at the influence of the length of probation on general recidivism. We believe that as probation entails supervision, that longer supervision will help keeping recidivism at bay. In other words, we research whether juvenile sex offenders who are supervised for longer have a lower chance of committing any offence than juvenile sex offenders who are on probation for a shorter period of time. The variable `probation` indicates the length of time of the probation and has a possible score

Figure 4.15: Frequencies of categories `probation`

supervision

		Frequency	Percent	Valid Percent	Cumulative Percent
Valid	0 months	6	1,2	1,2	1,2
	3 months	20	4,0	4,0	5,2
	6 months	59	11,8	11,8	17,0
	9 months	100	20,0	20,0	37,0
	12 months	144	28,8	28,8	65,8
	15 months	82	16,4	16,4	82,2
	18 months	54	10,8	10,8	93,0
	21 months	28	5,6	5,6	98,6
	24 months	7	1,4	1,4	100,0
	Total	500	100,0	100,0	

of 0 to 8 (0=0 months, 1=1–3 months, etc.). When we multiply the score for `probation` by three we know the number of months the probation lasted. Figure 4.15 and Figure 4.16 give the frequency distribution and the descriptives of the variable `probation`, as can be requested using the following syntax commands:

```
FREQUENCIES probation.
DESCRIPTIVES probation.
```

As Figure 4.15 shows, most juvenile sex offenders (28,8%) are on probation for one year. Only six juvenile sex offenders are not placed on probation and seven are on probation for two years. The `probation` variable has a relatively normal distribution, as we can see in Figure 4.16, with an average of 4 and a standard deviation of around 1.6. In order to calculate the effect of probation length on recidivism we need to first carry out a logistic regression, the recidivism variable is after all dichotomous (0=no recidivism, 1=recidivism). This is done using the following SPSS syntax, which produces the output seen in Figure 4.17.

```
LOGISTIC REGRESSION VARIABLES recidivism_general
     /METHOD=ENTER probation
     /CRITERIA=PIN(.05) POUT(.10) ITERATE(20) CUT(.5).
```

Figure 4.16: Distribution of `probation`

Descriptive Statistics

	N	Minimum	Maximum	Mean	Std. Deviation
supervision	500	0	8	4,00	1,598
Valid N (listwise)	500				

Figure 4.17: Logistic regression of recidivism on length of probation

Variables in the Equation

		B	S.E.	Wald	df	Sig.	Exp(B)
Step 1[a]	supervision	-,021	,065	,105	1	,746	,979
	Constant	1,194	,281	18,061	1	,000	3,299

a. Variable(s) entered on step 1: supervision.

Figure 4.18: Measure of fit for the logistic regression of recidivism on length of probation

Model Summary

Step	-2 Log likelihood	Cox & Snell R Square	Nagelkerke R Square
1	560,022[a]	,000	,000

a. Estimation terminated at iteration number 4 because parameter estimates changed by less than ,001.

Figure 4.17 seems to show a slight negative effect of length of probation on the chance of recidivism. In other words the longer the probation lasts the lower the chance that a juvenile sex offender will relapse into offending. However, this effect if far from significant. The Nagelkerke R^2 of 0 (see Figure 4.18) indicates that length of probation explains none of the variation in general recidivism.

Figure 4.19: Endogeneity bias in the relationship between length of probation and recidivism

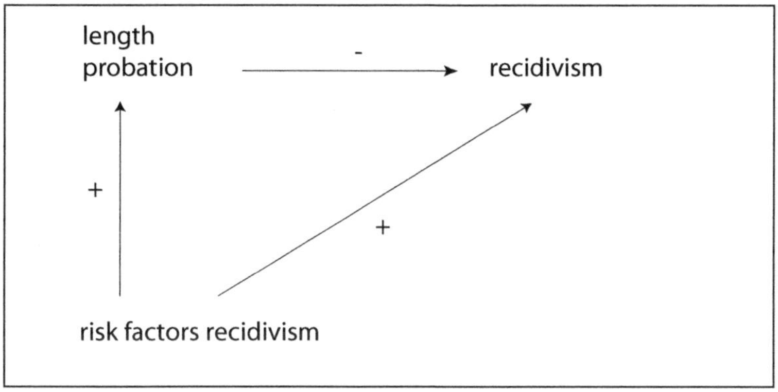

So from these first analyses it seems that the length of probation has no influence on the chance of recidivism. However it is entirely possible that confounding factors are influencing both the length of probation and the chance of recidivism. Juvenile offenders who have a higher chance of recidivism are also likely to be those who are placed on probation. Risk factors for recidivism, for example a lack of empathy, poor self image, psychopathology, impulsivity, and a history of sexual abuse, are likely used to determine how long a sex offender is placed on probation, and therefore influence the length of probation as well as chance of recidivism. This is illustrated in the diagram in Figure 4.19. These risk factors may have a distorting effect, resulting in endogeneity bias. By employing the instrumental variables method we will be able to filter out this endogeneity bias and we can investigate whether length of probation actually does have a significant effect on general recidivism.

4.3.1 Choosing an instrumental variable

Before carrying out the instrumental variables method we need to first find an instrumental variable which meets the two conditions discussed earlier. As we are using an existing dataset we are unable to allocate scores at random on an instrumental variable to the juvenile sex offenders. We therefore need to search for an existing variable. This variable needs to correlate with length of probation, and should only relate to chance of recidivism through length of probation.

Figure 4.20: Length of probation by sex offender type

Report

supervision

type_offender	Mean	N	Std. Deviation
child abuser	4,41	222	1,433
peer abuser	4,01	153	1,686
group offender	3,25	125	1,501
Total	4,00	500	1,598

In the previous chapter we saw in Figure 3.5 that offender type correlated with chance of treatment: group offenders were treated least often whilst child abusers were treated most often. Perhaps type of offender also correlates with length of probation. We can use the following SPSS syntax to ask for the average probation length for the three types of offenders. We can see from Figure 4.20 that type of offender does indeed correlate with length of probation.

```
MEANS TABLES=probation BY type_offender.
```

Figure 4.20 shows that group offenders are on average on probation for the shortest period of time, with an average score of 3.25, which relates to nearly 10 months. Peer abusers are on probation for longer: on average their score was 4.01, indicating that they are on probation for about a year. Child abusers however are on probation for longest, with an average score of 4.41, indicating a period of around 13 months.

Perhaps offender type is a suitable instrumental variable for our model. If we look at the two conditions instrumental variables need to meet we can see that offender type meets the first condition: as we saw in Figure 4.20, the instrumental variable (offender type) and the intervention (length of probation) correlate with each other. Whether it also meets the second condition of exogeneity is doubtful. It is possible that scores on `type_ offender` are not independent from length of probation. Empirical research on juvenile sex offenders has found that group offenders and solo offenders significantly differ on personal characteristics, such as neuroticism, impulsivity, extraversion and sensation seeking (Hendriks and Bijleveld, 1999). Furthermore child and peer offenders also appear to differ significantly on neuroticism, psychopathology, and self image, amongst others (Hendriks,

Bijleveld and Muizer, 2002). Because these characteristics are likely to also correlate with length of probation, the influence of offender type on length of probation is probably not entirely exogenous. Besides this, these characteristics also relate to chance of recidivism, whereby offender type influences recidivism via variables other than length of probation (e.g. neuroticism, impulsivity, extraversion, psychopathology, self image). Furthermore a direct effect of offender type on recidivism cannot be ruled out. Group offenders would, for example, be less likely to relapse into offending if they are removed from their gang of delinquent friends. The condition of exogeneity is thus not met. We can therefore conclude that `type_offender` is not a suitable instrumental variable for our research.

Besides offender type the other individual and background characteristics in the dataset (see Table 3.1) do not appear to be suitable instrumental variables, as these are also likely to have a direct effect on recidivism or relate to recidivism via other variables than the length of probation. We therefore need to search for a variable that does not originate from the individual dossiers of the juvenile sex offenders. In previous research looking at the effect of length of detention on work and income, judges have been used as instrumental variables to estimate length of detention (Kling, 2006). In our dataset whilst we do not have any information about the judges who presided over the juvenile sex offenders' trials, we do know at which court they were tried. Using the following SPSS syntax command we can examine whether the courts differed in the length of probation they handed out to the juvenile sex offenders.

```
MEANS TABLES=probation BY court.
```

This SPSS syntax gives us the output in Figure 4.21. From this output we can see that there are large differences in average length of probation handed out to the juvenile sex offenders between the 19 courts. On average the 500 juvenile sex offenders score 4 on `probation`, meaning that they are on probation for an average of one year. Sex offenders who were tried in the courts in Maastricht and Den Bosch were however, on probation for a much shorter time period, with average scores of 2.50 and 2.91 respectively. Sex offenders tried in the courts in Almelo, Middelburg, Leeuwarden, Arnhem, Zutphen, Roermond, and Groningen also received a relatively short probation period. On the other hand sex offenders tried in Amsterdam were on probation for the longest period, with an average score on the variable `probation` of 5. Sex offenders tried in the courts in Assen, Haarlem, Rotterdam, Utrecht, Dordrecht, Alkmaar, Breda, Zwolle, and The Hague were also on average placed on probation for a relatively long period.

There are obviously large differences between the different courts on how long they place juvenile sex offenders on probation. The variable `court` is therefore a possible instrumental variable. It appears at least to meet the relevance condition.

Figure 4.21: Length of probation period per jurisdiction

Report

supervision

court	Mean	N	Std. Deviation
's-Hertogenbosch	2,91	32	1,653
Breda	4,38	24	1,313
Maastricht	2,50	18	1,855
Roermond	3,85	20	1,424
Arnhem	3,56	34	1,618
Zutphen	3,56	27	1,476
Zwolle	4,18	40	1,448
Almelo	3,15	20	1,599
's-Gravenhage	4,06	16	1,436
Rotterdam	4,67	27	1,240
Dordrecht	4,50	20	1,235
Middelburg	3,28	32	1,746
Amsterdam	5,00	28	1,217
Alkmaar	4,45	33	1,523
Haarlem	4,74	23	1,214
Utrecht	4,58	24	1,501
Leeuwarden	3,33	21	1,528
Groningen	3,87	23	1,517
Assen	4,79	38	1,234
Total	4,00	500	1,598

Given the differences on average score of the `probation` variable for each court seen in Figure 4.21 we can expect a strong correlation between this instrumental variable and the intervention variable. The condition of exogeneity is also met, as the court where someone is tried is not dependent on the length of probation they are placed on. Furthermore, there is no direct effect of the court where someone is tried on their chance of re-offending. Both conditions for an instrumental variable are therefore met. The court where the juvenile sex offender is tried appears to be a suitable instrument to estimate the effect of length of probation on general recidivism. We will therefore use this variable to carry out the next steps of our instrumental variables model.

As the variable `court` is a nominal variable we cannot simply plug it into our analyses without first recoding it. The '*monotonicity* assumption' (see for example Rhodes, 2010) requires that we recode the different courts so that they are rank ordered from lowest average score to highest, or vice versa, on the `probation` variable. In our example we will order the courts from lowest to highest. The juvenile sex offenders tried in Maastricht consequently get the lowest score on the instrumental variable (score 1), followed by those who were tried in the court Den Bosch (score 2), Almelo (score 3), Middelburg (score 4) and so on, up to those juvenile sex offenders tried in Amsterdam, who are given the highest score (score 19). We can use the following syntax command to create this new variable:

```
RECODE court (3=1)(1=2) (8=3) (12=4) (17=5) (6=6)
      (5=7) (4=8) (18=9) (9=10) (7=11) (2=12) (14=13)
      (11=14) (16=15) (10=16) (15=17) (19=18)
      (13=19) INTO court_IV.
```

Some readers might be wondering why in this example the categorical variable court is used as an interval variable. Whilst it is possible that using it as a categorical variable would result in a better fitting model, using the simpler approach of an interval variable is sufficient to demonstrate the principles at work here.

4.3.2 The instrumental variables model

Our instrumental variable indicates whether the different courts placed the juvenile sex offenders on probation for a long or short period of time. This instrumental variable is used to estimate the intervention variable, length of probation, as shown in the equation below (4.12). Because the variable `court_IV` in equation (4.12) is an exogenous variable, the estimated length of probation is also partly exogenous. The estimated length of probation is then used to estimate the chance of general recidivism, as shown in equation (4.13).

$$\text{Estimated length of probation}_i = a + b\ \text{court\_IV}_i \tag{4.12}$$

$$\text{General recidivism}_i = c + d\ \text{Estimated length of probation}_i \tag{4.13}$$

The variable `court_IV` is not included in equation (4.13), as this variable is only used to extract the exogenous part of length of probation. Because confounding

Figure 4.22: Regression analysis in the first step: measures of fit

Model Summary[b]

Model	R	R Square	Adjusted R Square	Std. Error of the Estimate
1	,422[a]	,178	,176	1,450

a. Predictors: (Constant), court_IV

b. Dependent Variable: supervision

factors, such as risk factors for recidivism, do not correlate with the exogenous part of length of probation, their distorting effect has been filtered out of equation (4.13). As the variable `recidivism_general` is dichotomous, in the second stage of our model we carry out a logistic regression. The error term e_i is not included in the logistic regression equation (4.13), for reasons explained in section 2.3.

4.3.3 Instrumental variables using SPSS

We will now estimate the above model using SPSS. There are two possibilities in SPSS for estimating a 2SLS model. First, two separate models can be run. The first step is to run the model for the first stage, by using the instrumental variable (`court_IV`) to estimate the intervention variable (length of probation). This is done using the following SPSS syntax for running a OLS regression analysis.

```
REGRESSION
     /MISSING LISTWISE
     /STATISTICS COEFF OUTS R ANOVA
     /CRITERIA=PIN(.05) POUT(.10)
     /NOORIGIN
     /DEPENDENT probation
     /METHOD=ENTER court_IV
     /SAVE PRED.
```

The command `/SAVE=PRED` is is added to the syntax in order to automatically save the estimated scores for length of probation under the variable name `PRE_1`. This syntax generates a number of relevant tables.

The output in Figure 4.24 shows that the court where a sex offender is tried has a significant effect on the length of probation. Juvenile sex offenders tried at a

Figure 4.23: Regression analysis in the first step: *F* test

ANOVA[a]

Model		Sum of Squares	df	Mean Square	F	Sig.
1	Regression	226,632	1	226,632	107,758	,000[b]
	Residual	1047,368	498	2,103		
	Total	1274,000	499			

a. Dependent Variable: supervision

b. Predictors: (Constant), court_IV

Figure 4.24: Regression analysis in the first step: regression model

Coefficients[a]

Model		Unstandardized Coefficients		Standardized Coefficients	t	Sig.
		B	Std. Error	Beta		
1	(Constant)	2,742	,137		19,946	,000
	court_IV	,122	,012	,422	10,381	,000

a. Dependent Variable: supervision

court with a higher score on the variable `court_IV` score higher on the variable `probation` than juvenile sex offenders tried at a court with a lower score on the variable `court_IV`. The *adjusted* R^2 of .176 in Figure 4.22 indicates that the court at which a juvenile sex offender is tried explains 17.6% of the variation in length of probation. Furthermore, the F test statistic of 107.758 in Figure 4.23 is high and well above the critical value of 10. We can therefore conclude that this is not a weak instrument. This also indicates that the relevance condition is met.

The second step is to use the estimated length of probation to predict the risk of recidivism. Because our dependent variable is dichotomous we will use a logistic regression analysis to do this. In this analysis committing or not committing an new offence is the dependent variable. Our independent variable in this analysis is the variable we just created `PRE_1`, i.e. the estimated length of probation. The SPSS syntax is as follows:

Figure 4.25: Regression analysis in the second step: fit measures

Model Summary

Step	-2 Log likelihood	Cox & Snell R Square	Nagelkerke R Square
1	544,727[a]	,030	,045

a. Estimation terminated at iteration number 4 because parameter estimates changed by less than ,001.

Figure 4.26: Regression analysis in the second step: regression model

Variables in the Equation

		B	S.E.	Wald	df	Sig.	Exp(B)
Step 1[a]	PRE_1	-,617	,161	14,755	1	,000	,539
	Constant	3,622	,673	28,933	1	,000	37,395

a. Variable(s) entered on step 1: PRE_1.

```
LOGISTIC REGRESSION VARIABLES recidivism_general
     /METHOD=ENTER PRE_1
     /CRITERIA=PIN(.05) POUT(.10) ITERATE(20) CUT(.5).
```

This syntax reports the output shown in Figure 4.25 and Figure 4.26.

The regression coefficient for `PRE_1` is -.617 and significant with an α of 0.001. This means that the longer a juvenile sex offender is placed on probation the lower the chance is that he will re-offend. We now see a significant negative effect of length of probation on risk of recidivism, whilst earlier we did not find any effect due to confounding factors.

We have shown how to estimate the instrumental variables model by carrying out two separate regression analyses manually. In the literature, however, this method has been reported to generate incorrect standard errors (see for example Angrist, 2006) and it is therefore not generally used. Software programmes, such as Stata and SPSS therefore offer the possibility to estimate the model in one process, automatically adjusting for these incorrect standard errors. In SPSS the 2SLS procedure can be carried out using the following command:

```
2SLS Y WITH W
     /INSTRUMENTS Z
     /CONSTANT.
```

The name of the dependent variable should replace *Y*, the name of the endogenous intervention variable(s) should replace W, and the name of the instrumental variable(s) should replace *Z*. This procedure in SPSS does however have several disadvantages. First the analysis of the first stage is not reported in the 2SLS analysis output. Because of this we are not able to see whether the instrumental variable has a significant effect on the endogenous intervention variable. Neither do we know whether we have a weak instrument and we cannot test whether our instrumental variable is relevant. A second disadvantage is that when using the 2SLS procedure no exogenous independent or control variables can be included in the model. In practice the influence of several variables is often tested at the same time, and this is just not possible using the 2SLS procedure in SPSS. Finally, the 2SLS procedure includes the intervention and dependent variables in the model as interval variables. In other words, it is not possible to distinguish between an OLS regression and a non-linear regression analysis. As we are using a dichotomous dependent variable (general recidivism) the 2SLS procedure in SPSS is not suitable. We will therefore estimate our instrumental variables model using Stata. The instrumental variables procedure in Stata does not have these disadvantages and it still adjusts the incorrect standard errors.

4.3.4 Instrumental variables with Stata

In contrast to the 2SLS procedure in SPSS, Stata can be used to estimate our instrumental variables model with a dichotomous outcome variable. In Stata we use the `ivprobit` command. As the name suggests, this command makes use of a probit regression analysis. This probit regression looks very similar to a logistic regression, with the exception that the link function is a little different. With a probit regression a steeper S-shaped curve for the odds ratio, i.e. bending more sharply on the left and right hand side of the distribution, is fitted than with a logistic regression (see Figure 2.1). This probit regression is only used to estimate the second regression equation; the first regression equation simply employs a OLS regression which assumes that the intervention variable is measured at the interval level. The Stata command `ivprobit` is used as follows:

```
ivprobit Y (W=Z) X, first
```

In this command the dependent variable name replaces *Y*. Between the brackets the endogenous intervention variable(s) replaces the *W*, and the instrumental variable(s) replace *Z*. If we want to include one or more exogenous independent or control variables in the model these are placed where *X* is. The addition of 'first' to the command ensures that the results of the first regression equation are reported. In our case the command is as follows:

```
ivprobit recidivism_general (probation=court_IV),
    first
```

Putting this command into Stata produces the output shown in Figure 4.27. At the top of Figure 4.27 the results of the second stage are given. Again we see that there is a significant negative effect of length of probation on general recidivism. The coefficients are however different from those produced in SPSS. This is because Stata calculates a probit regression, whereas in SPSS we carried out a logistic regression. The next rows show the results of the first stage, and these are pretty much identical to the results from SPSS. Of all the other parameters shown in the output (/lnsigma, /athrho, sigma, rho) rho is of importance. When this parameter equals zero this means that our endogenous intervention variable in not endogenous at all but exogenous. This is not the case in our model, where we have a score of 0.529 with a confidence interval of 0.307-0.696. The *Wald-test of exogeneity* at the bottom of the output examines whether the rho is significantly different to 0. In Figure 4.27 the rho differs significantly from 0, indicates that the length of probation is indeed partly endogenous, and that we have therefore correctly employed instrumental variables.

In this detailed example we have shown how instrumental variables can be used to estimate the effect of probation on general recidivism for juvenile sex offenders. In the original OLS model we did not find a significant effect, and this was likely due to the distorting effect of confounding factors. By using the court where the juvenile sex offenders were tried as an instrumental variable we could however show that there was a negative effect of probation on recidivism. The longer a juvenile sex offender was on probation the less likely he was to re-offend. Critics might argue, however, that our instrumental variable is not suitable because the court where someone is tried is not randomly allocated. They might for example contend that juvenile sex offenders tried in the courts in Amsterdam, Rotterdam and Utrecht have more chance of coming from a large city than those tried in Assen, Zutphen or Middelburg. If the risk of recidivism is higher in cities than in villages, then the court could also influence chance of recidivism of juvenile sex offenders via urbanisation. As the condition of exogeneity cannot be tested empirically it falls to the researcher to justify and defend their choice of instrumental variable.

Figure 4.27: Stata output from `ivprobit`

```
Probit model with endogenous regressors            Number of obs   =       500
                                                   Wald chi2(1)    =     21.55
Log likelihood = -1165.5279                        Prob > chi2     =    0.0000
```

	Coef.	Std. Err.	z	P>|z|	[95% Conf.	Interval]
recidivism_general						
probation	-.310196	.0668262	-4.64	0.000	-.441173	-.1792189
_cons	1.838838	.2438399	7.54	0.000	1.36092	2.316755
probation						
court_IV	.1224376	.0117711	10.40	0.000	.0993666	.1455086
_cons	2.741831	.1371891	19.99	0.000	2.472946	3.010717
/athrho	.5885061	.1386242	4.25	0.000	.3168076	.8602045
/lnsigma	.3697138	.0316228	11.69	0.000	.3077343	.4316933
rho	.5288203	.0998578			.3066175	.696363
sigma	1.44732	.0457683			1.360339	1.539863

```
Instrumented:  probation
Instruments:   court_IV

Wald test of exogeneity (/athrho = 0): chi2(1) =    18.02 Prob > chi2 = 0.0000
```

4.4 Software

In the previous section we used a detailed example to show how the instrumental variables method can be carried out manually. As we stated earlier this manual procedure leads to incorrect standard errors, and therefore allowing the software programme to estimate the procedure in one step is usually preferred. As we discussed in section 4.3.3 the 2SLS procedure in SPSS has its disadvantages, and we therefore prefer to use Stata. In the previous section we outlined how to carry out an instrumental variable analysis with a dichotomous outcome variable using `ivprobit`. In this section we will demonstrate how to carry out instrumental variable analysis in Stata when we have a dependent variable measured at interval level.

The standard Stata command to carry out instrumental variables analysis is `ivreg`. However, a different command `ssc install ivreg2` downloads the add on `ivreg2`. We recommend doing this as the `ivreg2` procedure and accompanying add ons provide more information than the `ivreg` procedure. The following command shows how `ivreg2` should be used:

```
ivreg2 Y (W=Z) X, first
```

In this command *Y* again indicates the dependent variable. Between the brackets replace *W* with the endogenous intervention variable, and replace *Z* with the instrumental variable(s). One or more extra exogenous independent variables can be included in the model, and these should be placed where *X* is. Adding `first` to the command again ensures that the results from the first regression equation are reported. To make things simpler in the following example we use the same variables as in section 4.3.4, and we assume now that `recidivism_general` is an interval variable rather than dichotomous. The intervention variable is again `probation` and the instrumental variable is again `court_IV`. Including these variables in the command shown above produces the output shown in Figure 4.28. The top of Figure 4.28 gives the results of the first regression equation. These results are the same as those from the first regression equation we saw in section 4.3.3 and section 4.3.4. In Figure 4.28 however, as we used `ivreg2` we get some extra information. In the first table 'Partial R-squared of excluded instruments' and 'test of excluded instruments' are reported. In this example the *partial* R^2 and F test statistic for the 'excluded instruments' are equal to the R^2 and F test statistic reported in the top right of the figure. This is because there are no other exogenous independent variables included in the model. When this is the case the *partial* R^2 and F test statistic for the excluded instruments indicate how well the instrumental variables predict the intervention variables, excluding the influence of any exogenous independent variables.

In Figure 4.29 the results of the second stage regression equation are shown. Under this table the so called *Sargan statistic* is reported. This test can in some cases be used to examine whether the instrumental variable is exogenous. Earlier in this chapter we stated that exogeneity cannot be tested empirically and that whether the condition is met therefore needs to be justified theoretically by the researcher. However, this is not always true. When we have an *over-identified* model, i.e. there are more instrumental variables than endogenous variables, this condition can be tested using the *over-identification test*. This test examines whether the different instrumental variables produce roughly the same estimates, as we would expect if they were exogenous. In Figure 4.28 we have a *just-identified model* and so this *over-identification test* cannot be carried out. If we were to have an *over-identified model* and the *p* value for the *Sargan statistic* was significant, this would indicate that the estimates of the different instrumental variables were not similar, and that one or more of the instrumental variables was not exogenous. If this were the case not all of the instrumental variables would meet the exogeneity condition.

Figure 4.28: Stata output from `ivreg2`: first stage of 2SLS

```
First-stage regression of probation:

Ordinary Least Squares (OLS) regression
---------------------------------------

                                                      Number of obs =       500
                                                      F(  1,    498) =    107.76
                                                      Prob > F      =    0.0000
Total (centered) SS     =          1274              Centered R2   =    0.1779
Total (uncentered) SS   =          9274              Uncentered R2 =    0.8871
Residual SS             =   1047.368108              Root MSE      =      1.45

------------------------------------------------------------------------------
   probation |      Coef.   Std. Err.      t    P>|t|     [95% Conf. Interval]
-------------+----------------------------------------------------------------
    court_IV |   .1224375   .0117948    10.38   0.000     .0992639    .1456112
       _cons |   2.741832   .1374644    19.95   0.000      2.47175    3.011913
------------------------------------------------------------------------------
Partial R-squared of excluded instruments:   0.1779
Test of excluded instruments:
  F(  1,   498) =   107.76
  Prob > F      =   0.0000
```

Finally, we saw in section section 4.3.4 that `ivprobit` produces a *Wald-test of exogeneity* which indicates whether the intervention variable is indeed endogenous. When using `ivreg2` this test is not reported. We can however ask for the *Wu-Hausman F test* and the *Durbin-Wu-Hausman* χ^2 *test* to be reported. This F test and χ^2 test indicate whether a standard OLS regression, where the effect of W on Y is estimated, leads to the same conclusions as analysis using the instrumental variables. When this true the intervention variable is not endogenous, i.e. using the original intervention variable W produces the same results as using the exogenous $\hat{W}$. These tests are reported by Stata by using the `ivreg2` command followed by the command `ivendog`. If these tests produce a significant p value the intervention variable(s) are indeed endogenous, and the decision to use instrumental variables was therefore correct.

Figure 4.29: Stata output from `ivreg2`: second stage of 2SLS

```
Instrumental variables (2SLS) regression
----------------------------------------

                                                   Number of obs =        500
                                                   F(  1,    498) =      13.04
                                                   Prob > F      =     0.0003
Total (centered) SS     =        93.248            Centered R2   =    -0.1585
Total (uncentered) SS   =           376            Uncentered R2 =     0.7127
Residual SS             =   108.0294213            Root MSE      =      .4648

------------------------------------------------------------------------------
recidivism~l |      Coef.   Std. Err.      z    P>|z|     [95% Conf. Interval]
-------------+----------------------------------------------------------------
   probation |  -.1117104   .0308763    -3.62   0.000    -.1722269   -.051194
       _cons |   1.198842   .1252424     9.57   0.000      .953371   1.444312
------------------------------------------------------------------------------
Anderson canon. corr. LR statistic (identification/IV relevance test):  97.941
                                                   Chi-sq(1) P-val =    0.0000
------------------------------------------------------------------------------
Sargan statistic (overidentification test of all instruments):           0.000
                                                 (equation exactly identified)
------------------------------------------------------------------------------
Instrumented:          probation
Excluded instruments:  court_IV
------------------------------------------------------------------------------
```

4.5 Advantages and limitations

In this chapter we have seen how the instrumental variables method can be used to counteract endogeneity bias. The instrumental variables method has several advantages over that of propensity score matching, described in chapter 3. First, propensity score matching only offers a solution for endogeneity bias caused by (observed) confounding factors. The instrumental variables method in contrast, can also solve the problem of endogeneity bias caused by simultaneous causality or measurement error in the intervention variables. Second, we saw in chapter 3 that the propensity score matching method can only make the experimental and control group comparable in the basis of observed variables. In other words, propensity score matching can only be used to solve problems of overt bias. The instrumental variables method however offers a solution for hidden as well as overt bias, as explained in section 4.2.2. Finally, the instrumental variables method does not lead to the loss of respondents unlike the propensity score matching method. In propensity score matching we often lose respondents when we match them one to one.

There are of course some disadvantages to the instrumental variables method. First, there obviously needs to be a suitable instrumental variable which meets the necessary conditions. Is such a variable is available we then of course need data on this instrumental variable in order to employ the method. A second disadvantage is that the exogeneity of the instrumental variable cannot be tested empirically. Whether this condition is met can therefore only be argued on theoretical grounds. If we incorrectly assume that this condition is- met, the instrumental variable method can cause more problems than it solves, as we explained in section 4.2.4. Third, the instrumental variable method is not as suitable for cases where endogeneity bias is high. In such cases the variation in W is mostly endogenous, with only a small part being exogenous. Logically the exogenous instrumental variable can therefore only predict a small part of the variation in W and we consequently have a weak instrument. As we saw in section 4.2.4 using a weak instrument leads to not only biased but also noisy results.

So when there is a question of limited endogeneity bias using the instrumental variables method is a good solution. But remember using an instrumental variable to remove endogeneity bias is always done at the expense of accurate estimations. Thus the researcher always has to weigh up the advantages of removing the bias against the loss of accuracy in the estimations.

4.6 Further reading

In this chapter we have attempted to explain the instrumental variables method in an accessible way, without using too many formulas instead employing concrete examples. In the majority of the, mainly econometric, literature on instrumental variables the reader is bombarded with formulas, making the texts unreadable. One more readable piece on instrumental variables is a chapter by Bushway and Apel (2010) on the use of instrumental variables in criminology and criminal law. In addition the chapter on instrumental variables in the econometrics textbook written by Stock and Watson (2010) is also to be recommended.

As we have already mentioned in this chapter the difficult part of this method is finding a suitable instrumental variable. Once the instrumental variable has been found everything appears so logical you may ask yourself how you did not come up with it earlier. When searching for your instrumental variable it is therefore a good idea to read other articles where instrumental variables have been used as inspiration. In Table 4.1 we have provided a list of most of these articles together with the instruments used. A similar table can be found in Angrist and Krueger (2001), which summarises non-criminological studies with the instrumental variables used.

Table 4.1: Criminological studies with instrumental variables

Dependent variable	Endogenous variable	Instrumental variable	Reference
Arrest	Treatment	Random assignment treatment	Angrist (2006)
Crime and school achievement adolescents	Work adolescents	Employment law	Apel (2008)
Criminality	Prison capacity	Court decision	Levitt (1996)
Number of prisoners in the 1990s	Crime rate in the 1990s	Number of abortions in the 1970s	Listokin (2003)
Recidivism	Treatment	Judge	Rhodes (2010)
Employment and school	Test of drug use	Random assignment to test	Kilmer (2008)
Employment	Length of prison sentence	Judge	Kling (2006)
Recidivism	Treatment programme for abusers	Local unemployment rate; availability of victim support; perception of arrest risk resulting from recidivism	Jones and Gondolf (2002)
Crime rate	Number of police officers	Law enforcement spending	Worrall and Kovandzic (2010)
Civil conflicts in developing countries	Economic growth	Weather and vegetation	Miguel et al. (2004)
Crime rate	Number of police officers	Law enforcement spending	Worrall and Kovandzic (2010)
Property crime and violence in the 1800s	Price of rye	Rainfall	Mehlum et al. (2006)
Youth crime	Mandatory school attendance	Holidays due to teacher training	Jacob and Lefgren (2003)
Recidivism	Treatment programme for abusers	Local unemployment rate; availability of victim support; perception of arrest risk resulting from recidivism	Jones and Gondolf (2002)
Violent offending	Social capital	Number of telephones and radios per resident	Lederman et al. (2002)
Crime rate	Employment	Oil price and military spending at state level	Raphael and Winter-Ebmer (2001)
Migration from the city	Crime rate in city	Punitive criminal law system	Cullen and Levitt (1999)

Chapter 5

The regression discontinuity design

In this chapter we discuss the regression discontinuity design, or RDD for short. The regression discontinuity design is not suitable for all types of data. However, if the data have the right properties, the RDD is one of the most powerful methods available for causal inference from non-experimental data. The concept on which this method based is relatively easy to understand.

We will begin with a discussion of what the design involves in section 5.1. In section 5.2 we will then go into more detail, discussing a number of conditions which need to be met in order to get reliable results. In section 5.3 we illustrate the method using an example with SPSS commands. We end with a summary of the strengths and weaknesses of the design (section 5.4), as well as a short description of some further reading (section 5.5).

5.1 The regression discontinuity design

The regression discontinuity design has perhaps conceptually most in common with propensity score matching, discussed in chapter 3. In propensity score matching we try to make our two groups, those who have received an intervention and those who have not, as comparable as possible, given that they are likely to differ on characteristics related to the intervention and the outcome measure. In order to do this we match pairs of respondents, or units of analysis, who have and have not received the intervention, but who have a similar chance of receiving the intervention given their background characteristics. With a regression discontinuity design we are trying to reach the same end point, but we use different means to get there.

The regression discontinuity design can be employed if there is an underlying continuous measure which determines whether an intervention is allocated or not. For example, if you break the speed limit in an area where police are carrying out speed controls, you will be fined. If you are not breaking the speed limit, you will not be fined for speeding. In some American states if you earn less than a certain income (a certain threshold income) you are entitled to food vouchers. If you earn 1 dollar more than the threshold income you are not entitled to food vouchers. So, scoring above or below a certain cut-off point determines whether you receive an intervention or not: only people driving over the speed limit get fined, only people earning under a certain income get food vouchers.

In each of these cases we are interested in the effect of an intervention on an outcome variable. For example, do people who break the speed limit and receive a fine subsequently break the law less often? Are food vouchers beneficial for the health of children of low-income parents? Here again we encounter the problem we have repeatedly faced in this book: the people who receive the intervention are in some way different from those who did not receive the intervention. We assume that parents with good incomes have the means to feed their children healthily, and so it may not be not informative to compare the health of children of poorer parents with those of richer parents.

The regression discontinuity design makes use of the fact that there is a cut-off that decides whether the intervention is allocated. The design assumes that although those who do and do not receive the intervention clearly differ, that those who are just under the cut-off probably do not differ meaningfully from those found just above the cut-off. The design assumes that on this cut-off or '*threshold*', allocation of the intervention occurs pretty much at random. Given this assumption we can use the regression discontinuity design to measure the effect of an intervention for people who fall on the cut-off point.

In this way regression discontinuity design resembles propensity score matching. In propensity score matching we also use a certain area, the area of common support, to determine the effect of an intervention. However, whilst in propensity score matching we look at an area, with regression discontinuity design we are strictly speaking just interested in differences at the threshold itself. However, in practice a small area around the threshold is often used.

The regression discontinuity design was introduced in 1960 by Thistlethwaite and Campbell. The design has, however, not been widely used in the social sciences. It is only in the last few years that it has become more popular, perhaps partly due to Imbens and Lemieux's (2008) more theoretical publication on the topic. Researchers that have used it have mainly looked at education, taxes, and voting behaviour. In a quite readable historical article, Cook (2008) describes how the design after its initial formulation was forgotten, only to be rediscovered by economists in the 1990s.

5.2 Illustration of the regression discontinuity design

As described above, if we want to use the regression discontinuity design we need to have a variable on which people can score a value. If their score falls above or below a certain cut-off point or threshold on this variable they receive an intervention, at the other side of the cut-off the reverse applies. This continuum is sometimes referred to as the *running variable*.

We will use an example to illustrate its use. Say, for example, we want to know whether punishing people for breaking the speed limit turns them into well-behaved citizens. We will use the Dutch system whereby people driving more than 30 km per hour quicker than the speed limit receive a criminal record. This is a more serious sanction than a fine, for which no criminal record results. Because it is a more serious punishment we would expect it to have a preventative effect, i.e. preventing law breaking in this area, but perhaps as well across other domains, not just speeding. We will use the hypothetical example illustrated in Figure 5.2. The x axis shows the number of kilometers per hour above the speed limit each respondent was caught doing. The x axis therefore constitutes the running variable. The y axis shows the total number of new criminal offences.

Just from eyeballing the graph we can see that there appears to be a difference between those people who did not receive a criminal record, i.e. scoring under the 30 km per hour threshold, and those people who did receive a criminal record, i.e. scoring above the 30 km per hour threshold. There appears to be a 'kink' in the cloud of points at around the 30 km per hour threshold. We can inspect the difference between the two groups by drawing a regression line through the scores of those people found under the threshold. Where this line crosses the threshold we find the estimated number of new offences we would expect for people who did not receive the intervention and who drove 30 km per hour over the speed limit. Obviously in reality this group does not exist, and so what we actually consider are values directly to the left of the threshold rather than on the threshold itself. If we draw a regression line through the scores on the right of the threshold we find the estimated number of new offences for people who received the intervention and were driving at exactly 30 km per hour too fast.The difference between these two values is referred to as the *local treatment effect* (see Figure 5.3). This is in essence the regression discontinuity design. In essence, this is the regression discontinuity

The regression discontinuity design was presented by Thistlethwaite and Campbell in 1960. Whilst Donald Thistlethwaite was and still is a less well known scientist, Donald Campbell quickly achieved fame.
After a short career working on a turkey farm, Campbell went to the University of California, Berkeley, to study psychology. It quickly became obvious that he was a scientific omnivore. He published on topics from psychology to sociology and anthropology, from biology to philosophy. He was an great advocate of interdisciplinarity, and believed, similarly to Karl Popper, that the scientific process should be Darwinian: theories should either survive or die out. His collaborative model allows much room for creativity and in fact Campbell had a loathing for research carried out in small, isolated cliques of researchers.
In 1966, together with Julian Stanley, he published 'Experimental and Quasi-Experimental Designs for Research', and in 1979 'Quasi-Experimentation: Design and Analysis Issues for Field Settings', together with Thomas Cook. Both these publications would go on to become classics. They have been of enormous importance to the social sciences, fostering many research evaluations. They analyse the possibilities of drawing conclusions from experimental style studies carried out in situations with different levels of control. These classic texts therefore more than deserve a mention in this book.

Figure 5.1: Donald Campbell (1916-1996)

Figure 5.2: Illustration of regression discontinuity design: number of new offences by speed limit violations

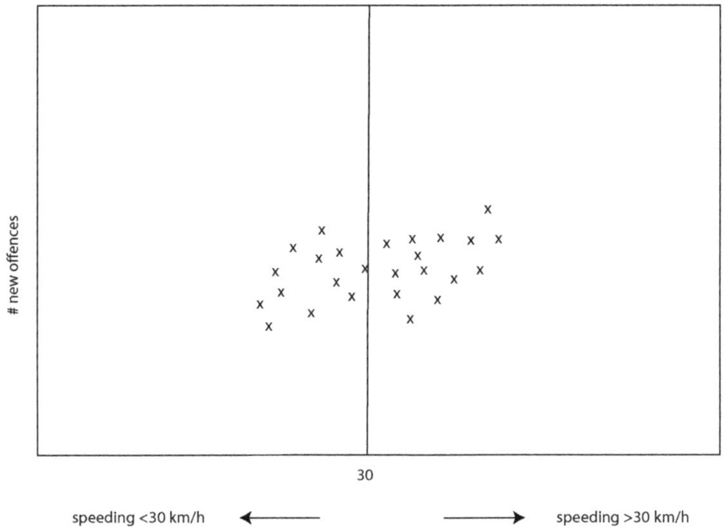

method. We compare scores on the outcome variable of respondents just above the threshold with scores on the outcome variable of respondents just below the threshold. Assuming that these people differ only marginally, this will give us an unbiased estimate of the treatment effect.

The manner in which we have described the regression discontinuity design thus far, is in the literature generally referred to as the *parametric* regression discontinuity design. Because a regression model is estimated, determining the size of the treatment effect is based on the parameters from this regression model.

Some authors distinguish also a *non-parametric* version of the regression discontinuity design. In this non-parametric version, one compares the mean scores of respondents just below and just above the threshold. This can be done using a simple t-test or even any other suitable non-parametric test. An issue to be decided is of course how many of these respondents we include in our comparison: if we take all respondents below the threshold and compare them with all respondents above the threshold, we will not get an unbiased estimate as those far removed from the threshold will also differ on other (confounding) variables besides the intervention itself. Ideally we would like to compare those júst below the threshold with those júst above it. Obviously, we may run into power problems as our sample size dwindles when we select a too narrow bandwidth. We will return to this is-

Figure 5.3: Determining the effect of the intervention at the threshold

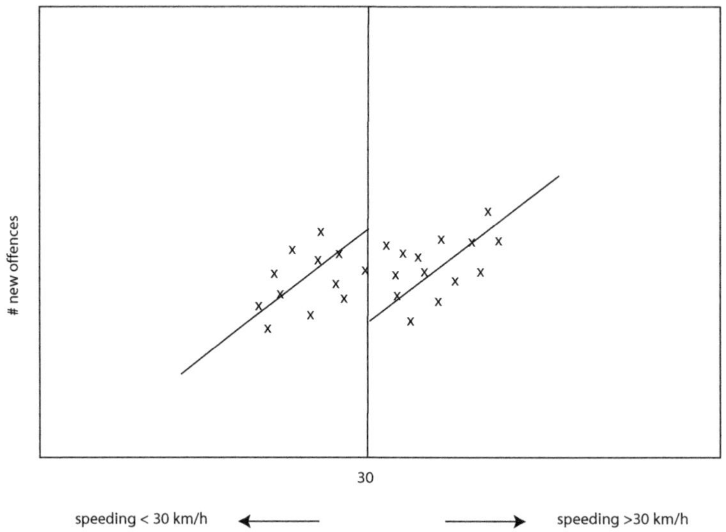

sue later on, as the issue of bandwidth selection also plays a role in parametric regression discontinuity analyses.

A number of general remarks need to be made before we can move to the practicalities of the application of the regression discontinuity design. The first thing to note is that the model assumes that people just above and just below the threshold do not systematically differ. But this need not be always true. It is possible that those drivers found just below the '30 km per hour over the speed limit' threshold are clever, or skilled enough to drive at exactly 29.99 km per hour. If this were the case we would have an endogeneity problem. We then cannot estimate the true effect of the treatment because it is confounded with other individual characteristics of our respondents.

There are several ways of examining whether the allocation of scores around the threshold is 'random' or not. Here the term random is enclosed in quotation marks because the intervention clearly cannot be randomly allocated in the true sense of the word. However, the idea is that allocation is independent of background characteristics and therefore 'random'. A first way to check whether allocation is 'random' is by visually inspecting the distribution of scores (analyses using the regression discontinuity design involved quite a bit of good visual scrutiny of your data).

Figure 5.4 depicts a distribution for which we might suspect that intervention allocation was *not* random. This figure shows the distribution of exam marks.

Figure 5.4: Example of a non-random distribution around the threshold

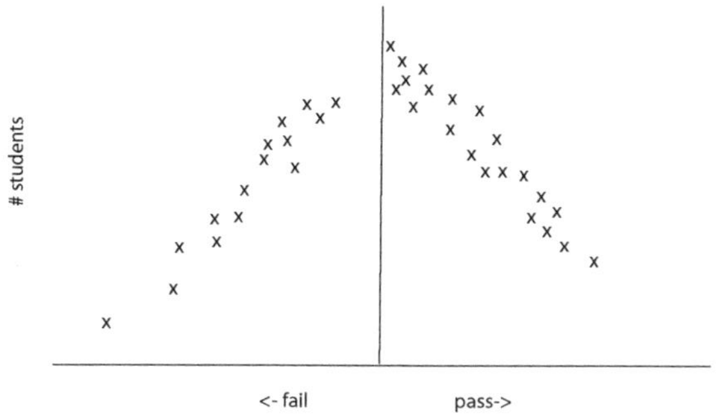

There is a sizeable group of data points just above the pass threshold of 6 (in reality often 5.5, with 5.4 a 'fail' and 5.5 rounded to 'pass') that is common in the Netherlands. It might be that this bunch of students went to the teacher, urging them to change their mark, persuading them of the amount of work they had put into the exam, that they had done their best, and so on. If one spots this kind of bulge just above or below the threshold this should be seen as an indication that the intervention allocation may not have been random and that respondents may have been able to influence it. In the example above, the students' individual characteristics likely played a role in determining whether they scored just above a 6.

An additional way to check whether the intervention was randomly allocated is to examine whether those people just above and just below the threshold differ on observed background characteristics. In doing this, we can of course only check for measured heterogeneity, that is, for variables that we have observed. This test will not help if respondents differ on characteristics we have not measured, such as in the above example: we are unlikely to have a measure of 'effort that students are willing to put in to persuade the teacher to pass them following a mark of 5.2'.

A second remark to be made is that the user should be aware that the estimation of the effect size in the parametric model depends on the model being correctly specified. We will illustrate this again using an example. In Figure 5.5 we can see that the relationship between the number of km per hour over the speed limit and the number of new offences is not linear but curvilinear. If we were to carry out a linear regression, drawing two straight lines through the data points to the left and right of the threshold we would end up with a clearly incorrect estimation of the local treatment effect. In Figure 5.5, it can easily be gleaned that we would then estimate it wrongly: we would likely estimate a negative effect as we would infer from comparison of the levels at which the regression lines cross-sect the threshold

Figure 5.5: Example of a misspecification of the regression discontinuity model

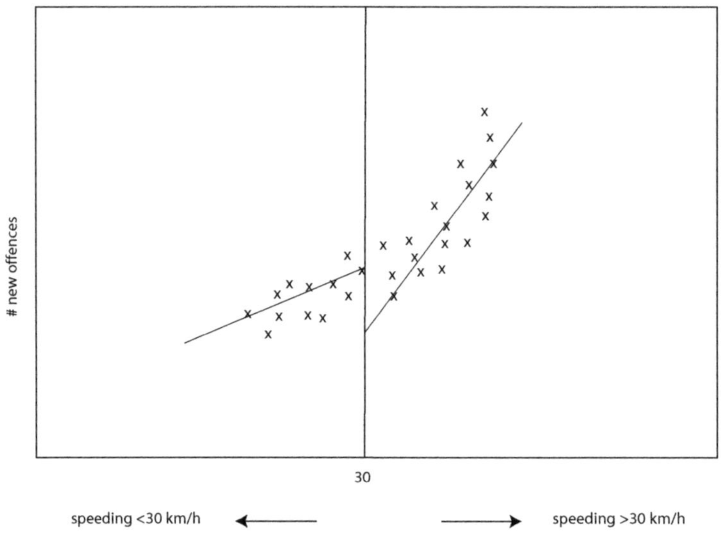

that those who received a criminal sanction for speeding more than 30 kms per hour committed fewer offences than those just below the threshold. However, as visual inspection of the cloud of points shows, the outcome variable here has a curvilinear relationship with the running variable: if we had fitted a curvilinear line through the points we might even have found no effect at all. It does appear therefore as if in this example the linear regression model has been specified incorrectly.

One way to inspect this is to extend the model with a curvilinear term: instead of regressing the outcome variable on the running variable itself, it could be regressed on its square as well (or any other function that visual inspection of the data suggests). We will return to this later in this chapter. More complicated models can be built for cases where the regression lines appear to change slope at the cut-off.

A third point to consider is that the size of the effect is dependent on the bandwidth employed around the threshold. In the example just discussed we fitted regression lines through the area to the left and to the right of the threshold. If we had used a wider range of values either side of the threshold or a smaller range either side, it is possible the effect would have been different: the regression lines could have pointed slightly more upward or downward. It is therefore advisable to estimate the treatment effect not only using several (non-linear) specifications of the regression model, but also using different ranges or bandwidths around the cut-off value. If the estimated effect size of the treatment is relatively stable, that is: if it is approximately the same across varying bandwidths, we can be fairly certain of our conclusions. If it does fluctuate, our estimations are clearly dependent on an arbitrary range chosen for examining the experimental and control groups. Using varying bandwidths to determine the effect of the intervention is advisable both for parametric and non-parametric versions of the regression discontinuity design.

Bandwidth impacts power, however. If we choose a narrower bandwidth (which is desirable from the point of view of having as little as possible confounding distorting our conclusions) we end up with smaller subsamples to compare, more instability, and likely also less power: differences will sooner turn up non-significant. If we want to increase our power, we may select a broader bandwidth around the threshold. The downside is then that bias may seep in: those further removed from both sides of the bandwidth cannot be said to differ by chance from each other and are more likely to differ on confounders as well. There is therefore a clear trade-off between power and bias (just as with propensity score matching). While some authors have developed nifty guidelines for the determination of bandwidth based on sample size, it should be stressed here that our interest is not as much choosing a particular 'right' bandwidth but showing that our conclusions are robust and independent of a particular bandwidth choice. The fact that we would like to have as narrow as possible a bandwidth makes for the fact that regression discontinuity designs perform best with large sample sizes.

All in all, we recommend that, when estimating a treatment effect using the regression discontinuity design, a number of checks is carried out. First, it is advisable to check to what extent the treatment is likely to have indeed been allocated randomly. For that, one should first generate a scatterplot of the number of cases against the running variable. That scatterplot should not show evidence of a sudden 'heaping up' just above or just below the threshold (as we discussed, Figure 5.4 gives an example of a situation where such a suspicious cluttering does occur and may lead one to suppose that the treatment was not (entirely) exogenous at the threshold). In addition, one should test whether the respondents (just) below or above the threshold do not differ markedly on their measured characteristics. If both these checks are negative (not cluttering of scores and no differences between respondents just below and just above the threshold) then one may for the time being proceed under the assumption that the treatment was (at least in part) exogenous.

Second, model specification and robustness checks should be performed. While these are not exactly the same, we nevertheless mention them in one breath as they can be closely interrelated here. These checks come in three shapes. To start with, one should generate a scatterplot of the outcome variable against the running variable. The cloud of points should show a clear jump or kink around the

Donald Thistlethwaite studied the psychology of reasoning at, like Campbell, the University of California, Berkeley. He worked at several universities, and his later research examined ways of changing people's attitudes. At VanderBilt University he supervised several PhD students, including Sam McFarland, who would later write his eulogy. McFarland spoke of how Thistlethwaite was well known at VanderBilt for his homemade wine.

Figure 5.6: Donald Thistlethwaite (1922-1997)

threshold. If there is an effect, one may see a jump before and after the threshold, as in Figure 5.2. Visual inspection of the graph also gives an indication what kind of parametric modeling would be suitable. Next, when using parametric regression discontinuity models, different specifications of the model should be estimated. For instance, a model with linear and non-linear terms for the running variable, or a model with interaction terms to accommodate changes in slope, may be used. If the findings on the size of the effect are robust, that is, the are substantively the same regardless of particular model specifications and hold for instance also when non-linear terms are included, we can be fairly sure that we have identified an effect and are not left with some quirk of one particular model specification.

Then, as discussed already above, the results should be computed for varying bandwidths, whether one uses a parametric or non-parametric approach. Last, some authors conduct so-called placebo tests, where they investigate whether they also find a significant impact of treatment at non-existing thresholds. What is meant by this is the following. Suppose that the real threshold value was 100, and that before that value of 100 respondents did not receive the treatment and that from 100 they did. One now estimates N models with hypothetical thresholds at, say, 95, 90, 85, 80, ..., and at 105, 110, 115, 120, ... These 'placebo'-thresholds should now *not* turn up significant (that is, only 5% out of 100 should...).

5.3 Example: Treatment and number of arrests

Just as in previous chapters we will illustrate how to use the regression discontinuity design using our example dataset of 500 fictional juvenile sex offenders. Similarly to in chapter 3, we will test how effective the treatment of these offenders is. In chapter 3 we saw that 173 offenders were treated and 327 were not. In the following sections we will explain how RDD analysis can be carried out using SPSS. The appendix also has the syntax commands for carrying out this analysis in Stata.

Following matching on their propensity scores, the treated offenders appeared to have significantly lower sex offending recidivism rates than untreated offenders. In this chapter we will use the regression discontinuity design to examine whether treatment of juvenile sex offenders also leads to a decrease in the overall number of arrests, irrespective of the type of offence. We are therefore not just looking at sex offences, but at the general level of criminal activity following treatment.

The dependent variable used in this chapter is the variable `arrests`. This gives the average number of arrests per year over the observation period post treatment, Figure 5.7 shows the distribution of scores on this variable. It appears to be relatively normally distributed with a mean of 0.48 and a standard deviation of 0.22.

Using a t-test we can examine whether the treated and untreated sex offenders score differently on this variable. We do this using the following syntax:

```
T-TEST GROUPS=treated(0 1)
     /MISSING=ANALYSIS
     /VARIABLES=arrest
     /CRITERIA=CI(.95).
```

Figure 5.8 shows the results of the t-test. The juvenile sex offenders who did not receive treatment were arrested on average 0.38 times a year. The treated sex offenders were arrested far more often, on average 0.67 times a year. This difference is significant. Based on these results researchers might conclude that treat-

Figure 5.7: Histogram of the variable 'arrests'

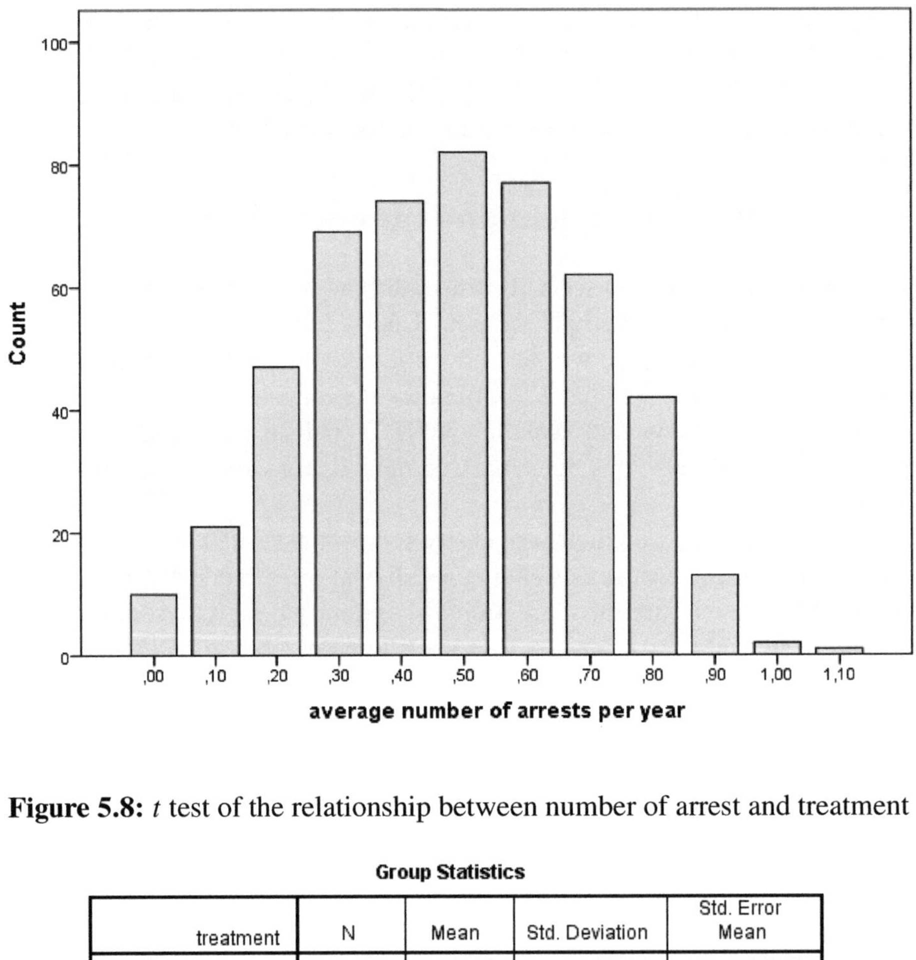

Figure 5.8: *t* test of the relationship between number of arrest and treatment

Group Statistics

	treatment	N	Mean	Std. Deviation	Std. Error Mean
arrests	no	327	,3817	,17749	,00982
	yes	173	,6705	,14626	,01112

ment has the opposite effect to that desired as it appears that juvenile sex offenders are arrested more often following treatment than after no treatment was imposed.

Of course, as the reader probably recalls, treatment was not allocated at random. Juvenile sex offenders judged to have a higher (sexual) recidivism risk were more likely to be treated than those judged to have a low (sexual) recidivism risk. It is therefore not so surprising that treated offenders, despite their treatment, are on average arrested more often than untreated offenders. In order to correctly determine the effect of treatment on general recidivism we will use the regression discontinuity design.

5.3.1 The underlying continuum

In order to use the regression discontinuity design we need to have an underlying continuous objective measure. Scores on this measure should have been used to determine whether an intervention is allocated or not. We can then use the design to compare respondents falling just above and just below the cut-off point.

In the dataset the variable `JSOAP` indicates the juvenile sex offenders' scores on the s0-called J-SOAP scale. The J-SOAP (Juvenile Sex Offender Assessment Protocol) is a structured risk assessment tool, used to estimate a juvenile sex offender's chance of re-offending. A J-SOAP score is calculated from a questionnaire, with 28 items relating to sexual impulses and preoccupation, impulsivity and anti-social behaviour, interventions, and adaptations to society. The scores on these 28 items are summed and then divided by the maximum score to give a percentage (Prentky and Righthand, 2003). The higher this percentage, the greater the risk a juvenile sex offender will re-offend. Scores on the J-SOAP scale are very well suited to a regression discontinuity design: the scale is namely used to determine whether a juvenile sex offender receives treatment. Those with a score of 50 or higher are all treated. Those with lower score are not treated. The cut-off point is therefore a score of 50 on the J-Soap scale.

Using the following syntax commands SPSS calculates the descriptives for the variable `JSOAP`. These are given in Figure 5.9.

```
DESCRIPTIVES VARIABLES=JSOAP
     /STATISTICS=MEAN STDDEV MIN MAX.
```

Figure 5.9 shows that the 500 juvenile sex offenders have an average score of 44.17 on the J-SOAP scale, with a standard deviation of 18.77. The lowest score is 2.2 and the highest score is 95.8. We know that 173 offenders were treated and therefore must have a J-SOAP score of above 50. The remaining 327 untreated offenders will have scored less than 50 on the scale.

5.3.2 Regression discontinuity design using SPSS

Now that we have determined that the variable `JSOAP` can be used as our underlying continuous measure, we will first draw a scatter plot to examine the relationship between this underlying continuous measure and our dependent variable, average

Figure 5.9: Descriptives for the variable `JSOAP`

Descriptive Statistics

	N	Minimum	Maximum	Mean	Std. Deviation
JSOAP	500	2,20	95,80	44,1720	18,76867
Valid N (listwise)	500				

number of arrests per year. Using the following syntax we ask SPSS to draw the plot in Figure 5.10.

```
GRAPH
     /SCATTERPLOT(BIVAR)=JSOAP WITH arrests
     /MISSING=LISTWISE.
```

As we can see in Figure 5.10, there is a clear relationship between J-SOAP scores and number of arrests per year. The higher the J-SOAP score, the more often a juvenile sex offender is arrested. This is a logical finding given that the J-SOAP is a risk assessment tool which estimates chances of recidivism. In Figure 5.10 we have drawn a line through the cut-off point at which offenders get allocated to treatment, right at the value of 50, the threshold J-SOAP score. All those sex offenders to the left of the line were not treated, those to the right were treated. As the *t*-test in Figure 5.8 already showed, the treated sex offenders are arrested on average more often than untreated offenders. Nevertheless, it looks like there is a break of sorts in the mass of points around the cut-off score of 50. The plot appears to show that treated offenders a little beyond the cut-off point are arrested less often than untreated offenders just before the cut-off point.

Now to use regression discontinuity design to determine how effective treatment is, we need to select respondents from around the cut-off point of 50. In this example we will include all sex offenders with a J-SOAP score between 40 and 60. The following syntax ensures that only these respondents are included in any further analyses.

```
USE ALL.
COMPUTE filter=(JSOAP >= 40 & JSOAP  <  60).
FILTER BY filter.
EXECUTE.
```

We are now left with 174 juvenile sex offenders. Of these offenders, 86 are treated and 88 untreated. The regression continuity design now works with the assumption that the treatment allocation for this selected group is not related to any

Figure 5.10: Scatter plot of 'arrests' and `JSOAP`

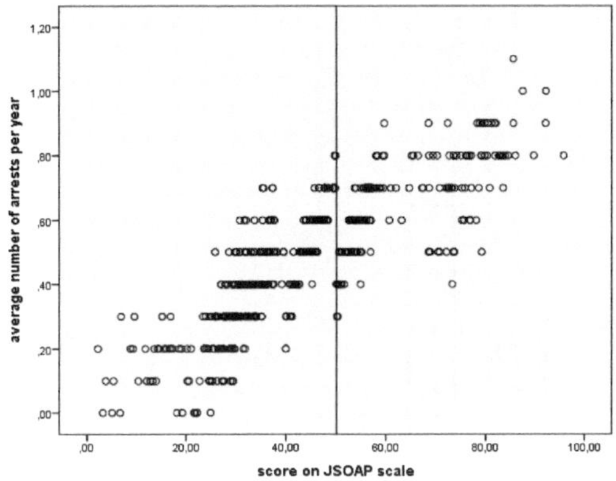

background characteristics, and is therefore not confounded. As described above, we can investigate this in two ways. First, we can examine whether the distribution of respondents on the underlying continuous measure is relatively smooth at the cut-off point. We gave an example in Figure 5.4 of a distribution where this was not the case. There we saw a bunching of respondents directly above the threshold. What we want to see here then, is a distribution that is fairly smooth, indicating a more or less random allocation of the scores around 50. The second test is to examine whether treated and untreated sex offenders, within our chosen range, differ from each other on certain background characteristics. If this is the case a relationship may exist between the intervention and the background characteristics, making it more difficult to correctly estimate the effect of the intervention.

First let us look at the distribution of J-SOAP score more closely. The distribution of `JSOAP` is illustrated in Figure 5.11, using the following syntax:

```
GRAPH
 /HISTOGRAM=JSOAP.
```

From the histogram in Figure 5.11 we can see that the distribution of scores on both sides of the cut-off is equal. It does not appear therefore that sex-offenders scoring just above or below 50 were deliberately or systematically given a higher or lower score to ensure they were treated or not treated. The histogram in Figure 5.11 therefore indicates that unrelated observed or unobserved characteristics do not seem to play a role in treatment allocation for this group of respondents.

We next examine whether the treated and untreated sex offenders differ significantly on the background characteristics measured. Using t-tests, or χ^2-tests for

Figure 5.11: Histogram of the `JSOAP` variable

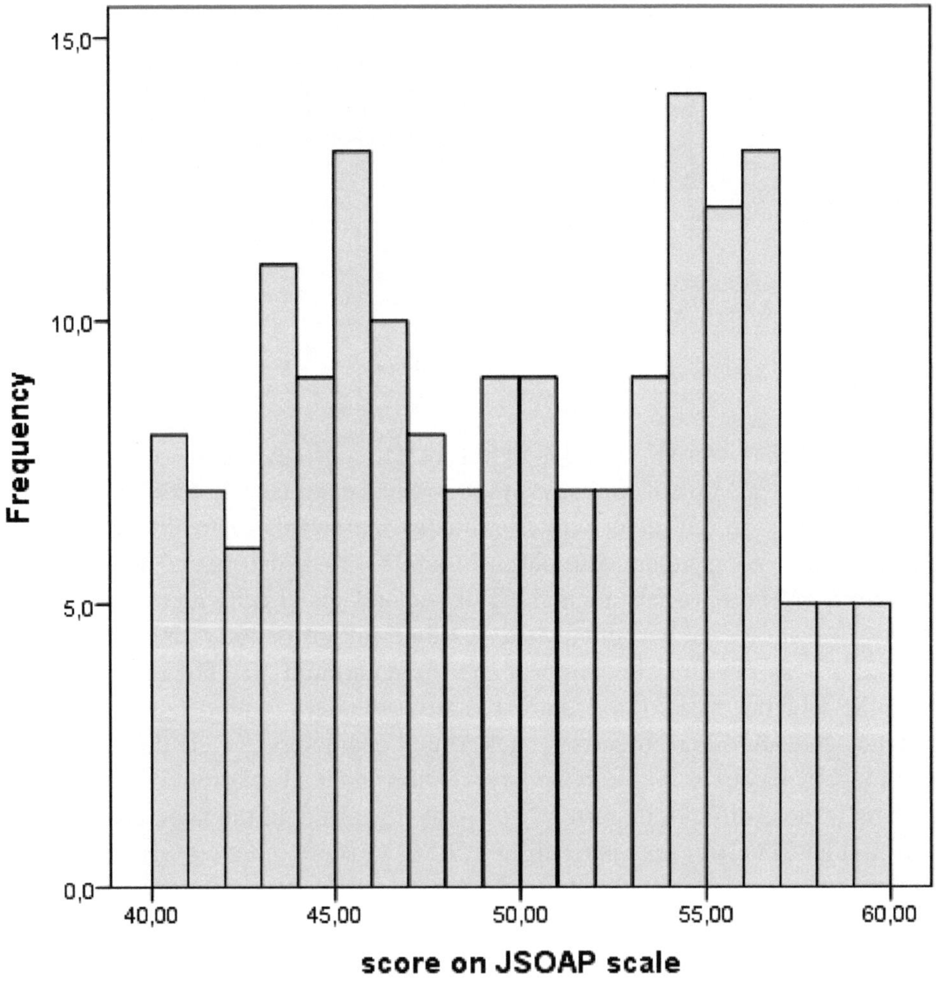

nominal variables, the scores of sex offenders in both groups can be compared. We have already seen in chapter 3 that the whole group of 500 treated and untreated sex offenders differ on the following variables: contact_peers, age_offence, IQ, neuroticism, impulsivity, ethnicity, type_offender en previous_sexoffence. We can now test whether there are significant differences between treated and untreated offenders in our selected sub-sample, those who score between 40 and 60 on the J-SOAP scale, on these variables. The following syntax is used to do this:

```
T-TEST GROUPS=treated(0 1)
     /MISSING=ANALYSIS
     /VARIABLES=IQ neuroticism impulsivity
     contact_peers age_offence
     /CRITERIA=CI(.95).

CROSSTABS
     /TABLES=treated BY ethnicity
     previous_sex offence type_offender
     /FORMAT=AVALUE TABLES
     /STATISTICS=CHISQ
     /CELLS=COUNT
     /COUNT ROUND CELL.
```

The output resulting from this syntax (not shown) indicates that our sub-sample of treated and untreated sex offenders with J-SOAP scores between 40 and 60 do not significantly differ on background characteristics. Based on the results from these tests, as well as the histogram in Figure 5.11, we feel confident to assume that treatment allocation around the cut-off point of 50 is not confounded by measured or unmeasured background characteristics.

As a next step we centre scores on the underlying continuous measure, in our case the J-SOAP score, around the cut-off point. By doing this it becomes easier to determine the effect of treatment for respondents in our dataset with a J-SOAP score that falls exactly on the cut-off point. Centering around the cut-off point is done by subtracting 50 from the original `JSOAP` score, using the following syntax command:

```
COMPUTE JSOAP_c=JSOAP-50.
EXECUTE.
```

The variable `J-SOAP_c` is now a centered variable.

We are now ready to carry out the regression discontinuity analysis. To begin with we will carry out a parametric regression discontinuity analysis, doing it in a rather long-winded fashion. The advantage of the rather more cumbersome method is that it is easy to see what happens. Following that, we carry out the analysis in one step. This second method is more efficient. The results of both analyses will, however, be exactly the same.

Using the long-winded method of regression discontinuity design we need to carry out two separate regression analyses. In these the number of arrests per year is estimated using the centered J-SOAP variable. One regression analysis is carried out on all the treated sex offenders and one on all the untreated sex offenders.

Figure 5.12: Results of the regression analysis for the untreated sex offenders

Coefficients[a,b]

Model		Unstandardized Coefficients		Standardized Coefficients	t	Sig.	95,0% Confidence Interval for B	
		B	Std. Error	Beta			Lower Bound	Upper Bound
1	(Constant)	,755	,013		58,840	,000	,729	,780
	JSOAP_c	,043	,002	,895	18,608	,000	,038	,047

a. treatment = no

b. Dependent Variable: arrests

Using the following syntax command we first ask SPSS to split the datafile into the treated and untreated respondents, and then ask for the regression analyses to be calculated. The results of these analyses are shown in Figure 5.12 and Figure 5.13.

```
SORT CASES BY treated.
SPLIT FILE SEPARATE BY treated.

REGRESSION
     /MISSING LISTWISE
     /STATISTICS COEFF OUTS CI(95) R ANOVA
     /CRITERIA=PIN(.05) POUT(.10)
     /NOORIGIN
     /DEPENDENT arrests
     /METHOD=ENTER JSOAP_c.
SPLIT FILE OFF.
```

Figure 5.12 gives the results for the regression analysis in which the number of arrests per year is predicted for untreated sex offenders. The results reflect our suspicions based on Figure 5.10, namely that a higher score on the J-SOAP scale leads to a significantly higher number of arrests per year. In order to determine the local treatment effect we need to examine the predicted number of arrests for an untreated sex offender with a score of 50 on the J-SOAP scale. Because we centered the J-SOAP scores, the number of arrests for an untreated offender with a score of 50 is simply the regression coefficient of the constant in Figure 5.12. The constant in a regression analysis is the estimated value on the dependent variable when the score on all the independent variables is zero. When we centered this variable we subtracted 50 from the J-SOAP scores, and so a centered J-SOAP score of 0 is the same as the original score of 50. The average number of arrests for an untreated sex offender with a J-SOAP score of 50 is therefore estimated to be 0.755 arrests per year.

Figure 5.13: Results of the regression analysis for the treated sex offenders

Coefficients[a,b]

Model		Unstandardized Coefficients B	Unstandardized Coefficients Std. Error	Standardized Coefficients Beta	t	Sig.	95,0% Confidence Interval for B Lower Bound	95,0% Confidence Interval for B Upper Bound
1	(Constant)	,416	,014		28,935	,000	,388	,445
	JSOAP_c	,039	,003	,842	14,287	,000	,034	,045

a. treatment = yes

b. Dependent Variable: arrests

Figure 5.13 gives the results for exactly the same analysis, but then carried out on the treated sex offenders. Again the J-SOAP score has a significant positive relationship with number of arrests: also for treated sex offenders a higher J-SOAP score predicts a higher number of arrests per year. In order to determine the local treatment effect we need to know how often treated offenders with a J-SOAP score of 50 are arrested per year. Once again, because we centered the variable, we look at the regression coefficient of the constant. This tells us that the treated sex offenders with a J-SOAP score of 50 are on average arrested 0.416 times a year.

Now, to calculate the local treatment effect we simply subtract the average number of arrests per year for treated offenders with a J-SOAP score of 50 from that of untreated offenders with a J-SOAP score of 50: 0.755 - 0.416 = 0.339. Treatment therefore leads to a decrease of 0.339 in number of arrests per year for a sex offender who scores 50 on the J-SOAP scale. This effect is illustrated in Figure 5.14. The question is of course, is this difference significant? Instead of investigating this, using additional tests, we will answer this by carrying out the regression discontinuity design using the one-step method. Before we do so, however, we will carry out a couple of robustness checks.

To rule out the possibility that our treatment effect is dependent on a coincidental threshold bandwidth, i.e. J-SOAP scores between 40 and 60, we repeat the analyses using other bandwidths. This is done by simply selecting smaller and larger groups of sex offenders based on a narrower or wider range of J-SOAP scores. If we reduce the range of J-SOAP scores to 42 to 58, for example, the results remain the same. We still find that treated offenders with a J-SOAP score of 50 are arrested less in the following years than untreated offenders with a J-SOAP score of 50. The effect size does decrease slightly when applying this narrower range, to 0.313. However, when an even narrower range is selected, 45-55, the effect of treatment remains more or less the same size: treated sex offenders are on average arrested 0.330 fewer times than untreated sex offenders. Next we try setting the range to be wider. Using a range of 38-62 the results again remain more

Figure 5.14: Results of the combined regression analyses for all sex offenders

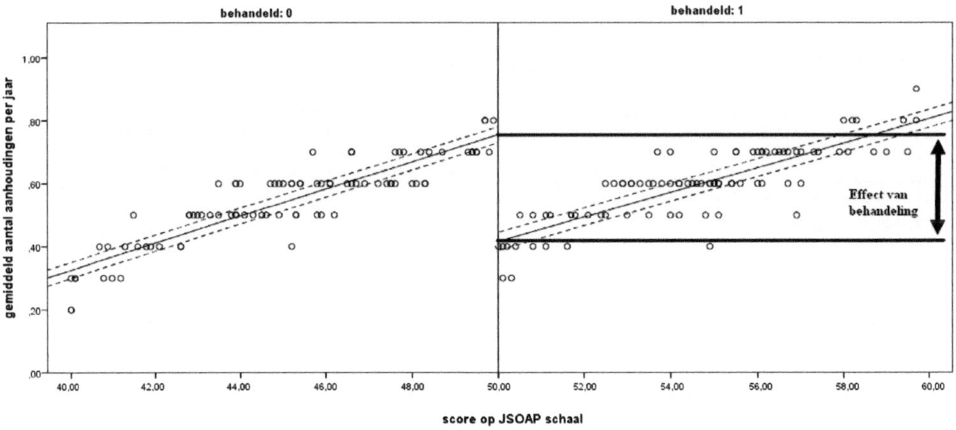

or less the same, 0.306 fewer arrests per year. Only when the range is widened to include all respondents with a J-SOAP score of between 35 and 65, does the effect size get considerably smaller. For this range a treated sex offender with a J-SOAP score of 50 is only arrested 0.189 times fewer than an untreated sex offender with a score of 50. This smaller effect size is not surprising given that a much wider range of respondents is included in the analyses. Respondents with scores lying further away from the threshold have been included and these are, of course, less similar to each other. What makes us feel confident is that the effect does not disappear when the bandwidth becomes smaller.

Finally, with the help of Figure 5.14, we check whether the model has been correctly specified. Looking at Figure 5.14 it appears that the model is not misspecified: visual inspection does not lead us to expect that a curvilinear model would fit better or that the regression lines on both sides would have different slopes. The distribution of scores to the left and right of the threshold supports a linear regression line on both sides, and there is no indication that a bent line would fit the distribution of the scores better.

Having carried out these controls it appears that the necessary conditions for a regression continuity design have been met and that the effect we found is robust. We therefore conclude that treatment is effective in reducing the number of arrests amongst sex offenders. This conclusion, however, only holds for those sex offenders who scored on the cut-off point for receiving or not receiving treatment. It can therefore only be generalised to sex offenders with a J-SOAP score of 50, and not to the entire group of sex offenders.

As we stated above, this analysis can also be carried out in one step.[1] In the cumbersome approach we had carried out two regression analyses. We predicted the number of arrests Y using the J-SOAP score X for sex offenders twice: once for those with scores below the cut-off point of 50, and once for those with scores on or above the cut-off point of 50:

$$Y = a_1 + b_1 X \quad \text{if } X < 50$$
$$Y = a_2 + b_2 X \quad \text{if } X \geq 50$$

with X the running variable J-SOAP. The formulas indicate that the difference between the treated sex offenders, X score of 50 or higher, and untreated sex offenders, X score of less than 50, is equal to the difference between the two intercepts, a_2 - a_1, exactly as we saw when carrying out our first method of analysis. What the formulas also demonstrate is that the regression coefficients are not necessarily equal. Because we carry out two regression analyses, one on respondents above and one on respondents below the cut-off, the regression coefficients are unrestricted, and can therefore differ. In our example they indeed differed slightly, one regression line had a b of 0.43, the other of 0.39.

We can however combine the two regression equations, to carry out the regression discontinuity method in one step. For that, we first assume that the regression coefficients are equal, i.e. $b_1 = b_2 = b$. Second, we define the treatment effect τ as a_2 - a_1. We can now write the two equations in the following manner:

$$Y = a_1 + \tau W + bX$$

where W is equal to 0 if X is smaller than 50 and W is equal to 1 if X is greater or equal to 50.

We can now estimate the effect of the intervention at the cut-off point of 50 in one step, by carrying out a regression analysis with two variables. The first variable is W, in our case `treated`, and the second is X, the original J-SOAP variable. The estimated τ is the estimated effect of the intervention.

To do this in SPSS we first select all the respondents with a J-SOAP score between 40 and 60. The following syntax is then used to carry out the analysis in one step

```
REGRESSION
     /MISSING LISTWISE
     /STATISTICS COEFF OUTS R ANOVA
     /CRITERIA=PIN(.05) POUT(.10)
```

[1]Here again we will use a J-SOAP score range of 40 to 60. This does not however need to be indicated in the formulas.

Figure 5.15: Results of the one step method of RDD analysis

Coefficients[a]

Model		Unstandardized Coefficients B	Unstandardized Coefficients Std. Error	Standardized Coefficients Beta	t	Sig.
1	(Constant)	-1,301	,080		-16,277	,000
	JSOAP	,041	,002	1,757	23,193	,000
	treatment	-,339	,019	-1,339	-17,670	,000

a. Dependent Variable: arrests

```
/NOORIGIN
/DEPENDENT arrests
/METHOD=ENTER JSOAP treated.
```

Note that we no longer need to use the centered J-SOAP variable. The results of the analysis are shown in Figure 5.15.

From the figure we can see that the effect of the intervention is 0.339, exactly as we found in the previous analysis results. We can now also see that, as we suspected, this effect is significant. Besides being more efficient, carrying out the analysis in one step calculates the significance of the treatment effect by using the whole sub-sample of treated and untreated. If we wanted to calculate this when using two separate analyses, we would have to examine whether the confidence intervals of the two sub-samples overlapped. We would carry out two tests, each on a smaller section of the data. This test would consequently be *underpowered*. The *power* is therefore less than when we use the whole sub-sample, and consequently this method is unnecessarily conservative. Another advantage of using the one step method is that we can include extra variables in the model. Although we assume that any distorting effects, b, have been weeded out by using a RDD, we can nonetheless include variables that we think might affect the intervention allocation or the dependent variable in the model:

$$Y = a_1 + \tau W + bX + \gamma_1 C_1 + \gamma_2 C_2 + \cdots + \gamma_k C_k$$

In this way we can control for any variables which may still distort our findings. We end up with the effect of the intervention W controlling for the effect of X and any other possible confounding variables $C_1, C_2, \ldots$.

When using the one step method, the controls we carried out previously when using the long-winded method also need to be performed. First, testing for the effect of threshold range should be done by repeating the analysis with different ranges. Next, correct model specification should be tested for. In our model we had restricted the model further, i.e. not only did the relationship need to be linear, but also the *b*s on the left and right hand side of the cut-off needed to be equal. Testing whether these two restrictions are justified can be carried out by adding interaction terms to the model. To test for any nonlinear effects, a nonlinear version of the running variable can be added. This is done by specifying the model as follows:

$$Y = a_1 + \tau W + bX + cX^2$$

Other versions are possible too, such as cubic versions of the running variable, its square root, etc.

Including an interaction term in the model, X by W, can be done by first centering the running variable X (i.e. subtracting 50 from each X: $X'=X-50$) to make the model easier to interpret, and then specifying the model as follows:

$$Y = a_1 + \tau W + bX' + cX'W$$

which will enable us to see whether the slopes are indeed identical left and right of the threshold value. If neither of these additional terms turn up significant in the extended models, we may conclude that the association between X and Y is linear and that there is no difference in the effect of X on either side of the cut-off point.

We tested whether nonlinear regression models of the number of arrests on the J-SOAP score gave different results if we added nonlinear version of the running variable, or added an interaction term to the model. None of these were the case. First, a quadratic version of the running variable was added to the model; this variable had a regression coefficient that was not significantly different from zero (b = -0.00003, p = 0.093) and changed the value of τ only marginally to -0.337. Next we added an interaction term to the model. Also this interaction term was not significant (p = 0.337), and the value of τ was again hardly affected at τ = -0.338.

The most important information from any of these alternative specifications of the regression discontinuity model and from the various bandwidths we can use is whether the estimate of τ remains substantively the same. If τ turns up more or less the same from these different specifications of the model, we can conclude that estimate of the effect of the intervention is robust. As the examples show, this is indeed the case for our data.

5.3.3 Regression discontinuity design with Stata

We have provided an example of how to carry out regression discontinuity design using SPSS. Even though SPSS does not have any special procedures to do these analyses, it is fairly easy and straightforward to do a RDD in SPSS. Using the one step method the analysis can be carried out quickly, using one regression analysis followed by a number of separate controls.

In Stata, the same regression procedures and control tests can be carried out as in SPSS for regression discontinuity analysis. In the appendix at the end of the book we give the syntax for carrying out regression discontinuity analysis in Stata using the same 'manual' procedure that we employed using SPSS.

Stata also has several tailored procedures for carrying out regression discontinuity analysis. Examples of 'pre-fab' procedures for carrying out RDD in Stata using are rd and rdrobust, and modifications of these procedures are regularly made available in Stata. These do not always give (exactly) the same outcomes as manual procedures do, as for instance specific, so-called *kernel* methods are used for fitting the regression lines before and after the threshold.

5.4 Strengths and weaknesses of the regression discontinuity design

Of all the possible methods described in this book for drawing causal conclusions from non randomised data, regression discontinuity design is perhaps the strongest. Given the assumptions described above, the regression discontinuity design is able to estimate the effect of the intervention on the threshold point. The regression discontinuity design method is therefore also often referred to as the '*local randomized design*'. The *internal validity* of the design is strong. Comparisons made between the RDD and randomised clinical trials (Berk et al., 2010) show that the results of both are practically the same.

In contrast, the *external validity* of the regression discontinuity design is more limited. Causal conclusions based on results using this method pertain only to respondents with scores *on* the threshold. This might not seem to be too much of a problem. If we consider our breaking the speed limit example, we do not really need to know the effect of the intervention for people who always drive too fast, because we are unlikely to be able to influence their behaviour. Similarly, we do not need to know the effect of the intervention for people who never break the speed limit, because they will never need the intervention. Nevertheless, strictly speaking, conclusions as to the effect of the intervention can only be made for those scoring *on* the threshold, and not those just above or below the threshold. This is a limitation, as we are arguably interested in the effect of the intervention for those people somewhat below and above the threshold as well. In other words, if the *range* becomes too narrow the results are not really very useful.

The *power* of the regression discontinuity design is also less than that in a Randomized Controlled Trial (RCT). This is unsurprising given that we only use those respondents with scores close to the threshold. Consequently, the chance of making a type II error looms. In order to compensate for this a larger N is needed for this design compared to a Randomized Controlled Trial.

There is one more point to be considered with regression discontinuity design. The design is based on the assumption that the research units above and below the threshold do not differ on observed or unobserved characteristics. We can of course only test whether they differ on characteristics that we have measured. If however, we only include a very narrow range of research units from around the threshold, we are left with a small subset of our sample. Due to the resulting decrease in power, our tests are more likely to be non-significant. All in all, if we make the range very narrow the fact that our respondents do not differ may also be due to this lack of power, rather than due to a lack of actual differences. For this reasons we recommend testing for differences in background characteristics also using several different ranges.

Finally, as we have discussed, identification of the correct treatment effect is dependent on correctly specifying the model. As noted above, misspecification can lead to entirely the wrong conclusions.

5.5 Further reading

In the literature one comes across a variation on the RDD, called '*fuzzy regression discontinuity design*' or FRD. Fuzzy RDD is generally used when there is a cut-off point, but some room is allowed for discretion in allocating the treatment. For example, the chance of getting a criminal record when driving 30 km per hour too fast does not instantly jump from 0 under the threshold of 30 km per hour to 1 above 30 km per hour, but instead increases more gradually the closer one gets to the 30 km per hour cut-off. In another example, people might receive a welfare allowance if they score above a given poverty indicator, but not everyone receives this, and some people who score below the given poverty indicator may also receive the allowance. Treatment allocation is therefore 'fuzzy': it is spread out a bit around the threshold. Consequently, the underlying continuous variable correlates with treatment just as an instrumental variable does. This fuzzy regression discontinuity design is therefore similar to the instrumental variables approach discussed in chapter 4.

Another variation is '*kinked regression*'. This method estimates the local treatment effect using the change in the gradient of the regression lines. For more details see Berk (2009). Berk (2009) demonstrated that regression discontinuity designs can be used with both a dichotomous outcome variable and an outcome variable with a non-standard distribution, such as a Poisson distribution, without too much difficulty. Variations also exist for designs with multiple thresholds.

Lee and Lemieux (2015) provide a more formal but nevertheless comprehensible introduction to the regression discontinuity design. The journal Advances in Econometrics (2017) recently published a set of articles, edited by Cattaneo and Escanciano, some more theoretical and others more applied, with the most recent state of the art in regression discontinuity analysis.

Chapter 6

Fixed effects panel models

6.1 Introduction

In this chapter we will discuss fixed effects panel models. These models are increasingly employed in empirical research. They are mainly used to analyse data relating to different points in time from a sample of different individuals, companies or other research units. This kind of data is also referred to as longitudinal or panel data. The overarching advantage of these models is that the distorting effects of observed, as well as unobserved, differences between the research units can be pretty much avoided. This probably all sounds rather cryptic, and so we will first describe the idea behind the method using a simple example. This method offers an elegant solution to the troublesome problem that non-experimental research designs face, namely that we want to compare dissimilar groups. The method does however have its limitations.

The type of panel model we will describe in this chapter is just one of many versions of this method. We will briefly outline the other versions towards the end of the chapter. We follow Brüderl (2005)'s method of explaining fixed effects panel models. As in previous chapters we will outline how to perform the analysis using the available software, providing a thoroughly worked through example. We will conclude with suggestions for further reading.

6.2 Analysis method for longitudinal data

Fixed effects panel models are mainly used to analyse data on N research units collected at T points in time. In the social sciences N is usually people, but these could for example be companies. This kind of data is called longitudinal data. Mostly T is small and N is large, i.e. we have a substantial sample of research units N, for which we have data at a limited number of T time points. Often this kind of data is the result of a research design which collects information from the research units at different points in time, the so-called prospective panel design. Panel data can however also be collected at one time point using a retrospective design, i.e. data concerning a period of time in the past are collected.

In longitudinal data scores on the dependent variable can vary over time. We express this as y_{it}, whereby subscript i stands for the individual research units and subscript t for the time points. This kind of variable is referred to as a time varying variable. An example of a time varying variable in criminology is the number of offences an individual commits in one year. Besides time varying dependent variables we also have time varying independent variables, for example education, addiction, employment, or depression. We can use these to try and explain y_{it}.

Let us take employment as an example. In one year an individual may be employed, and in the following year they may no longer be employed. Due to the time varying character of this kind of independent variable we express this, similarly to the dependent variable, as X_{it}. Here we use a capital X to indicate that this can refer to several independent variables. Of course not all variables vary over time. We also have time-invariant or time constant independent variables. These variables, such as gender, do not differ from one time point to the next. We express these as X_i. They can of course vary between research units, but they do not vary within research units over time.

A example of a longitudinal dataset is given in Table 6.1. To keep things simple we have presented fictional data from just 4 individuals measured at 6 time points. The data are presented in long format, i.e. for every research unit a separate row is used for each point in time. Longitudinal data can also be saved in wide format. In this case each research unit is represented by just one row, and scores on the different variables relating to each time point are presented in separate columns. Most software used for estimating panel models assumes that data are in long format, hence our choice for this format here. We have four variables: `ID`, `time`, `crime` and `work`. The first variable identifies the research units and the second the time point of the measurement. The third variable indicates the number of offences committed per year and the fourth variable indicates whether the individual was employed in that year.

If we wanted to know whether committing criminal offences is related to being employed, this fictional dataset should be able to help us answer the question. The number of criminal offences and employment status vary between individuals, as well as within individuals, over time. It is exactly this within individual variation over time which sets longitudinal data apart from cross-sectional data. Cross-sectional data only provide information on differences between individuals. Panel data provide two sources of variation, differences between individuals (inter-individual) and differences within individuals (intra-individual). Fixed effects panel models allow us to examine the extent to which these intra-individual differences, i.e. within research units over time, can be explained. The goal of fixed effects panel models is basically to examine the extent to which changes in X leads to changes in Y, given that all else remains the same. This goal seems to be very similar to that of the classic experiment discussed in section 1.2. We will however see that whilst fixed effects panel models are a worthy method to use when attempting to determine causal effects, the method still pales in comparison to the classic experiment.

If we wanted to research the causal effect of employment on criminal behaviour using a classic experiment we would have to randomly assign individuals into two groups. The experimental group would receive the *treatment* of employment, and the control group would remain unemployed. If we then found that the control group committed more offences than the experimental group we could rightly conclude that employment causes people to commit less crime. Whilst in a classic experiment we can randomly place people in either the experimental or control group, in our example dataset looking at employment this cannot and has not been done, as soon becomes obvious when we examine the data in Figure 6.1.

To make things easier we have drawn lines connecting the scores of the four individuals at different time points, and so we can quickly see how the scores for each individual change over time. For each individual at each time point we can see whether they were employed (diamond) or unemployed (circle). It is quite clear from the figure that employment was not randomly allocated, as the height of the different lines appears to differ systematically. The two uppermost lines, i.e. those individuals who committed the most offences, are the only ones for which we see any unemployment. These 2 individuals are only employed in the later years. Employment therefore appears to be strongly related to the number of criminal offences committed.

But are we able to conclude that employment causes a decrease in criminal behaviour? As we have not conducted an experiment we cannot entirely rule out the possibility that the relationship between employment and criminal behaviour is spurious. As we saw in section 1.1 an underlying variable can cause two variables to relate to each other. In our current example it might be that people with limited self control commit more criminal offences and also have more trouble finding employment. If we have no measure of self-control in our dataset, as would often be the case when using official data sources, the estimation of the effect of employment on criminal behaviour would be distorted. In this kind of situation we have unmeasured or unobserved heterogeneity which can potentially lead to bias in our results.

Table 6.1: Example of longitudinal data

ID	time	crime	work
1	1	0	1
1	2	0	1
1	3	1	1
1	4	0	1
1	5	1	1
1	6	0	1
2	1	2	1
2	2	2	1
2	3	3	1
2	4	2	1
2	5	2	1
2	6	2	1
3	1	5	0
3	2	4	0
3	3	5	0
3	4	3	1
3	5	4	1
3	6	3	1
4	1	7	0
4	2	6	0
4	3	6	0
4	4	8	0
4	5	5	1
4	6	5	1

6.3 A naive analysis of panel data

When analysing longitudinal data we need to be on the look out for unobserved heterogeneity. It would be easy to draw the wrong conclusions if we used a naive and simple regression analysis method. We will illustrate why using the fictional data

Figure 6.1: Longitudinal data number of offences by employment

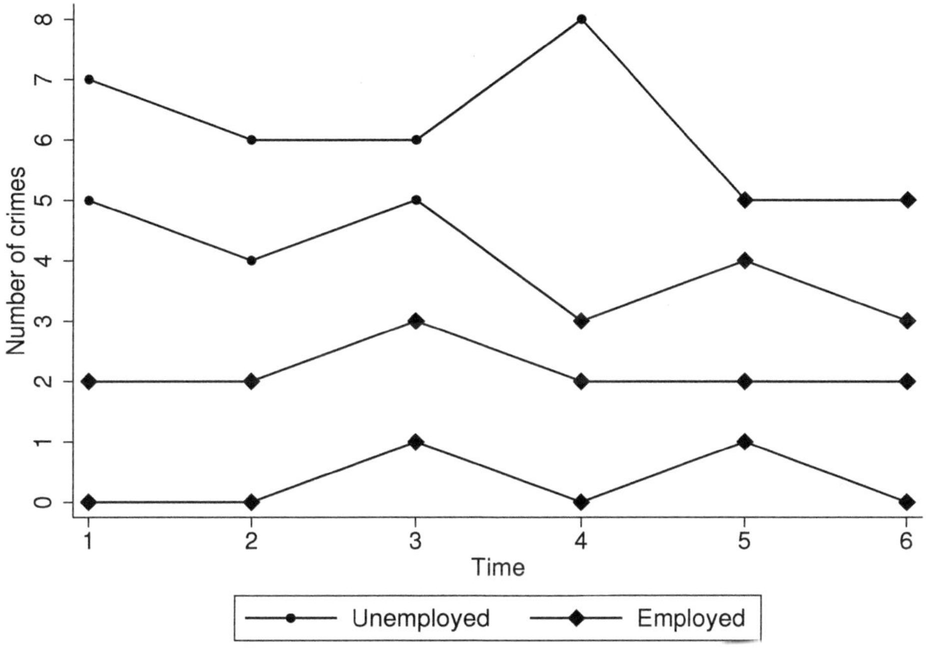

concerning employment and criminal behaviour presented in the previous section. Let us examine what the OLS estimate for the relationship between employment and criminal behaviour for this fictional dataset would be. We estimate the standard OLS regression model given in equation (6.1), with just one independent variable x_{it}, `work`.

$$y_{it} = b_0 + b_1 x_{it} + e_{it} \tag{6.1}$$

The OLS estimate for the effect of employment b_1 is -3.8. In other words, based on the OLS regression model we would conclude that being employed reduces the number of offences committed by 3.8. However, in section 2.2 we stated that the OLS regression model assumes that individual observations are independent of each other. In our OLS regression we have therefore incorrectly assumed that we are dealing with 24 independent observations. Of course, we know that we actually have 4 individuals each measured at 6 time points, and therefore not 24 independent observations. That these observations are not independent is also obvious looking at Figure 6.1. The scores for the different individuals appear to strongly relate to each other over time, i.e. individual 1 scores consistently low on number of offences, whilst individual 4 scores the highest number of offences at each time point.

Recall that we are trying to determine the extent to which changes in employment lead to changes in criminal behaviour, i.e. an intra-individual effect. The value -3.8 appears to be a gross overestimation of the negative effect. After all we do not see such a large drop in the number of offences committed by the two individuals who go from being unemployed to being employed. So why does the OLS regression estimate indicate such a strong effect? The answer lies in the fact that the OLS regression does not distinguish between inter- and intra-individual differences. As Figure 6.1 illustrates the differences in criminal behaviour are much greater between individuals than within individuals over time. The OLS regression estimates the effect of employment on criminal behaviour using the average score for the employed versus the average score for the unemployed. However, differences in criminal behaviour may result from differences between the individuals other than simply different employment statuses. If we had measurements of all the possible causes of these individual differences we could include these in the model as control variables. By including these controls we would get a better estimate of the effect of employment on criminal behaviour. However, we can of course only include these control variables if we have data on them. As we argued in chapter 1 there is no statistical way to guarantee that we have removed all bias by controlling for distorting factors in this way. It is highly likely that the cause of differences between individuals is unobserved. In our example we do not need to include any control variables in the model for it to be obvious that differences between individuals are already present at the first time point in the panel data.

6.4 The fixed effects panel model

So how should we go about estimating the effect of changes in employment status on criminal behaviour? The fixed effects panel model offers a solution by focussing on intra-individual differences and ignoring all stable inter-individual differences. This is possible because using panel data we are able to separate these two different sources of variation. In just a couple of steps we can expand the OLS regression equation, transforming it into a fixed effects panel model. Whilst the algebra is relatively simple it may be rather difficult to follow for those not used to working with formulas. We will therefore illustrate each step by demonstrating what it does to our fictional dataset.

First we separate the error term from the OLS regression equation (6.1) into two parts: (a) error specific to each individual ν_i and (b) error specific to each individual at each point in time ε_{it}. This is shown in equation (6.2).

$$e_{it} = \nu_i + \varepsilon_{it} \tag{6.2}$$

The first error term ν_i is simply the extent to which an individual on average differs from the grand mean, the overall average across all individuals. In the example the average number of offences per year is 3.17. We can see that the individual with the highest scores commits on average 3 offences more than this, whilst the individual with the lowest scores commits on average nearly 3 offences below this. The extent to which an individual's average score deviates from the overall average score is given by ν_i. This refers to the average deviation per individual over the entire period, and therefore the index t is not included, as this individual specific error does not change over time. Each person therefore has a fixed value (fixed effect) on ν_i. A person's self-control score is an example of a time-invariant, unmeasured characteristic that would be included in ν_i. Individuals with low self control would have a high ν_i (after all, on average they commit more offences) and individuals with high self-control would have a low ν_i. The second error term ε_{it} indicates the extent to which each individual, indicated by index i, deviates from their own average at each point in time, indicated by index t. For example, we can see that the first (=7) and the fourth (=8) observations of the highest scoring individual were above their own average (=6.17) and the four remaining observations for that individual were below their own average.

Given that our ultimate goal is to discover whether changes in employment influence the number of offences an individual commits, we are not really interested in the absolute differences between individuals. Of course some people will commit more offences than others, but in determining the effect of employment what we really want to know is how much people's criminal behaviour changes as they move from unemployed to employed and vice versa, regardless of the level of criminal behaviour they started out at. It should be obvious therefore that what we actually want to do is to get rid of the average individual differences included in ν_i. We will show how this is done using some linear algebra.

To start with we replace the OLS error term from (6.1) with the split OLS error terms from equation (6.2). In doing this we end up with the so-called error-components model indicated in equation (6.3).

$$y_{it} = b_0 + b_1 x_{it} + \nu_i + \varepsilon_{it} \tag{6.3}$$

Next we carry out two transformations. First we average equation (6.3) per individual across all time points. The resulting equation is (6.4).

$$\bar{y}_i = b_1 \bar{x}_i + \nu_i + \bar{\varepsilon}_i \tag{6.4}$$

Equation (6.4) indicates that every individual's average dependent variable ($\bar{y}_i$) is a function (b_1) of the average individual score on an independent variable ($\bar{x}_i$) plus individual error ($\bar{\varepsilon}_i$).

This transformation is easier to understand if we expand Table 6.1 to include our two transformed variables. Table 6.2 includes the average scores on number of offences per year (y), as well as on the work variable (x), for each individual, `M(crime)` and `M(work)`. Interpreting these variables is easy. For example, on average across all 6 years the third individual committed 4 offences, whilst they were only employed for half of those years.

In the next step we need to subtract equation (6.4) from equation (6.3). We can also illustrate this step using our two extra variables. As we can see in equation (6.5), an individual's average score on the dependent variable, $\bar{y}_i$, is subtracted from the dependent variable, y_{it}. The resulting score is then the deviation from the individual average. The same happens for each independent variable ($x_{it} - \bar{x}_i$).

$$y_{it} - \bar{y}_i = b_1 (x_{it} - \bar{x}_i) + \varepsilon_{it} - \bar{\varepsilon}_i \tag{6.5}$$

In our example this results in two new variables, namely two individual mean centred variables. Table 6.3 is an extension of 6.2 including the two centred variables, `W(crime)` and `W(work)`.

These two transformations mean that ν_i from equation (6.3) is no longer included in equation (6.5). By subtracting the average over time of all the variables in the model the only differences we are left with are intra-individual differences. And so we no longer have to deal with any unobserved, time-invariant heterogeneity. As a result of these transformations our results are no longer susceptible to any differences that are constant over time, such as differences in propensity to commit crime or gender differences. Equation (6.5) is therefore the fixed effects panel model.

We can now estimate the intra-individual effect of employment on criminal behaviour by regressing `W(crime)` onto `W(work)` using an OLS regression. The estimated intra-individual effect of employment on criminal behaviour (b_1) now amounts to -1.5. In other words, our fictional data indicate that when an previously unemployed person is employed, in that year the average number of offences they will commit will drop by 1.5. Where our original OLS regression model incorrectly indicated that employment had a very large effect on criminal behaviour, b_1 was estimated to be -3.8, we now see a far more conservative effect. The OLS regression overestimated the effect of employment because all the between individual differences were included in the estimation of the effect. The fixed effects

Table 6.2: Example of longitudinal data including individual specific average scores

ID	time	crime	work	M(crime)	M(work)
1	1	0	1	0.33	1.00
1	2	0	1	0.33	1.00
1	3	1	1	0.33	1.00
1	4	0	1	0.33	1.00
1	5	1	1	0.33	1.00
1	6	0	1	0.33	1.00
2	1	2	1	2.17	1.00
2	2	2	1	2.17	1.00
2	3	3	1	2.17	1.00
2	4	2	1	2.17	1.00
2	5	2	1	2.17	1.00
2	6	2	1	2.17	1.00
3	1	5	0	4.00	0.50
3	2	4	0	4.00	0.50
3	3	5	0	4.00	0.50
3	4	3	1	4.00	0.50
3	5	4	1	4.00	0.50
3	6	3	1	4.00	0.50
4	1	7	0	6.17	0.33
4	2	6	0	6.17	0.33
4	3	6	0	6.17	0.33
4	4	8	0	6.17	0.33
4	5	5	1	6.17	0.33
4	6	5	1	6.17	0.33

panel model, in contrast, removes all the stable observed and unobserved differences between individuals from the OLS estimation, thereby estimating an effect which controls for all time-invariant, observed and unobserved, heterogeneity.

Table 6.3: Example of longitudinal data including individual specific averages and centred variables

ID	time	crime	work	M(crime)	M(work)	W(crime)	W(work)
1	1	0	1	0.33	1.00	-0.33	0.00
1	2	0	1	0.33	1.00	-0.33	0.00
1	3	1	1	0.33	1.00	0.67	0.00
1	4	0	1	0.33	1.00	-0.33	0.00
1	5	1	1	0.33	1.00	0.67	0.00
1	6	0	1	0.33	1.00	-0.33	0.00
2	1	2	1	2.17	1.00	-0.17	0.00
2	2	2	1	2.17	1.00	-0.17	0.00
2	3	3	1	2.17	1.00	0.83	0.00
2	4	2	1	2.17	1.00	-0.17	0.00
2	5	2	1	2.17	1.00	-0.17	0.00
2	6	2	1	2.17	1.00	-0.17	0.00
3	1	5	0	4.00	0.50	1.00	-0.50
3	2	4	0	4.00	0.50	0.00	-0.50
3	3	5	0	4.00	0.50	1.00	-0.50
3	4	3	1	4.00	0.50	-1.00	0.50
3	5	4	1	4.00	0.50	0.00	0.50
3	6	3	1	4.00	0.50	-1.00	0.50
4	1	7	0	6.17	0.33	0.83	-0.33
4	2	6	0	6.17	0.33	-0.17	-0.33
4	3	6	0	6.17	0.33	-0.17	-0.33
4	4	8	0	6.17	0.33	1.83	-0.33
4	5	5	1	6.17	0.33	-1.17	0.67
4	6	5	1	6.17	0.33	-1.17	0.67

Figure 6.2 illustrates the relationship between the transformed variables, as well as the fixed effects estimation. From the figure we can see that only those individual who switch from being unemployed to being employed contribute to the estimation of the intra-individual employment effect. The individuals with unchang-

Figure 6.2: Illustration of a fixed effects estimation

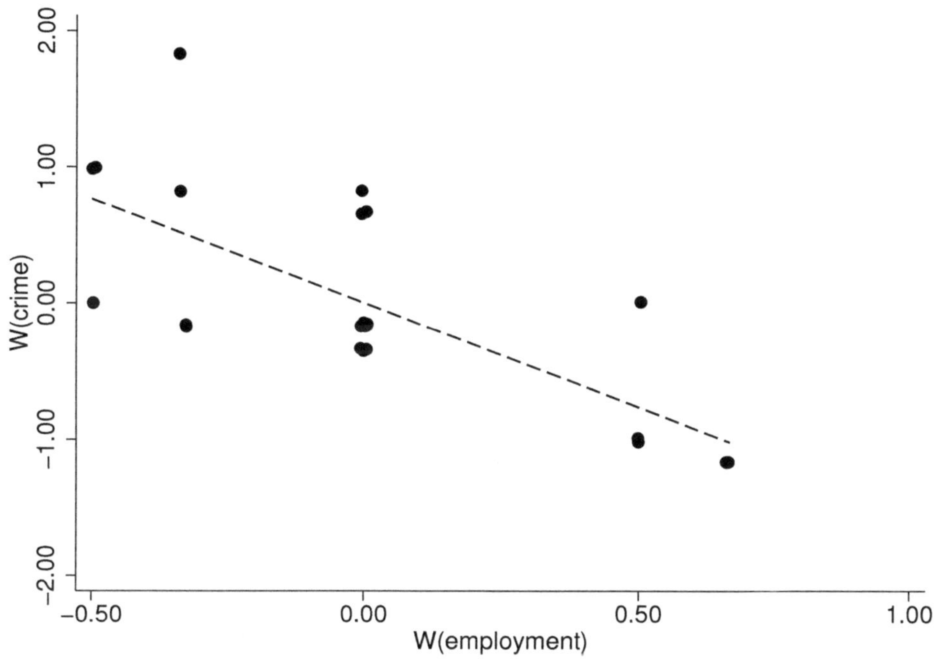

ing employment scores do not contribute anything to the fixed effects estimation. Their scores for `W(work)`=0.00. The position of the remaining individuals' scores determines the position of the regression line. So, only individuals whose scores vary on at least one of the independent variables contribute to the effect estimation. If we removed from the dataset all individuals who do not vary at all on any of the independent variables the resulting regression line would be exactly the same. Variation on the dependent variable is not necessary when the dependent variable is continuous, as in our illustrated model. Moreover, individuals with a constant score on the dependent variable, but with scores that vary on at least one of the independent variables, will have a substantial influence on the effect estimations. Later we will see that when carrying out a logistic fixed effects panel model variation on the dependent variable is necessary. For now the regression line, or fixed effects estimation, in the figure is simply a comparison of criminal behaviour scores for individuals before they were employed and after they were employed.

6.5 Software

As we have seen the fixed effect panel model for a continuous dependent variable can simply be estimated by first transforming the original variables and then applying an adjusted OLS regression. Consequently estimating these models is possible using any of the available software, R, SAS, SPSS, Stata, and so on. Of course when estimating fixed effects panel models we do not have to carry out all these transformations by hand. In many of the software programmes there are procedures which simply carry out the model estimation for the researcher. In this chapter however we want to illustrate what happens behind the scenes in these estimation procedures. As a result it is possible to estimate a fixed effects panel model even without access to the appropriate software. However, when the fixed effects panel model is estimated by hand, by transforming the variables oneself, the standard errors are under-estimated. This increases the chance that we incorrectly conclude that we have a statistically significant effect. This is because the OLS regression assumes that we have $N \times T - k$ degrees of freedom. However, the transformations, which result in the time-invariant unobserved heterogeneity being removed, mean that N degrees of freedom are discarded.

In this chapter we will outline the procedure for estimating fixed effects panel models in Stata. This procedure is very simple and automatically estimates the correct standard errors using $N \times (T-1) - k$ degrees of freedom. Furthermore, more advanced fixed effects panel models can also be implemented in Stata, making it possible to analyse discrete dependent variables, i.e. dichotomous or count variables. These non-linear models cannot be estimated by carrying out simple transformations of the data. The reader may have been wondering whether it was actually correct of us to analyse number of criminal offences as if it were a continuous variable. After all, in chapter 2 we saw that for this kind of count variable Poisson models are better suited. For reasons of simplicity we chose not to use a Poisson model in our example. In section 6.6 we will use some concrete data on criminal behaviour to demonstrate how Stata estimates a logistic fixed effects panel model.

To use Stata to estimate fixed effects panel models the data need to be in long format and there needs to be a unique identifying variable for each research unit. To learn how to convert data from wide to long format in Stata see section 6.6. Once the data are in the correct format the `xt` series of commands can be used to analyse the panel data. Rabe-Hesketh and Skrondal (2008) provide an extensive description of the analysis options in Stata, including those concerning estimation of fixed effects panel models. For now the following commands will suffice. First:

```
xtset IDvariabele
```

tells Stata that the present data are panel data, and that all rows with the same score on `IDvariabele` relate to the same research unit for which we have several measurement over time.

After the `xtset` command we can ask Stata to estimate a fixed effects panel model. In order to estimate a *linear* fixed effects panel model we use the `xtreg` command[1]. We replace `y` with the name of the dependent variable, `x1` with the name of the first time-varying independent variable, and `x2` with the name of a second time-varying independent variable, and so on. Next, after the comma, `fe` is entered to indicate to Stata that we want to estimate a fixed effects panel model, as shown below.

```
xtreg y x1 x2, fe
```

If we want Stata to estimate a *non-linear* fixed effects panel model the procedure is slightly different. The first command needs to be adjusted to indicate the type of non-linear model we want estimated. For a dichotomous dependent variable (0/1) we recommend using `xtlogit` and for a count dependent variable we recommend using `xtpoisson`. The command for a logistic model is as follows:

```
xtlogit y x1 x2, fe
```

and for a Poisson model:

```
xtpoisson y x1 x2, fe
```

Whilst we learnt in chapter 2 that over-dispersed count data can be analysed using a negative binomial model, and Stata does have the command `xtnbreg`, this command does not estimate a fixed effects negative binomial panel model we would expect it to. The command `xtnbreg` estimates a model with individual specific variance in the dispersion parameter, instead of individual specific variance in the size of the score. It is clear that this model is not equivalent to the other `xt` models by the fact that the time-invariant independent variables can be included in a `xtnbreg` model. We therefore do not recommend using the `xtnbreg` model. Allison and Waterman (2002) provide possible solutions for estimating a fixed effects panel model using over-dispersed count data.

[1]Another way to estimate a fixed effects panel model for a continuous dependent variable is by estimating an OLS regression using the original, untransformed variables, and controlling for N dummies, without estimating the intercept. This provides the correct fixed effects estimation with accurate standard errors. Of course this method results in much higher degrees of freedom. When there are a large number of research units in the data there will be many parameters to estimate, slowing the procedure down considerably.

6.6 Example: Effects of marriage, parenthood, and work on criminal behaviour

Once again we will illustrate our analysis method using a concrete example. We will use Stata to analyse our dataset containing 500 fictional, juvenile sex offenders. When using Stata any comments are preceded by a '*'. It is good practice to add comments in this way, as the commands needed can be quite complicated. By adding comments it becomes much easier to reconstruct analyses at a later date. First the dataset needs to be opened, in this example the dataset is in the root folder of the C-drive.

```
* Opening data file VM-JSO.dta

global DATAMAP "C:\"
use "${DATAMAP}VM-JSO.dta", clear
```

The data in the data file `VM-JSO.dta` are in wide format and therefore need to be transformed into long format for analysis. This is done using the following commands:

```
* idnumber is identification variable
reshape i idnumber
* year is time variable
reshape j year
* offence_ work_ marriage_ and child_ vary between
* persons and over time
reshape xij offence_ work_ marriage_ child_
reshape long
```

Whilst the data file includes a variable indicating number of offences per year this count variable is so skewed and the variable contains so many zeros that we have chosen to examine the chance that an offence is committed in a given year, rather than the number of offences committed in a given year. We want to examine the extent to which being employed, being married, and having a child affect the chance of offending. We will therefore estimate a logistic fixed effects panel model. First we need to dichotomise the dependent variable.

```
* Freq.distribution of the count dependent variable
tab offence_, mis
* Creating dichotomous dependent variable
gen offencedi=offence_>0 if offence_!=.
* Freq.distrib.  of the dichotomous dependent variable
tab offencedi, mis
```

We need to tell Stata that the present dataset is panel data. We do this using the following command:

```
* Indicate that the data are panel data
xtset idnumber
```

Next we need to tell Stata that all missing values need to be removed. We do this as follows:

```
 * Remove all missings from
 * work, marriage, and child
drop if work_==.|marriage_==.|child_==.|offencedi==.
```

Now we are ready to estimate our fixed effects panel model. To do this we use the following command. By adding ' `or`' after the comma Stata provides the effect estimates of the logistic fixed effects panel model as odds ratios. If ' `or`' is not included the effect estimates would be given as log-odds.

```
xtlogit offencedi work_ marriage_ child_, fe or
```

The results are given in Figure 6.3.

We can see from the first note in Figure 6.3 that some individuals have committed offences in several years. This is a warning that Stata automatically provides, which for our analysis is not a problem. Next, Stata indicates that 230 individuals, 1446 rows in the data file, are removed from the logistic regression analysis because their scores on the dependent variable do not vary. Here the logistic fixed effects panel model differs from the linear fixed effects panel model. When using the logistic version research units which do not vary on the dependent variable do not contribute to the effect estimates. For this reason Stata does not include them in the analysis. We can see that not all individuals in the data file have the same number of time points from the fact that the number of removed rows divided by the number of removed individuals is not a whole number. We therefore have an unbalanced dataset. The next part of the output in Figure 6.3 demonstrates that estimating a fixed effects panel model is an iterative process. In each iteration the estimation algorithm is trying to come up with a better solution. In our example 3 iterations were needed to produce the correct estimates. We can also see that 163 individuals were included in the analysis, comprising 1225 rows in the data file. On average the individuals included in the analysis thus appear 7.5 times in the data file. We can again see that we have an unbalanced dataset by the fact that the number of years that individuals appear in the data file varies from 3 to 15. This is not a problem for estimating panel models. A balanced dataset, where each individual has an equal number of observations, is not a requirement.

Figure 6.3: Results of logistic fixed effects panel model

```
note: multiple positive outcomes within groups encountered.
note: 230 groups (1446 obs) dropped because of all positive or
      all negative outcomes.

Iteration 0:   log likelihood = -435.60943
Iteration 1:   log likelihood = -434.89656
Iteration 2:   log likelihood =  -434.8962
Iteration 3:   log likelihood =  -434.8962

Conditional fixed-effects logistic regression   Number of obs      =      1225
Group variable: idnumber                        Number of groups   =       163

                                                Obs per group: min =         3
                                                               avg =       7.5
                                                               max =        15

                                                LR chi2(3)         =      9.08
Log likelihood  =  -434.8962                    Prob > chi2        =    0.0282

------------------------------------------------------------------------------
     crimedi |         OR   Std. Err.      z    P>|z|     [95% Conf. Interval]
-------------+----------------------------------------------------------------
        job_ |   .6519767   .1173556    -2.38   0.017     .4581589    .9277865
   marriage_ |   .4558782   .2657792    -1.35   0.178       .14541    1.429235
      child_ |   .8671215   .2932986    -0.42   0.673     .4468546     1.68265
------------------------------------------------------------------------------
```

Next we will discuss how to interpret the results of a logistic fixed effects panel model. The log-likelihood is estimated to be -434.8962. By itself this does not give us any useful information. The log-likelihood is a measure of the model fit and can only be used to compare the fit of nested models (see section 2.3). We can see the comparison with the null model in LR $\chi^2(3)$, i.e. the likelihood-ratio test for the estimated model, with 3 parameters, against the null model, without any parameters. The likelihood-ratio test has a value of 9.08. This statistic is calculated by multiplying the negative log-likelihood by 2 (=869.79239) and subtracting this from the null model's negative log-likelihood multiplied by 2 (=878.87418). This difference has, approximately, a χ^2 distribution, meaning that it is possible to test whether the given model is statistically significantly better fitting the data than the null model. This is the case, and we can see this in the test result that Stata reports: Prob $> \chi^2 = 0.0282$.

Now we will interpret the effect estimates. The estimated odds ratio for `work` is .65. This is statistically significantly different from an odds ratio of 1, and so we can conclude that employment decreases the chance that a sex offender will commit an offence. Basically, when an individual moves from being unemployed to being employed the odds of them committing an offence (odds: $P_{Y=1}/P_{Y=0}$) decrease by 35 percent. This can also work in the opposite direction, meaning that losing a job results in a more than 50 percent increase in the chance of committing an offence ($= 1/.65$). Being married and having children do not have any statistically significant effect on chances of offending. This is despite a substantial effect of marriage in this sample, i.e. the odds of offending are reduced by 55 percent after marrying. However, because of the relatively high unreliability of the estimated effect, indicated by the standard errors for the estimator, we cannot confidently conclude that this effect is generalisable to the sample population.

This example illustrates an analysis estimating the effects of certain events, i.e. getting a job, getting married, and having a child. Fixed effects panel models can also be used to estimate the effect of continuous independent variables. The effect in such as case would be interpreted as estimated changes in Y resulting from a one unit increase in X.

6.6.1 Period effects: Two-way fixed effects panel models

In the examples above we have repeatedly focussed on removing observed and unobserved time-invariant between individual differences. It is however possible that period effects play a role, whereby individual scores are correlated with unobserved time characteristics. For example, this would be the case if the four people in Figure 6.1 all started to commit more offences from time point 4 onwards. Imagine that all scores from that point on were noticeably higher, and that it was obvious that this sudden change was also connected to being employed. As a result the estimated effect of work on number of offences would change. Such period effects actually come down to person constant, or person invariant, between time point differences. These effects, just as with time-invariant between person differences, are removed from the estimations by using fixed effects, except now the differences are between time points rather than individuals. In the models described above by applying fixed effects to the individual specific constants, we actually control for all between person variation in the model. Using an analogous method we are able to simultaneously apply fixed effects for time specific constants, thereby controlling for all between time point variation. When we simultaneously control for between individual and between time point differences we refer to a *two-way* fixed effects panel model. In these models, any variation in scores caused by period effects, for example a general trend in the population, and by between individual differences is removed.

We illustrate the importance of controlling for period effects using the results of our example. In our data it seems that the average chance of an individual committing an offence decreases as the years go by. However, the chance of being employed, getting married, and having a child increases as the years go by. It is therefore possible that the results in Figure 6.3 are influenced by these trends. By controlling for time dummies in this model we can estimate the effect of being employed, being married or having a child on the chance of committing an offence in a given year independently of these period effects. Note that controlling for time dummies has exactly the same effect as using person dummies to estimate fixed effects panel models as described earlier. The panel data however has far fewer time points than individuals, which means that we only need to include a few extra dummies into the model. To carry out this analysis we therefore need to make some period dummies. Because all cases with missing data on any independent variable were already removed, we are left with individuals aged 18 and older with valid scores on all the independent variables.

```
* Creating period dummies
tab year, gen(year_)
```

Next we estimate the same model, but now including the $T-1$ period dummies. We can use a shortened code for our dummy variables by inserting the ' –' symbol in our command. This indicates that all the variables between `year_2` and `year_15` should be included in the model. This only works if the variables are next to each other in the dataset.

```
xtlogit offencedi work_ marriage_ child_ year_2-year_15,
    fe or
```

The results are shown in Figure 6.4. We can see that the effects of work, marriage and child are now different to those in Figure 6.3. Previously, we found a statistically significant negative effect of work on chance of committing an offence (OR =.65). Now however, the estimated effect is not as strong (OR =.73), and moreover it is only statistically significantly different from an odds ratio of 1 in a one-sided significance test ($P > |z| = .09$). This means that on the basis of this analysis we can no longer conclude that being employed decreases the chance of committing a criminal offence. The other two effects remain statistically non-significant, although the effect of having a child reverses in direction. The fact that our results can look so different after controlling for period effects highlights the importance of controlling for these between time point differences.

6.6.2 A random effects panel model

Whereas a fixed effects panel model estimates effects based only on variation within units, a random effects panel model estimates effects based on variation within and between units. If one is interested in simultaneously estimating the ef-

Figure 6.4: Results of two-way logistic fixed effects panel model

```
Conditional fixed-effects logistic regression   Number of obs      =      1225
Group variable: idnumber                        Number of groups   =       163

                                                Obs per group: min =         3
                                                               avg =       7.5
                                                               max =        15

                                                LR chi2(17)        =     54.30
Log likelihood  =   -412.289                    Prob > chi2        =    0.0000
```

crimedi	OR	Std. Err.	z	P>|z|	[95% Conf.	Interval]
job_	.7315389	.1361006	-1.68	0.093	.5080119	1.053418
marriage_	.6146105	.3711275	-0.81	0.420	.1881954	2.007202
child_	1.460519	.5326156	1.04	0.299	.7146521	2.98483
year_2	.6751451	.1877674	-1.41	0.158	.3914407	1.16447
year_3	.6095643	.1610831	-1.87	0.061	.3631462	1.023193
year_4	.6808154	.181532	-1.44	0.149	.4037065	1.148135
year_5	.4224689	.1204448	-3.02	0.003	.2416125	.7387034
year_6	.418831	.1636822	-2.23	0.026	.1947077	.9009371
year_7	.5953656	.2045882	-1.51	0.131	.3035858	1.167578
year_8	.3765156	.1345922	-2.73	0.006	.1868555	.7586825
year_9	.3089653	.1189482	-3.05	0.002	.1452802	.657072
year_10	.2566541	.1060861	-3.29	0.001	.114159	.5770137
year_11	.0519698	.0543393	-2.83	0.005	.0066948	.403425
year_12	.0501494	.0524621	-2.86	0.004	.0064537	.3896922
year_13	.4593652	.2628933	-1.36	0.174	.1496298	1.410256
year_14	.1051139	.1121768	-2.11	0.035	.0129797	.8512483
year_15	1.42e-06	.0005876	-0.03	0.974	0	.

fects of time-varying and time-invariant variables a random effects model should be used.

$$y_{it} = b_0 + b_1 x_{it} + \nu_i + \varepsilon_{it} \tag{6.6}$$

Random effects models assume that there are no correlations between the time-varying independent variables (x_{it}) and the ν_i. A random effects panel model will only provide consistent effects if this assumption is met. If this assumption is violated this will result in biased estimators. However, there is no test for violation of this assumption. Furthermore, in most criminological and social science research this assumption is not very plausible, and so using a random effects model is generally not recommended. Besides, one has to wonder if estimating the effect of time-invariant variables is really that important. The advantage of panel data is specifically that the effects of time-varying variables can be estimated. We therefore do not recommend using panel data to estimate the effects of time-invariant variables, as analyses will be based on assumptions which cannot be tested and are likely to have been violated. It is far more useful to focus your attention on several time-varying variables, than to conduct an analysis of a list of determinants of the dependent variable.

Should you still want to carry out a random effects model there are tests which can be used to determine whether the estimates are biased or not. We will now use the same data as for the analysis in Figure 6.3 to estimate a random effects model controlling for all the time-invariant variables we have in the dataset. In Stata estimating a random effect model simply involves replacing the `fe` in the `xt` command with `re`.

However, we first need to make dummy variables for the nominal variable `type_offender` (this was not necessary previously as this is a time-invariant variable):

```
* Create dummy variables for type_offender
tabulate type_offender, gen(type_offender)
```

The procedure is then as follows:

```
xtlogit offencedi work_ marriage_ child_ ethnicity
    contact_peers psychopathology
     age_offence IQ neuroticism impulsivity
     type_offender2 type_offender3 previous, re or
```

The results of the random effects panel model are shown in Figure 6.5. We can see from the figure that the random effects model uses many more units in the analysis. The fixed effects logistic panel model only included those cases with variation on the dependent variable. In contrast, the random effects estimates are based on both within and between variation. Consequently, individuals whose scores on the dependent variable do not change are also included in the analysis. These results also demonstrate different effects for work, marriage and child than those seen in Figure 6.3. The estimated effect of work appears to be slightly stronger and that for child is in the opposite direction, although it is not statistically significant here either. The odds ratio for ethnicity is very large. Evidently people with a non-Dutch ethnicity have a far higher chance of committing an offence in a given year than native Dutch people, when controlling for being employed, being married and having a child, and all other variables in the model. We also see positive effects for all the remaining time-invariant control variables, with the exception of whether an individual has a previously registered sex offence. A number of the control variables have statistically significant effects, highlighting yet again the importance of controlling for these kinds of between individual differences.

Compared to the output from the fixed effects panel model in Figure 6.3, this output has a number of extra rows. The term `sigma_u` indicates how dispersed

Figure 6.5: Results of logistic random effects panel model

```
Random-effects logistic regression              Number of obs      =      2671
Group variable: idnumber                        Number of groups   =       393

Random effects u_i ~ Gaussian                   Obs per group: min =         1
                                                               avg =       6.8
                                                               max =        15

                                                Wald chi2(13)      =     98.82
Log likelihood  = -860.90885                    Prob > chi2        =    0.0000
```

crimedi	OR	Std. Err.	z	P>|z|	[95% Conf.	Interval]
job_	.490617	.0760844	-4.59	0.000	.3620255	.6648842
marriage_	.4629027	.2299499	-1.55	0.121	.1748437	1.225546
child_	1.52916	.4026273	1.61	0.107	.9127079	2.56197
ethnicity	3.453485	.6774262	6.32	0.000	2.351193	5.072557
peercontact	1.157627	.1608371	1.05	0.292	.8816686	1.519959
psychopath~y	1.416858	.2862363	1.72	0.085	.9535972	2.105172
crimeage	1.031326	.0605807	0.53	0.600	.9191699	1.157167
IQ	1.127828	.1060643	1.28	0.201	.9379797	1.356102
neuroticism	1.210078	.1014014	2.28	0.023	1.026798	1.426073
impulsivity	1.239886	.0978278	2.73	0.006	1.062238	1.447246
offenderty~2	1.911109	.4266917	2.90	0.004	1.233782	2.960278
offenderty~3	1.649801	.4003808	2.06	0.039	1.025317	2.654635
priorsexof~e	.7393858	.1923905	-1.16	0.246	.4440029	1.231279
/lnsig2u	-.112089	.2696404			-.6405745	.4163965
sigma_u	.9454971	.1274721			.7259405	1.231457
rho	.2136712	.0453039			.138069	.3155171

the research units are, given as a standard deviation. We can interpret this as the extent to which individuals vary on their *Y* scores. This is the dispersion we saw in Figure 6.1, where the four individuals clearly differed in the number of offences they committed. In the present case we have not estimated number of offences, but a logistic random effects panel model. The idea is the same though. The `sigma_u` indicates the extent to which the different individuals on average score differently. The term `lnsig2u` is simply the same distribution presented as the logarithm of the variance ($ln(.9454971^2) = -.112089$). Next, `rho` indicates the proportion of the variance which can be attributed to the differences between individuals. In the literature concerning multilevel models this is also referred to as the intra-class correlation, see Snijders and Bosker (2012). Equation (6.7) shows how `rho` is calculated:

$$\rho = \frac{\sigma_v{}^2}{\sigma_v{}^2 + \sigma_\varepsilon{}^2} \tag{6.7}$$

In the logistic model σ_ε^2 is set to be $\pi^2/3$; in a linear random effects panel model this variation is estimated and indicated in the Stata output as `sigma_e`. In our example `rho` is therefore calculated as: $\frac{.9454971^2}{.9454971^2+pi^2/3} = .2136712$. This is a substantial intra-class correlation, indicating relatively high between person variation. This is a consequence of the fact that some individuals committed offences in many years, whilst others committed hardly any offences. The last line in Figure 6.5 gives the result of the test of whether the intra-class correlation significantly differs from 0. Unsurprisingly, this is clearly the case.

6.6.3 Fixed effects versus random effects panel models

In addition to describing the output of the logistic random effects panel model in the previous section, we will also demonstrate how to determine whether there are important differences between the fixed effects panel model and the random effects panel model. Given that the random effects panel model is based on a strong assumption, the violation of which can lead to biased estimates, it is important to check whether we can trust the estimates from the random effects model. If we can, the random effects estimates are preferable, given that the random effects panel model produces more efficient estimates. Moreover, we would then be able to interpret the effect of time-varying and time-invariant variables.

The Hausman test can be used to compare the results of the random effects panel model with those of the fixed effects panel model. What the test does is to examine whether there are statistically significant differences between the effects. When this is the case, i.e. H_a is true, because the fixed effects panel model always provides consistent estimates, the conclusion is that estimates from the random effects panel model are inconsistent. If the differences are not statistically significant, i.e. H_0 is true, we can conclude that the random effects panel model also provides consistent estimates, and therefore the random effects model is preferred because its estimates are more efficient (see chapter 2.6.2). This evaluation of the Hausman test is illustrated in Table 6.4.

It is possible to carry out the Hausman test in Stata. First, one needs to estimate a fixed effects panel model, saving the results in Stata's memory. In our example this is done using the following commands:

```
xtlogit offencedi work_ marriage_ child_, fe or
estimates store fixedlogit
```

Next the random effects panel model needs to be estimated, and then the Hausman test compares the results of the two. This is done using the following commands:

```
xtlogit offencedi work_ marriage_ child_ ethnicity
```

Table 6.4: Evaluation of the Hausman test results

	H_0 is waar	H_a is waar
RE estimate	consistent & efficient	inconsistent
FE estimate	consistent & inefficient	consistent

Figure 6.6: Results of the Hausman test

```
              ---- Coefficients ----
             |      (b)          (B)            (b-B)     sqrt(diag(V_b-V_B))
             |  fixedlogit        .          Difference          S.E.
-------------+----------------------------------------------------------------
        job_ |   -.4277464    -.7120914         .284345        .0913805
   marriage_ |   -.7855295    -.7702385       -.0152911        .3051684
      child_ |   -.1425761     .4247185       -.5672946        .2123258
------------------------------------------------------------------------------
                           b = consistent under Ho and Ha; obtained from xtlogit
            B = inconsistent under Ha, efficient under Ho; obtained from xtlogit

    Test:  Ho:  difference in coefficients not systematic

                  chi2(3) = (b-B)'[(V_b-V_B)^(-1)](b-B)
                          =       25.29
                Prob>chi2 =      0.0000
```

```
    contact_peers psychopathology
    age_offence IQ neuroticism impulsivity
    type_offender2 type_offender3 previous, re or
hausman fixedlogit
```

The results of the Hausman test are shown in Figure 6.6.

We see in Figure 6.6 a comparison of the estimated parameters, in so far as they appear in both models (this is why the effect of all time stable variables are not included). The last few lines of the output indicate what our conclusion should be. Clearly H_0 is rejected in favour of H_a. So we conclude that the random effects estimates are inconsistent and that the fixed effects estimates from Figure 6.3 are therefore preferred.

6.7 Limitations of fixed effects panel models

The strength of the fixed effects panel model is that it is an excellent method for estimating intra-individual effects controlling for all time-invariant unobserved heterogeneity. However, because all differences between research units which do not vary over time are removed from fixed effects panel models, it is impossible to use these models to estimate the effect of time-invariant variables. Estimating the effect of gender, for example, is not possible. Moreover, it is not exactly obvious what the effect of such a time-invariant variable would mean. After all, how can a variable that does not change over time result in a change in an individual's dependent variable score?

The fixed effects panel model can only estimate effects of time-varying independent variables. Time-invariant independent variables can however still play a role in a fixed effects panel model in another way, namely if we are interested in moderating effects. Imagine that we wanted to test whether the effect of employment on criminal behaviour differed for men and women. We can include a product term, the interaction effect, between gender (a time-invariant variable), and work (a time-varying variable) in the fixed effects model alongside the main effect of work. We can of course not estimate a main effect of gender, as we would when examining interaction effects in a regular OLS regression, as it is a time-invariant variable. A fixed effects panel model is able to estimate the effect of this product term, as the product term is a time-varying variable.

Just because fixed effects panel models can only estimate the effect of time-varying variables, this does not mean that they can be used to estimate all effects that theoretically vary over time. The fixed effects panel model can only estimate an effect for variables that actually do vary over time in the data. Some variables, whilst in theory time-varying, in reality show very little variance over time. For example, it would be very difficult to estimate the effect of employment on criminal behaviour amongst pensioners. After all, most pensioners have left the labour market, and so if we followed them over time we would not see any changes in their employment status. Furthermore, only a few pensioners are still criminally active, and so in panel data on pensioners we would find very little variation over time. The result of fixed effects estimations of the effect of employment would result in very large standard errors. In order to reliably estimate the effect of employment on criminal behaviour among pensioners we would therefore need a very large sample size. Without this the chance of making a Type II error, i.e. incorrectly concluding that the null hypothesis should be accepted, is considerable. This is because fixed effects panel models, in controlling for all time-invariant unobserved heterogeneity, lose a lot of efficiency.

We have seen that fixed effects panel models are ideal for determining whether changes in Y relate to changes in X, whilst controlling for possible distortions from unobserved heterogeneity. Nevertheless, they should not be employed naively. The model is indeed excellent at controlling for all time-*invariant* unobserved heterogeneity, but this does not mean that there is no distorting heterogeneity remaining. The model cannot control for unobserved time-*varying* heterogeneity. If the time-varying independent variables included in the model correlate with this unobserved time-*varying* heterogeneity we can still end up with biased results. If one suspects that the analysis is susceptible to this problem more complex models need to be used, for example a fixed effect panel model in combination with the instrumental variables method. Apel and colleagues (2008) employed this kind of model to estimate the effect of employment on deviant behaviour in teenagers. They used differences in the maximum permitted employment hours for teenagers in the different American states as their instrumental variable. Finally, the fixed effects panel model does not control for time-*invariant* heterogeneity *for which the effect on Y varies over time*. It should therefore be obvious that using fixed effects panel models is not the answer to everything and that the limitations of these models should be considered when using them.

6.8 Final points

In this chapter we have focussed on the fixed effects panel model. We have shown it to be a powerful model for controlling for unobserved time-invariant heterogeneity when analysing panel data. Panel data offer far more possibilities for determining causal effects than cross-sectional data. When collecting prospective panel data however, attrition can play an important role. Some people lose interest and motivation in taking part in a research study as time goes by, others move house and cannot be traced, and inevitably some die. If at each measurement point a smaller percentage of people take part the total number of research units available for analysis can rapidly decrease. But even if enough units remain in the sample to be able to carry out statistical analyses, attrition can remain a problem. In panel studies attrition can, after all, be selective. This means that the research units which drop out of the study are not the same as those that remain in the study. This can of course be checked by examining characteristics observed at earlier time points. However, differences on unobserved characteristics cannot be checked for. Given that the fixed effects panel model controls for time-invariant unobserved heterogeneity selective attrition is not a problem for the internal validity of the research, as long as the attrition only relates to time-invariant observed and unobserved characteristics. However, if the attrition rate is high the external validity of the research may be called into question.

Fixed effects panel models are often used on panel data where research units are followed over time. The examples in this chapter all use this type of panel design. Fixed effects models can, however, be applied to a wider variety of panel designs. For example, these models can be used in sibling studies. Given that siblings share all kinds of family characteristics, which are often unobserved, fixed effects models can offer a solution when examining the effect of characteristics which differ between siblings.

6.9 Further reading

In this chapter we have mainly focussed on the fixed effects panel model. We have also briefly discussed the random effects panel model. In much of the, mainly econometric, literature which uses these models extensively the uninitiated reader will quickly get lost in a forest of formulas (see for example Baltagi, 2005). In this chapter, however, we have tried to focus on explaining the models at a conceptual level without using too many formulas. Halaby (2004) provides a relatively accessible explanation of panel models, as does Dugan (2010), who also outlines time series analysis. The econometric literature does however provide important variations on and extensions to the models discussed here. We will briefly mention one of these extensions. In this chapter we have only focussed on estimating the effects of independent variables on dependent variables. It is also possible that the score of a dependent variable at an earlier time point influences the score on the same dependent variable at a later time point. It should be immediately obvious than in such a situation the exogeneity assumption is violated. This complicates the correct estimation of the effects considerably, and more complex econometric models need to be used. In order to estimate effects like these so-called *dynamic panel models* have been developed. Averdijk (2011) provides a nice example of how these models can be used in criminological research, looking at the extent to which routine activities influence chance of being a victim of crime. And finally we would like to recommend a book which focusses on the estimation of panel models in Stata. It provides both a handy reference guide to the different Stata procedures, as well as clear and coherent examples (Rabe-Hesketh and Skrondal, 2008).

Chapter 7

Trajectory models

The methods discussed so far in this book have used a variety of techniques to control for selection effects or endogeneity bias. In propensity score analysis, for example, the effect of a treatment on respondents with near identical chances of receiving the treatment is calculated. Regression discontinuity design does a similar thing using a slightly different approach. The instrumental variables method tries to solve the problem by filtering out endogeneity from the predictors.

In the previous chapter we read about how fixed effects panel models also filter out possible bias. This method removes inter-individual differences, and simply analyses the remaining intra-individual changes. In other words, this technique controls for time-invariant, unobserved as well as observed, heterogeneity. For example, we can examine whether people commit fewer offences in periods when they are employed than in periods when they are not employed. This means that within-individual effects are explored, as each person is compared to themselves at a different point in time. This other version of themselves which exists at another time point is considered to be in another 'condition'. We assume all other circumstances to be equal in both 'conditions'. In other words, we assume that the individual, each single person, is a homogeneous unit. However, the price we pay for looking at within person differences is that we can no longer examine between person differences. For example, say that we have an individual in our dataset who worked for the entire research period. In the same period they did not commit a single criminal offence, because their employment had such a strong negative effect on their criminal behaviour. A fixed effects panel model will not pick up this effect. This model can only calculate the effect for individuals with scores that vary on at least one of the independent variables. In another example, imagine that employment has no effect on the criminal behaviour of chronic offenders, but does have an effect on the behaviour of low frequency offenders. A fixed effects panel model cannot demonstrate this effect, unless it is obvious before the analyses are carried out who is going to become a chronic offender and who a low frequency offender. When this is not known a priori the analysis just gives a global indication, i.e. the effect of employment across the entire research sample. These kinds of differences, between individuals or between offender groups, cannot be seen using the fixed effects panel model, unless extra information is available.

The method we are going to discuss in this chapter is slightly less strict. Rather than looking at within individual effects this technique estimates within *group* effects. The advantage of doing this is that differences between groups of people, such as the difference between chronic and low frequency offenders, can be examined. However, when using this method to draw causal conclusions we make an important assumption, namely that each group of individuals is homogeneous, i.e. all members within a group have the same characteristics.

This method is called the *group-based trajectory* model (Nagin, 2005). The most important advantage it has is that group membership is based on an a priori unknown function of age, that uses maximum likelihood to determine the model. The effects, for example of employment on delinquency, are now conditional on allocating an offender to one of the groups. In this way the model controls for the bias which can contribute to each group's specific developmental trajectory. Simply put, different effects can be estimated for different groups of research units.

We will begin with a general introduction to this method. This will be followed by a simple example which we will gradually extend to illustrate all the possibilities this method offers for analysing observational data. After providing details on the application and interpretation of the method in section 7.7 we will go on to address the main limitations of the method in section 7.8. We end with suggestions for further reading.

7.1 The trajectory model

Research into behavioural development is a prominent feature in the social sciences. For example, when do children start to form friendships? Do children in day care form these earlier than children who stay at home until they start school? When do people start to commit criminal offences? What factors influence this behaviour? When do people desist from criminal behaviour? And what events are correlated with this desistance? These kinds of questions, often related to developmental psychology or life course criminology, are the focus of the method we discuss in this chapter.

In previous chapters we have already read about how fixed effects panel models make use of longitudinal data. In this chapter we look specifically at the *shape* that behavioural development takes over time. Depending on the type of research and the data available behavioural development from childhood up into adulthood can be examined. Criminologists are mainly interested with three questions: How does criminal behaviour change with age and over time? Are there individual characteristics which correlate with the type of criminal career path people follow? And which events or interventions can lead to someone who looks to be following a certain criminal career path changing direction and committing fewer criminal offences?

The *shape* of the developmental pathway is therefore the focus. This pathway only becomes visible when we represent development as a trajectory (see Figure 7.1). To begin with it is important to understand that a trajectory describes an average course. A trajectory which describes the development of criminal behaviour within a population, i.e. the *age-crime curve*, will probably look different to a trajectory which describes the development within a subgroup of that population. For example, Figure 7.1 shows the development of criminal behaviour summarised into one trajectory. There is a clear peak at the age of 18 years. If we look closely, we also see that criminal behaviour never actually stops completely. The trajectory remains active as it were, never dropping to zero.

Figure 7.2 gives us more detail than Figure 7.1, and shows us what is actually happening. We can see that the curve in Figure 7.1 represents a heterogeneous rather than homogeneous group. The curve in Figure 7.1 is actually made up of two very different trajectories of delinquent behaviour. Figure 7.2 provides an alternative picture. One subgroup follows a trajectory that shows a peak in delinquent behaviour adolescence, before eventually dropping off and stopping all together in adulthood. The other subgroup is already offending at a persistent level at the age of 12 years, and they continue to do so into adulthood. Looking at the two figures, if we only had information from the first we would incorrectly conclude that no-one stops offending, or desists as it is often referred to in the literature. If we then attempted to explain this developmental pattern it is likely our explanations would be entirely wrong. The combined curve does not present the true situation. Figure 7.2 is in this case far more informative. We can see from this figure that there is *developmental heterogeneity* in this sample. There are in fact two subgroups whose criminal behaviour develops differently. It is likely therefore that we need two different explanations for these developmental trajectories.

The example we have just described looks very much like the two trajectories of criminal behaviour Moffitt outlines in her developmental theory of delinquent and anti-social behaviour (1993). In this theory she describes two kinds of offender. One type, the *adolescence-limited* offenders, the larger group, only displays delinquent behaviour during adolescence. In contrast, the *life-course persistent* offenders, the smaller group, remains delinquent into adulthood. Moffitt

Figure 7.1: Average development of criminal offending frequency

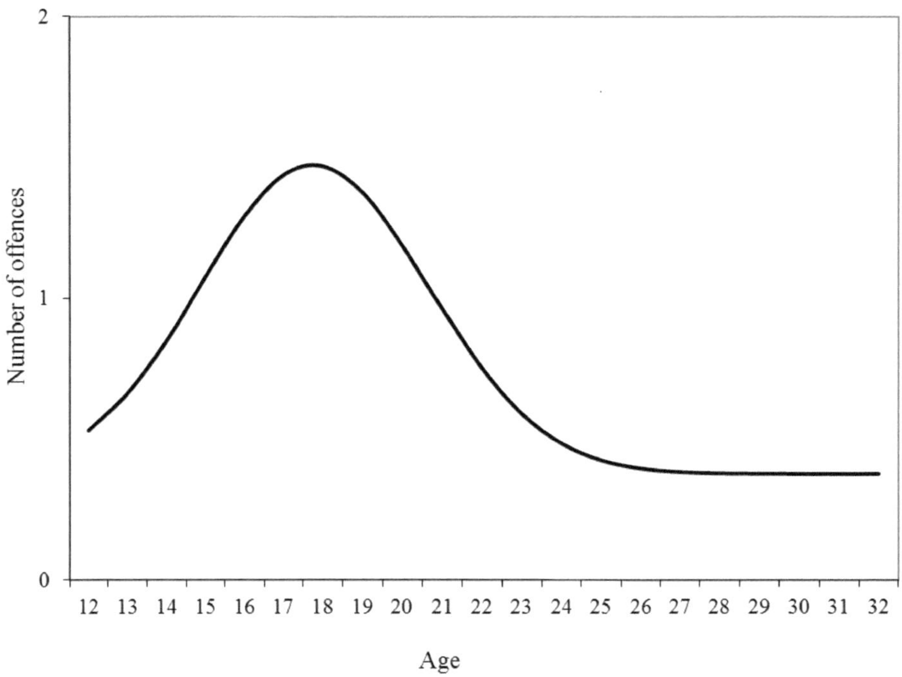

argues that the difference between these two developmental trajectories correlates with certain risk factors. The adolescent limited offenders, who mainly commit less serious offences, do so in response to a desire for autonomy and under the influence of delinquent peers. The life-course persistent offenders, however, show signs of neurological and psychological problems from a young age. It is these that lead to antisocial behaviour and later on more serious criminal offending.

Moffitt's theory demonstrates that if we want to explain the development of criminal behaviour over the life course, we cannot assume that all individuals follow the same path. Different psychological and psychosocial characteristics can play a role in the development of criminal behaviour, influencing the course a criminal career takes. Whether Moffitt's developmental taxonomy with just two pathways is sufficient remains to be seen. This model does not offer any explanation for the existence of other groups, such as late starters or offenders who desist in adulthood, that have been found in empirical criminological research.

Figure 7.2: Development of criminal offending frequency for two homogeneous subgroups

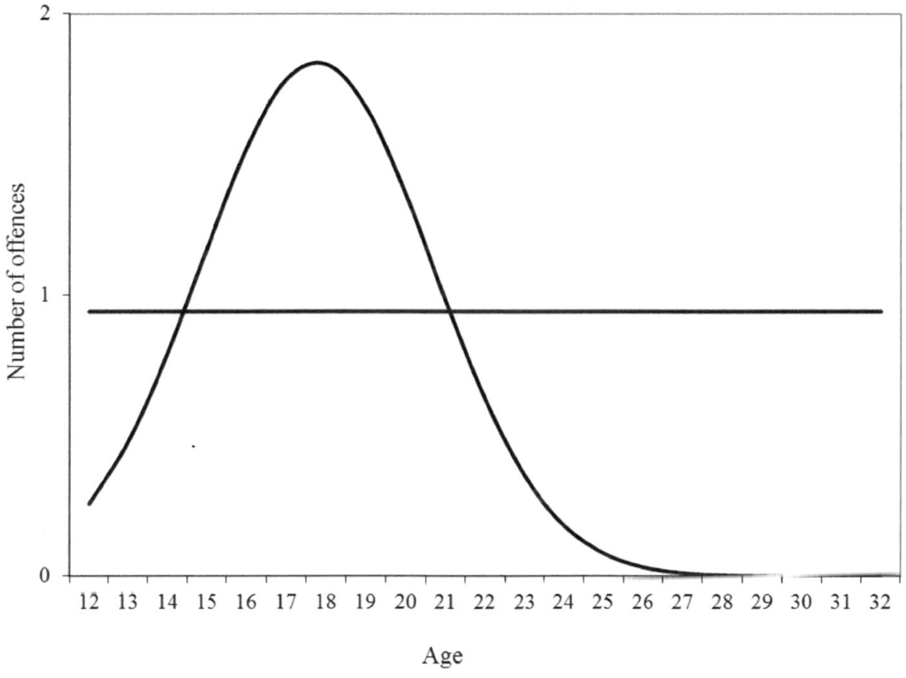

The trajectory model which we discuss in this chapter provides a unique solution to this problem. The model 'decides' how many different groups are needed to best describe the development of delinquent behaviour within the research sample. This method first looks for groups of individuals within the sample who follow roughly the same criminal career path. These *homogeneous subgroups* are therefore not decided on *a priori*, based on statistical characteristics such as intelligence or impulsivity, the so-called *ex ante* approach. Rather they are determined on the basis of the observed distribution of criminal career paths in the research sample, the so-called *ex post* approach. This method searches for the most parsimonious model, i.e. the fewer parameters the better, to distinguish between different homogeneous groups.

Daniel Nagin introduced the *group-based trajectory model* to criminology in the early 1990s. In a series of articles written with the leading scholars in developmental and life course criminology he showed how the model could be used to carry out empirical research into the most important questions in the field (Nagin and Land, 1993, Nagin et al., 1995, Laub et al., 1998). Over the years his work has really put this method on the map, within as well as outside of criminology (Nagin, 1999). He wrote the book Group-Based Modelling of Development (2005) in 2005. In 2006 Daniel Nagin was made professor of Public Policy and Statistics at Heinz College, Carnegie Mellon University in Pittsburgh. That same year he received the prestigious Edwin Sutherland Award from the American Society of Criminology for his contribution to the field.

Figure 7.3: Daniel Nagin (1948)

7.2 A closer look at the trajectory model

The trajectory model is extremely well suited to summarising and describing longitudinal data on behaviour or other such variables. It provides a comprehensive picture of how behaviour develops over time in different subgroups. We will now compare the model with the fixed effects model discussed earlier in this book.

Whilst standard methods for analysing longitudinal data examine whether individuals deviate from the average population, in the previous chapter we saw how fixed effects models examine whether individuals deviate from their own average. In this way the model corrects for between-individual differences. The deviations from the individual mean can be estimated as a function of age and/or other time-varying covariates. It is important to note that this function is the same for all individuals. What this means is that, for age, for example, if an effect is found we assume that all individuals at roughly the same age score either above or below their individual mean, i.e. we assume development is uniform. In the case of employment and criminal behaviour we assume that the effect of employment on criminal behaviour is the same for everyone.

However, in criminology there are strong indications that the development of criminal behaviour is *not* uniform, and that the effect of time-varying covariates, such as work, is *not* the same for everyone. The fixed effects model[1], therefore, treats apples and oranges as if they were the same, and thereby compromises the usefulness of the estimated effects. It would be better to take possible developmental differences into account, and include these differences when estimating an effect.

Here, however, we encounter another problem. On the one hand, we do not want to use one model for the whole group, whilst on the other hand we do not want to estimate *N* models for *N* individuals. Estimating a separate, and consequently incomparable, model for each individual would be absurd. Besides this being pretty much impossible to interpret, it would also mean that any change which could be attributed as a possible function of age would be corrected for, and consequently many effects would no longer be detectable. The solution for this problem is the trajectory model. This model does not simply estimate one model for the whole group, nor does it attempt to model a different model for each individual, but rather estimates separate models for a limited number of subgroups.

7.2.1 Trajectory model example

Figure 7.4 illustrates the group-based trajectory model (Van der Geest et al., 2011). This model uses data from research examining 270 high-risk boys placed in a treatment facility for juveniles in the early 1990s.

The dependent variable in this research was the number of convictions per year from age 12 to 32. The trajectory model indicated that five subgroups represented the best fit for this data. We will briefly describe these groups as seen in Figure 7.4.

[1]In the fixed effects model we can only distinguish between groups, *a priori*, on the basis of statistical data on characteristics such as intelligence or impulsivity. We cannot distinguish between groups *ex post* on the basis of criminal development.

Figure 7.4: Trajectories of the criminal careers of high-risk boys (Van der Geest et al., 2011): adolescence-limited offenders (AL), late-developers (LD), low frequency offenders (LFO), high frequency desisters (HFD), high frequency chronic offenders (HFC)

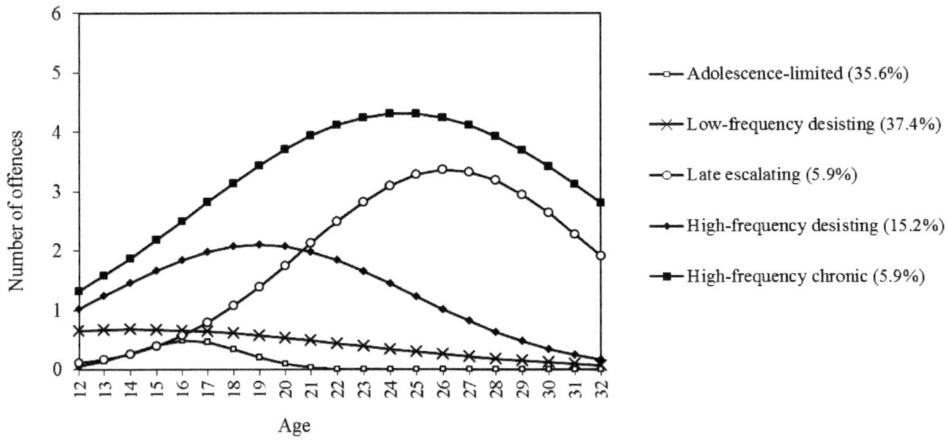

Nearly three quarters of the sample falls into either the 'adolescence-limited offender' group (35.6%) or the 'low frequency offender' group (37.4%). A third much smaller group is the 'late-starters' (5.9%), who appear to be following the same trajectory as the 'adolescence-limited', up until the age of 16 years. From then on however we see a noticeable increase in the number of convictions. Finally, we have two groups which from the beginning of the observation period demonstrate a higher number of convictions than the rest. Individuals in the 'high frequency desister' group (15.2%) have by the age of thirty near enough stopped offending, whilst the 'high frequency chronic offender' group (5.9%) continue to offend at a high rate. All the trajectories in Figure 7.4, however, sooner or later, demonstrate a drop in the number of offences per year.

As stated above, the idea behind trajectory models is that groups are not chosen at random. The individuals in the subgroups follow a similar criminal career path. In order to explain *why* the subgroups differ it is interesting to see whether their background characteristics also differ. Researchers have looked for differences in this sample of high-risk boys. Specifically, they examined whether subgroup classification (a nominal variable) correlated with certain characteristics, such as their treatment progression.

This information is shown in Table 7.1 (treatment characteristics were measured when the boys were 15-17 years old). The descriptive statistics are split into

Table 7.1: Treatment characteristics per trajectory group Van der Geest et al. (2007)

	AL	LFD	LB	HFD	HFC
General treatment characteristics					
Average age begin treatment	15.5	15.5	15.8	16.1	15.1
Average age end of treatment	17.3	17.4	17.4	17.5	16.7
% premature end to treatment	10.3	9.6	14.3	15.2	50.0
Average treatment score (0-5)					
Motivation	3.6	3.4	3.1	3.4	2.6
Understanding of consequences	3.2	3.0	2.8	2.7	3.0
Understanding of risk factors*	3.1	3.0	2.8	2.7	2.6
Empathy*	2.9	2.9	2.7	2.6	2.4
Treatment evaluation*	3.3	3.2	3.4	2.9	2.3
Risk of re-offending after treatment*	2.8	3.0	3.1	3.4	3.6
Average progression score (0-5)					
Positive change in control impulses*	3.0	3.0	2.9	2.8	2.3
Positive change in social skills*	2.4	2.5	2.3	2.3	1.9

**Anova p <.05*

the five subgroups. We can see, and importantly also test, whether these scores significantly differ between the subgroups.

We can see from the table that by far the largest percentage (50%) of those ending their treatment prematurely are classified as 'high frequency chronic' offenders. Offenders in this group also happen to score worst on nearly all of the treatment characteristics. In contrast, 'late developers' on average score positively on the treatment evaluation. Treatment officers judged their development to be 'normal' or even 'positive'. Up to the age of 16 years the 'late developers' look remarkably similar to offenders in the two groups with low levels of delinquency. They have very few convictions and their treatment runs relatively smoothly.

The two groups with high levels of delinquency are clearly differentiated from the rest. Besides having more convictions, their estimated recidivism risk is statistically significantly higher compared to the 'adolescent-limited' group. So what we see is that groups which follow different criminal career trajectories also differ on a number of outcome measures taken following their treatment in the treatment institute for juveniles, and that these differences can be interpreted i.e. they are theoretically meaningful.

7.3 Model selection

The trajectory model in the example above highlights interesting and coherent distinctions between the groups. Not only do the groups have different criminal career trajectories, but they also differ on treatment characteristics. Keeping in mind this example, we will now look in more detail at how to build a model like this.

The first decision to make concerns the distribution we need to use for our trajectory model based on what our dependent variable is. If the dependent variable is a count variable, we use a *zero-inflated Poisson* (ZIP) model. The prefix 'zero-inflated' indicates that the 'inflation parameters' (alpha) can be included in the Poisson model (see section 2.4.3 and Table 2.1). When dealing with longitudinal data, in which the criminal careers are often interrupted, i.e. there are years in which delinquency is zero, using this inflation parameter ensures that these interruptions do not directly influence the shape of the trajectory. This is very useful as delinquent behaviour is generally concentrated in a small section of the population. If the dependent variable is dichotomous, we use a *logistic model* (logit). And finally, if the dependent variable is a scale variable, for example a psychometric scale, then we use the *censored normal* distribution (cnorm). Depending on the distribution (ZIP, logit or cnorm), different link functions to 'link' behavioural (e.g.criminal) development to age are required. When using a Poisson model the logarithm of the number of offences (or the frequency, often given as lambda or λ) is written as a function of age:

$$\log(\lambda_{ijt}) = \beta_{0j} + \beta_{1j} * \mathrm{age}_{it} + \beta_{2j} * \mathrm{age}_{it}^2$$

The Y link function can, if needed, be expanded to a cubic or third degree polynomial, if the quadratic or second degree polynomial is not free enough to summarise the development of our dependent variable. In this chapter however we limit ourselves to the second degree function described above. Estimating the trajectory model with second degree polynomial functions gives us the following equation:

$$y_{it}^{j} = \beta_{0j} + \beta_{1j} * \mathrm{age}_{it} + \beta_{2j} * \mathrm{age}_{it}^2 + \mathrm{error}_{it}$$

The above equation simply states that every observed score, in subgroup j, for individual i, at time point t, is a per subgroup absolute function of age and individual error. If a trajectory is pretty much horizontal, for example see Figure 7.2, then $\beta_{1j} = 0$ and $\beta_{2j} = 0$. In this case the subgroup demonstrates chronic delinquent behaviour. If also $\beta_{0j} = 0$ then no delinquent behaviour at all is seen. When $\beta_{2j} < 0$ the trajectory demonstrates an upside down parabola, with behaviour peaking at a certain age.[2]

There are two choices to make when applying a group-based trajectory model. First we need to decide on the number of subgroups for which we want to estimate a trajectory. Next we need to decide on which polynomial function we want to use for each subgroup. This can be a third degree function, a quadratic function, a linear function or a constant. The model generates t-tests which indicate whether the coefficients are statistically significantly different from zero, and therefore contribute to the model. In general a second degree function is needed to estimate criminal career as a function of age.

In order to determine the number of groups in a trajectory model, usually indicated by the letter 'J', we need to use both objective and subjective model selection criteria. One test statistic suitable for selecting a model is the *Bayes Information Criterion* (BIC). In general, the model with the highest BIC score (or with trajectory models: the least negative score) is the best model (Nagin, 2005). However, formal criteria alone should not relied on for selecting the best model. When choosing the number of groups for our trajectory model subjective and substantial criteria need to be examined, alongside the statistics, to ensure that the model is interpretable. In some cases the BIC value keeps increasing as more groups are added to the model. If this is the case the researcher needs to decide whether the extra groups are theoretically interesting and whether they demonstrate genuinely different developmental paths (Nagin, 2005, p.74).

The calculation of the BIC value uses the maximum likelihood (L), the number of parameters in the model (k), and the sample size (N):

$$BIC = log(L) - 0.5klog(N)$$

In chapter 2 we saw that the maximum likelihood is an estimation method whereby the coefficients which have the highest chance of producing the observed scores are determined. Increasing the number of parameters (k) is not beneficial for the BIC value. So when adding an extra trajectory group one needs to weigh up the improvement in maximum likelihood against increasing the number of parameters. The number of parameters increases with every trajectory group added to the model.

When running the trajectory model two different BIC values are automatically reported. One BIC value is based on the number of observations ('N' in the Stata

[2]If $\beta_{2j} \geq 0$ the trajectory is a right-side-up parabola, but this shape is very rare in longitudinal behavioural research.

Table 7.2: Criteria for choosing the best model in trajectory analysis

2(ΔBIC)	indication that the model is better
0-2	no
2-6	yes
6-10	strong
10	very strong

output, or put formally $\sum_{i=1}^{N} T_i$, where T_i is the number of time points for which we have measurement of i persons). The other BIC value is based on the number of individuals (N individuals)[3]. When choosing the model we do not have to worry too much about this issue. Generally it does not matter which BIC we consider; in most cases both BIC values indicate the same number of groups.

Sometimes the BIC 'tipping point', whereby one model is clearly preferred over another, is not reached. If this is the case it is possible to look at differences in BIC between models. We will not go into the Bayesian statistics behind this approach here (for more information see Jones et al., 2001). When choosing a model all we need to know is that Δ BIC is a 'Bayes factor' estimator, a construct used to indicate how important the difference between the BIC of two models is. This is done as follows. We calculate the difference in BIC between one more complex model and an alternative simpler model. This is multiplied by 2, giving us 2(ΔBIC). The result indicates the level of support for the more complex model. Table 7.2 shows how to interpret the scores. These objective criteria are often a useful guide when choosing the number of groups in the model.

7.4 Posterior probabilities of group membership

Once we have selected our model, using the parameters, we can calculate the *posterior probability* that an individual will belong to one of the trajectory groups. This posterior probability tells us how sure we can be that the individual concerned will follow the criminal career path as indicated by one of the estimated trajectories. This probability is represented by a value of between 0 and 1. The reason

[3]In theory N is the number of independent observations in the sample. Which N is the best for longitudinal research is open to question. On the one hand we assume that repeat measures within individuals are dependent, and so the total number of observations over estimates N. On the other hand we can argue that, specifically in longitudinal research, repeat measures are partly independent, otherwise why bother carrying out repeat measures? If this is the case N is underestimated. The truth lies somewhere in between the two.

for the term 'posterior' is that this calculation is made *after* the model has been selected.

Each individual therefore has J posterior probabilities, equal to the number of trajectory groups. Together they add up to 1. The highest posterior probability an individual has, indicates the trajectory which best fits them. In an ideal world this probability would be 1, and the rest would then automatically be 0. By using the highest posterior probability (PP) we can now 'allocate' individuals to one of the trajectory groups. Next, for all the individuals assigned to a certain trajectory group J, the average posterior probability (AvePP) can be calculated (AvePP_j). As the degree of certainty with which we can assign individuals (PP) decreases, the AvePP also decreases. As a rule of thumb the AvePP should be .7 or higher for all subgroups. The AvePP is therefore used as a diagnostic tool for group allocation.

The posterior probability is somewhat different than the estimated probability of group membership $\hat{\pi}_j$. This $\hat{\pi}_j$ is the chance that a randomly picked individual will be allocated to a trajectory group (J). If we calculate the average posterior probability that an individual would be assigned to a group (J), regardless of the group they are actually allocated to, we get $\hat{\pi}_j$. In this way we calculate the proportion of the total sample allocated to a trajectory group (J). We need to be aware, however, that this calculation results in different group sizes to those resulting from 'forcing' individuals into groups on the basis of their highest posterior probability score.

As in the example trajectory model in section 7.1 trajectory groups are nearly always different in size. The $\hat{\pi}_j$ is therefore different for each trajectory group J. It is particularly useful to consider $\hat{\pi}_j$ when judging the effectiveness of group allocation if the underlying differences are large. For example, when $\hat{\pi}_j = 0.9$ for a subgroup, people can be allocated with more certainty for the simple reason that 9 out of 10 people are allocated into that group. So even if we put everyone into subgroup (J) the chance that we have correctly allocated people will be 9 to 1. This makes the AvePP less useful as a tool for diagnosing group allocation. If we want to take into account differences in group size we can use another measure of group allocation, namely the *odds of correct classification* (OCC). This measure is based on the AvePP_j, but includes the estimated proportion of persons in each subgroup J in the calculation ($\hat{\pi}_j$). The rule of thumb is that when OCC_j is larger than 5.0 for every subgroup group, allocation is accurate (Nagin, 2005). The OCC is calculated thus:

$$\text{OCC}_j = \frac{\text{AvePP}_j/1 - \text{AvePP}_j}{\hat{\pi}_j/1 - \hat{\pi}_j}$$

7.5 Adding independent variables to the trajectory model

Researchers carrying out trajectory model analysis are generally not only interested in the shape of the trajectories, but also in the influence of independent variables on the dependent variable they are modeling. Criminologists are not only interested in *how* criminal careers develop, but also in *why* they develop differently for different groups of offenders. Differing psychosocial or psychological characteristics can play a role in the development of delinquent behaviour and consequently correlate with the *shape* of a criminal career. In other words, when using trajectory models we want to examine whether the different trajectory groups differ on certain independent variables, or predictors.

In Table 7.1 we saw an example of high-risk boys who, on the basis of their highest posterior probability scores, were 'forced' into one of the trajectory groups. We can create a new variable in the dataset called 'group membership', ranging in score from 1 to J, and use this to look at the percentages, for example male or female, or averages, for example average number of offences, on different independent variables per trajectory group. Using conventional statistical methods, such as F- and χ^2-tests, the relationship between various predictors and group membership can be examined. For example, we could test whether certain groups of offenders are more intelligent or impulsive.

7.5.1 Statistical predictors

An alternative method can be used determine whether trajectory groups differ on observed characteristics. Rather than allocating individuals to subgroups on the basis of their maximum posterior probability scores, it is possible to test whether and to what extent predictors have an effect on the probability of group membership (π_j). The advantage of using this method is that discrete group allocation does not need to be assumed. This allocation into groups is namely a problem. By allocating people to groups in this way we assume that they definitely belong to that specific subgroup. We take away the element of uncertainty that is inherent in the posterior probability values. We can determine which predictors are related to certain developmental trajectories without 'forcing' people into subgroups.

An advantage of using this method is that several predictors can be included simultaneously, and that the effect of each predictor is calculated controlling for the effect of the other predictors, as in a regular multiple regression analysis. The predictors which are examined in this way are by definition static. When several predictors are included simultaneously the estimated coefficient is the effect relative to the 'contrast' group. So when interpreting the effect of (statistically significant) predictors their effect is always compared to the reference group. Consequently, the *risk profile* that this method results in is made up of characteristics on which individuals in a given trajectory group differ from individuals in the reference group.

7.5.2 Time-varying covariates

Time-varying covariates can also be added to the model to examine possible effects of changes over time or events which occur on the development of a trajectory. For example, the influence of certain transitions in someone's life, such as finding a job, getting married, becoming a parent, moving to a less desirable neighbourhood, on the development of the dependent variable in a trajectory can be examined.

In the introduction to this chapter we used the example of the effect of employment on criminal behaviour as something that can differ between different offender groups. It might be the case that chronic offenders do not get the same advantages from employment as other offenders, because they experience less social control in their work or they judge the risks associated with offending to be lower. In order to examine *what* the effect of employment is and *whether* this effect differs between offender groups we can include employment in our model as a time-varying covariate.

One of the advantages of including time-varying covariates in the trajectory model is that we can estimate *differential effects*, i.e. for each subgroup we get a different function with estimated β-parameters. For each β we can then test whether it statistically significantly differs from 0. The coefficients can be interpreted in the same way as for regular regression analysis. The assumption that each subgroup is a homogeneous group leads to the assumption that within each group the effect estimates are not distorted by selection. The trajectory model in this way offers a possible solution to the endogeneity problem.

A model with no covariates measures the average development of all the individuals in a given trajectory group, regardless of the changes which may lead to deviations from the average trajectory (such as finding a job). By including covariates in the model the estimated β-parameters for age must be interpreted differently: these indicate the shape of the trajectory when all covariates equal zero (in our example this would mean that someone was chronically unemployed). This means that if we add covariates which influence the trajectory to the model, the β-parameters for age will differ from those of the model without covariates.

7.6 Censoring, missing data and exposure

As we have seen, we can use the trajectory model to examine longitudinal data. A common problem in longitudinal research is that measurement does not start and stop at the same age for all people, i.e. data is censored. Another problem is that we often miss some measurement points for some people, i.e. we have missing data. People can die, emigrate or for other reasons be out of the picture either temporarily or permanently. The trajectory model is able to deal with these issues reasonably well most of the time. Nevertheless, there are two things which can cause problems.

If the data is *censored* and the number of people within the trajectory groups at the beginning or end of the period for which we have observations is relatively small then the shape of the trajectories can be partly influenced by the limited number of observations. If this is the case it is better to cut off the period on which trajectory model is based. There is no rule of thumb which helps decide when to cut off the observation period in this way. In addition, it is best to remove people from the dataset if they only have a few observation points due to, for example, their dying at a young age. Of course doing this will have an effect on the generalisability of the results.

The second issue which can cause problems is imprisonment. When people are in prison they are obviously less able to commit criminal offences, if at all. In other words their *exposure* is reduced. We need to take any decrease in delinquency we see as a result of someone's imprisonment into account. There are several ways to do this. For example, if someone is in prison for an entire observation period we can set their delinquency for that year to be missing. Alternatively, if someone is in prison for half a year and commits three offences in the remaining half of the year we can assume that their delinquency level for the entire year without imprisonment would be $3/0.5 = 6$. One of the disadvantages of carrying out this correction is that it can result in very large corrected values, see Van der Geest et al. (2009) for an alternative correction procedure. A final solution is to include a time-varying exposure variable, with a minimum score of 0 and maximum of 1, in the model. The model then corrects the dependent variable after the groups have been formed. So the shape of the trajectories for the years in which people are imprisoned will change, but the composition of the groups does not change.

7.7 Example: The influence of employment on criminal behaviour

In this chapter, as in previous chapters, we will illustrate the method using an example. Again we will be using the example dataset with 500 fictional juvenile male sex offenders. We have longitudinal data on the number of convictions and employment for each year from age 12 to 32 years. We also have statistics on several other individual characteristics.

The first task is to ensure the data is saved in the correct format. The trajectory model assumes a wide format. This means that every research unit, in our case each sex offender, is represented by one row of data, with their scores on each variable and at each time point recorded in separate columns. So, if we have data on their delinquency and employment from ages 12 to 32 years, as well on intelligence, we have 44 variables: `idnumber`, `offence_12` to `offence_32`, `work_12` to `work_32` and `IQ`. The first variable identifies the research units. Next we have 21 variables indicating the number of offences per year and 21 variables indicating employment, 0 or 1, per year. Finally, we have a statistical measure of intelligence. Due to the wide format we do not need to include a separate age variable. But, the analysis will only be carried out correctly if the variables are ordered consecutively by time points in the dataset.

The statistical programmes SAS and Stata can both be used to estimate trajectory models. We will only provide instructions to carry out the analysis in Stata[4]. For SAS instructions see www.andrew.cmu.edu/user/bjones. To estimate the trajectory model in Stata we first need to download the `traj` '*add-on*' using the following command:

```
net from http://www.andrew.cmu.edu/user/bjones/traj
net install traj, replace
```

We next need to indicate the age years for which we want the trajectories to be estimated. In our example these are the 21 measurement points (t1-t21) for ages 12 to 32. By dividing the ages by 10 the model can deal with the calculations needed for the iteration process more easily.

```
foreach val of numlist 1/21 {
gen t`val'=(`val'+11)/10
}
```

[4]Small differences in the output are possible, depending on the version of Stata used. Any differences will however be minimal and the interpretation of the output remains the same.

7.7.1 The trajectory model

The dependent variable in our example is the number of convictions per year of life. This is a count variable and so we will use a *zero-inflated Poisson* (ZIP) model. We are going to estimate the trajectory model on the basis of second degree polynomial functions (asked for using the command `order (2)`), including an *inflation parameter* (the alpha is asked for using the command `iorder (0)`). This alpha ensures that, in our case, breaks in the criminal career, i.e. years when delinquency is zero, do not directly influence the shape of the trajectories. Using the following syntax a model is estimated for one group. This gives us the average age-crime curve for the sample. The syntax command `trajplot` creates a plot of the model[5].

```
traj, model(zip) var(offence_12-offence_32) indep(t1-t21)
      order(2) iorder(0)
```

```
trajplot, xtitle("leeftijd/10")
      ytitle("number offences")
```

The Stata output (see Figure 7.5) shows that this model has a BIC value of -4513.35 (N=7491), based on the total number of person years, and -4507.93 (N=500), based on the number of respondents in the sample. The *likelihood* (L) is -4495.51. The β-parameters for age and the inflation parameter significantly differ from zero ($p <.001$). The line in Figure 7.6 illustrates the estimated curve for the number of convictions per year and the points indicate the average observed number of convictions per year.

We can now extend the model to estimate more groups. This is after all the reason for carrying out trajectory models. If we wish to estimate a 2 group model we estimate the second degree polynomial functions (`order (2 2)`) with an inflation parameter for each group (`iorder (0 0)`). For each command in the syntax we add a number which indicates how many parameters there are in the trajectory function:

```
traj, model(zip) var(offence_12-offence_32) indep(t1-t21)
     order(2 2) iorder(0 0)
trajplot, xtitle("age/10")  ytitle("number offences")
```

In comparison to the model with one group the BIC values for this model are closer to zero (BIC=-4118.51, N=7491; BIC=-4106.33, N=500) and the likelihood in less

[5]As we stated in section 7.6 it is also possible to include a time-varying exposure variable (minimum 0 and maximum 1) in the model: `traj, model(zip) var(offence_12-offence_32) indep(t1-t21) order(2) iorder(0) expos (expos_12-expos_32)`.

Figure 7.5: Coefficients for the one group model

```
500 observations read.
500 observations used in trajectory model.

                         Maximum Likelihood Estimates
                         Model: Zero Inflated Poisson (ZIP)

                                          Standard       T for H0:
Group   Parameter         Estimate          Error     Parameter=0    Prob > |T|

1       Intercept         -5.17231        0.51748          -9.995        0.0000
        Linear             5.27970        0.54582           9.673        0.0000
        Quadratic         -1.35935        0.13766          -9.875        0.0000

        Alpha0             0.73183        0.05972          12.255        0.0000

 Group membership

1       (%)              100.00000        0.00000

BIC= -4513.35 (N=7491)  BIC= -4507.93 (N=500)  AIC= -4499.51  L= -4495.51
```

Table 7.3: BIC values for increasing number of groups

Number of groups	BIC	2(ΔBIC)
1	BIC=-4507.93	
2	BIC=-4106.33	803.20
3	BIC=-4041.24	130.18
4	BIC=-4010.93	60.62
5	BIC=-3994.27	33.32
6	BIC=-4001.16	-13.78

negative (-4078.36). The model therefore is a better fit for the data than the first model. However, we are not finished yet. In Table 7.3 we can see an overview of the BIC values for trajectory models with an increasing number of groups, each estimated using second degree polynomial functions with an inflation parameter[6]. We can see that the 'tipping point' occurs for the model with 6 groups, meaning that based on the BIC we should select the 5 group model.

[6]Depending on the results one can also choose to leave out parameters which do not significantly contribute to the model out of the model (parameters are automatically tested with *t*-tests. Parameters with a *p* value smaller than .05 do not contribute significantly to the model). Trajectories where age has a linear function (or even constant) can then be estimated using fewer parameters.

Figure 7.6: Illustration of the model

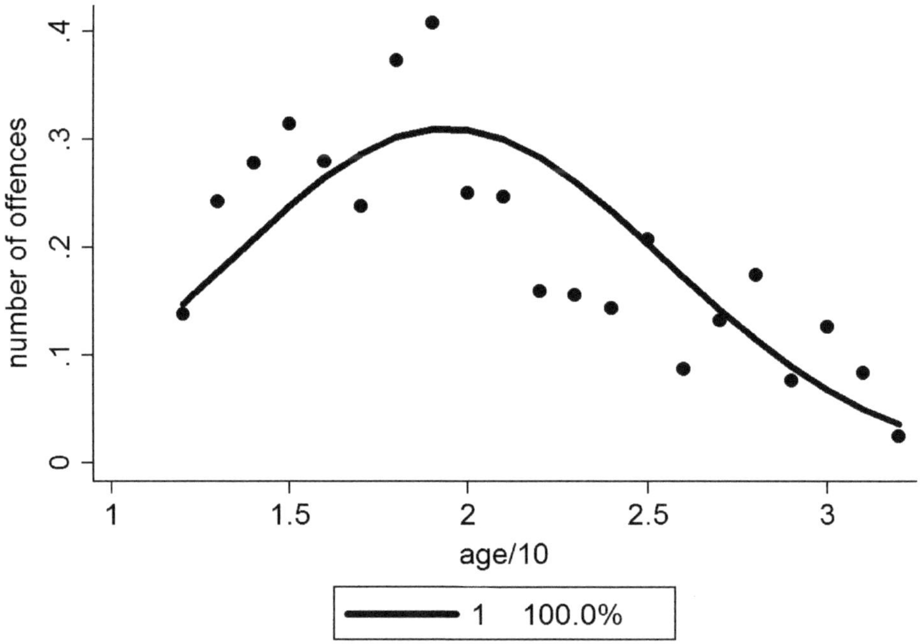

Again, using the syntax command `trajplot` a plot of the different trajectories is drawn, see Figure 7.8. All the coefficients are given in Figure 7.7.

```
traj, model(zip) var(offence_12-offence_32) indep(t1-t21)
     order(2 2 2 2 2) iorder(0 0 0 0 0)
trajplot, xtitle("Age/10") ytitle("N. of offences")
```

Illustrating the model, as in Figure 7.8, is an important part of the analysis. The curves indicate the estimated number of convictions per trajectory group J. The points indicate the average observed number of convictions per year. The legend indicates the estimated probability of group membership $\hat{\pi}_j * 100$. Stata assigns respondents to a trajectory group based on their highest posterior probability (PP) and saves these in the variable `_traj_Group`. The syntax command for displaying details of this 'forced' group assignment is:

```
tab _traj_Group
```

Figure 7.7: Coefficients for the 5 group model

Maximum Likelihood Estimates
Model: Zero Inflated Poisson (ZIP)

Group	Parameter	Estimate	Standard Error	T for H0: Parameter=0	Prob > |T|
1	Intercept	-6.25102	1.04815	-5.964	0.0000
	Linear	6.00065	1.04376	5.749	0.0000
	Quadratic	-1.29892	0.25181	-5.158	0.0000
2	Intercept	-2.54414	1.09154	-2.331	0.0198
	Linear	1.61781	1.14721	1.410	0.1585
	Quadratic	-0.39010	0.27932	-1.397	0.1626
3	Intercept	-35.32780	5.52973	-6.389	0.0000
	Linear	47.09330	7.58812	6.206	0.0000
	Quadratic	-16.25538	2.58562	-6.287	0.0000
4	Intercept	-19.13713	2.75590	-6.944	0.0000
	Linear	21.62181	3.20918	6.737	0.0000
	Quadratic	-6.14158	0.90540	-6.783	0.0000
5	Intercept	-33.58398	4.20151	-7.993	0.0000
	Linear	36.40549	4.40448	8.266	0.0000
	Quadratic	-9.36645	1.14798	-8.159	0.0000
1	Alpha0	-0.46451	0.16344	-2.842	0.0045
2	Alpha0	-0.01163	0.32146	-0.036	0.9711
3	Alpha0	-12.58303	86.36312	-0.146	0.8842
4	Alpha0	-2.06361	1.01917	-2.025	0.0429
5	Alpha0	-0.45340	0.29232	-1.551	0.1209
Group membership					
1	(%)	7.83862	1.53122	5.119	0.0000
2	(%)	25.09230	3.53947	7.089	0.0000
3	(%)	51.04414	2.89177	17.652	0.0000
4	(%)	13.90956	2.90098	4.795	0.0000
5	(%)	2.11538	0.74278	2.848	0.0044

BIC= -4026.75 (N=7491) BIC= -3994.27 (N=500) AIC= -3943.69 L= -3919.69

If we want to calculate the average posterior probability for each group separately, i.e. the average posterior probability for the respondents who are assigned to the trajectory groups, the following syntax is used:

```
mean _traj_ProbG1 _traj_ProbG2 _traj_ProbG3 _traj_ProbG4
    _traj_ProbG5, over(_traj_Group)
```

Figure 7.8: Illustration of the trajectories for the 5 group model

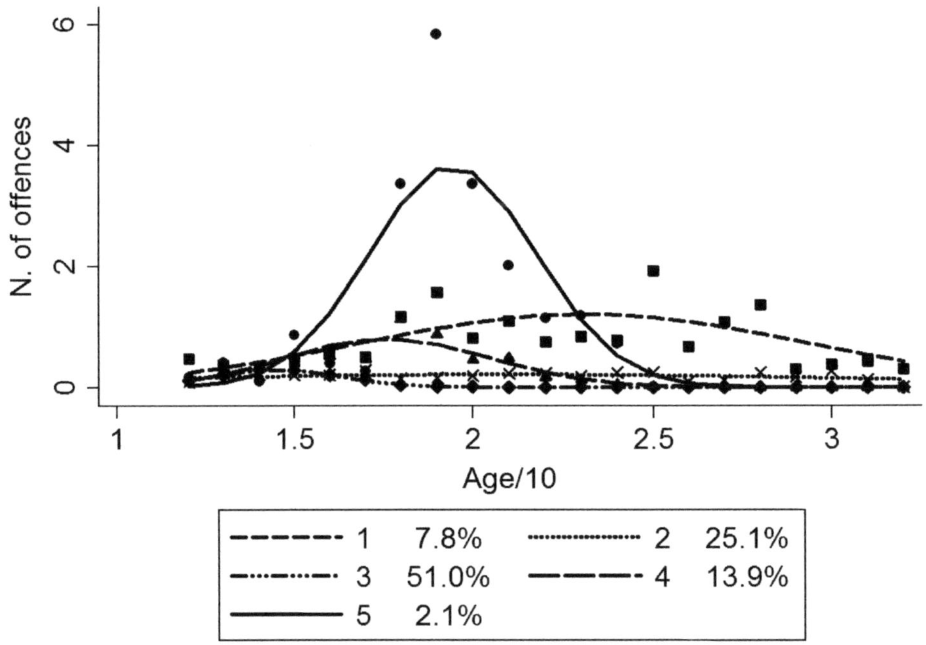

The output in Figure 7.9 now shows mean group probability per subgroup. Looking at group 1 we see the mean group probability of being assigned to group 1; for group 2 we see the mean group probability of being assigned to group 2; and so on. If each of these values is .7 or greater we can be confident enough in the group assignment. We can also now calculate the OCC for each of the groups. For example, for subgroup 3 (N=287) with AvePP=.88 and $\hat{\pi}_3 = .51$ the OCC is calculated as follows:

$$\mathrm{OCC}_j = \frac{.88/1-.88}{.51/1-.51} = 7.05$$

This value also is within the norm.

Finally, it is also possible to save the dataset with the additional variables `_traj_Group` `_traj_ProbG1` to `_traj_ProbG5`. The syntax for saving the dataset in an SPSS compatible format is:

```
saveold "C:\Data\Filenametest"
```

Figure 7.9: Mean group probabilities for the 5 group model

```
Mean estimation                         Number of obs    =     500

             1: _traj_Group = 1
             2: _traj_Group = 2
             3: _traj_Group = 3
             4: _traj_Group = 4
             5: _traj_Group = 5
```

Over	Mean	Std. Err.	[95% Conf.	Interval]
_traj_ProbG1				
1	.8980574	.0267199	.8455601	.9505547
2	.0253937	.0051844	.0152078	.0355795
3	.0028663	.0005616	.0017629	.0039698
4	.0892604	.0136599	.0624224	.1160983
5	.0206867	.0136626	-.0061566	.0475299
_traj_ProbG2				
1	.0534711	.0191013	.0159422	.091
2	.8294922	.0163821	.7973057	.8616787
3	.1012366	.003931	.0935134	.1089599
4	.1393519	.0154663	.1089648	.169739
5	.000642	.0004292	-.0002014	.0014853
_traj_ProbG3				
1	3.08e-14	1.72e-14	-2.90e-15	6.45e-14
2	.0260995	.0064583	.0134106	.0387884
3	.8766538	.0057326	.8653907	.8879168
4	.0141445	.0051912	.0039452	.0243439
5	3.67e-08	2.46e-08	-1.17e-08	8.52e-08
_traj_ProbG4				
1	.0348531	.012759	.0097851	.059921
2	.1181949	.0130011	.0926511	.1437386
3	.0189981	.0023181	.0144437	.0235524
4	.7535823	.0198738	.7145357	.7926289
5	.0940467	.0532725	-.0106194	.1987129
_traj_ProbG5				
1	.0136184	.0055147	.0027836	.0244533
2	.0008198	.0001483	.0005285	.0011111
3	.0002452	.0001074	.0000342	.0004563
4	.0036609	.0019589	-.0001878	.0075096
5	.8846246	.056607	.7734071	.9958421

It is not necessary to add an file type extension as the file is automatically saved as a `*.dta` data file. This type of file can be opened in SPSS by going to `Open Files > Stata`.

7.7.2 The trajectory model with covariates

We will now show how to include predictors in the trajectory model. For example, if we want to know whether IQ has an effect on probability of group membership, we can include this variable as a predictor when estimating the trajectory model. The estimated coefficients for the different subgroups are relative to a 'contrast' group, and so when interpreting the effect of a predictor, we see the effect compared to the reference group. We can choose which group is the reference group using 'refgroup'. Usually the most active subgroup, in our case group 5, or the least active subgroup is chosen as the reference group. Estimating the effect of IQ in this way shows the extent to which individuals in a given trajectory group differ from those in the reference group. The syntax now looks as follows:

```
traj, model(zip) var(offence_12-offence_32) indep(t1-t21)
    order(2 2 2 2 2) iorder(0 0 0 0 0) risk(IQ)
    refgroup(5)
```

Often when adding predictors to the trajectory model we need to give the model a helping hand by providing the model with *starting values*. Essentially we are giving the model a push in the right direction, so that fewer iterations are needed to find the optimal results. These starting values are identical to the parameter estimates of the model without IQ. We can find these in the output. In this example with 5 subgroups we need 28 starting values: 5 second degree polynomial functions (5*3 parameters = 15 starting values), 5 inflation parameters (5 starting values), and constants and coefficients for IQ compared to the reference group (4*2=8). Because we do not yet know the constants and coefficients for IQ we use zeros as starting values. The syntax is expanded thus:

```
matrix strt = (-6.25102, 6.00065, -1.29892, -2.54414,
    1.61781, -0.39010, -35.32780, 47.09330, -16.25538,
   -19.13713, 21.62181, -6.14158, -33.58398, 36.40549,
    -9.36645, -0.46451, -0.01163, -12.58304, -2.06361,
   -0.45340, 0, 0, 0, 0, 0, 0, 0, 0)

traj, model(zip) var(offence_12-offence_32) indep(t1-t21)
    order(2 2 2 2 2) iorder(0 0 0 0 0) risk(IQ)
    refgroup(5) start (strt)
```

The output is shown in Figure 7.10. The reader will notice that the output looks different now that we have added the covariate to the model. The coefficients have changed slightly.

Finally we will demonstrate how to include *time-varying* covariates, or changes which occur during the observation period, in the model. In our example we will examine whether being in employment affects the number of offences committed. Again we help the model out by providing starting values. In our example with 5 subgroups we need to provide 30 starting values: 5 second degree polynomial functions with parameters for work (5*4 parameters = 20 starting values), 5 inflation parameters (5 starting values), and 5 estimated probabilities for group membership (5 starting values which add up to 1; the smallest probability in this case is 0.05). We do not know what the coefficients for work are, so here again we use zeros as starting values. The syntax command for adding a time-varying covariate is as follows:

```
matrix strt = (-6.25102, 6.00065, -1.29892, 0,
   -2.54414, 1.61781, -0.39010, 0,
   -35.32780, 47.09330, -16.25538,
   0, -19.13713, 21.62181, -6.14158, 0, -33.58398,
   36.40549, -9.36645, 0 , -0.46451, -0.01163,
   -12.58304, -2.06361, -0.45340, 0.076, 0.242,
   0.494, 0.149, 0.05)
```

```
traj, model(zip) var(offence_12-offence_32) indep(t1-t21)
    order(2 2 2 2 2) iorder(0 0 0 0 0)
    tcov(work_12-work_32) start (strt)
```

The output in Figure 7.11 now shows the entire estimated model, including estimated coefficients for work for each trajectory group. The syntax automatically generates *t*-tests to determine whether there is an effect of work on delinquency, and whether this effect differs per subgroup. We examine whether the effect of work is differential, i.e. do some groups of offenders profit more from work than other groups?

If we compare the estimated model with work coefficients with the model without work coefficients (Figure 7.7) we can see that adding the time-varying covariate changes the results slightly: the order of the groups has changed and the estimated probabilities of the 5 trajectory groups are different, for some groups more than others. The interpretation of the differential effects is therefore a tricky business. It can help to ask Stata to draw a plot, just as we did for the model without time-varying covariates.

Whilst this is possible using the command `trajplot`, the Stata version of the trajectory model is still in development. For reasons which we will not go into any

Figure 7.10: Coefficients for the 5 group model including IQ as covariate

Model: Zero Inflated Poisson (ZIP)

Group	Parameter	Estimate	Standard Error	T for H0: Parameter=0	Prob > |T|
1	Intercept	-6.20783	1.05515	-5.883	0.0000
	Linear	5.96151	1.05066	5.674	0.0000
	Quadratic	-1.28935	0.25338	-5.089	0.0000
2	Intercept	-2.56708	1.11383	-2.305	0.0212
	Linear	1.64136	1.16703	1.406	0.1596
	Quadratic	-0.38893	0.28446	-1.367	0.1716
3	Intercept	-35.26745	5.47524	-6.441	0.0000
	Linear	47.02022	7.51159	6.260	0.0000
	Quadratic	-16.23360	2.55900	-6.344	0.0000
4	Intercept	-18.19647	2.83327	-6.422	0.0000
	Linear	20.48653	3.31805	6.174	0.0000
	Quadratic	-5.80963	0.94041	-6.178	0.0000
5	Intercept	-33.79811	4.21180	-8.025	0.0000
	Linear	36.63355	4.41327	8.301	0.0000
	Quadratic	-9.42654	1.14949	-8.201	0.0000
1	Alpha0	-0.46820	0.16449	-2.846	0.0044
2	Alpha0	0.06736	0.31693	0.213	0.8317
3	Alpha0	-12.59387	86.70459	-0.145	0.8845
4	Alpha0	-2.01521	0.96066	-2.098	0.0360
5	Alpha0	-0.42118	0.28289	-1.489	0.1366
Group membership					
1	Constant	1.36591	1.06519	1.282	0.1998
	IQ	-0.04092	0.37361	-0.110	0.9128
2	Constant	2.16995	1.00635	2.156	0.0311
	IQ	0.09236	0.34290	0.269	0.7877
3	Constant	3.47970	0.91289	3.812	0.0001
	IQ	-0.12334	0.32190	-0.383	0.7016
4	Constant	2.69534	0.98279	2.743	0.0061
	IQ	-0.31260	0.35041	-0.892	0.3724
5	Constant	(0.00000)	.	.	.

BIC= -4042.79 (N=7491) BIC= -4004.89 (N=500) AIC= -3945.89 L= -3917.89

further a plot including a time-varying covariate is drawn in such as way as to make interpretation difficult. It is possible to use another method to draw an interpretable plot, we will not however go into this here. Hopefully in future versions of Stata this more complicated method will not be necessary for the trajectory model.

7.8 Strengths and limitations

Just as the methods discussed in previous chapters the trajectory model has its strengths and limitations. We need to be aware of these when choosing a method, as well as when interpreting the results. First, in the introduction to this chapter we mentioned that when using the trajectory model to make statements about causality, we assume that the individuals within a trajectory group are homogeneous, i.e. individuals within groups look like each other. Whilst individuals within the same trajectory group have similar developmental trajectories, we cannot know whether their background and individual characteristics are similar, and thus whether we really have removed endogeneity bias. Second, the number of groups that we end up with in the trajectory model is dependent on the N, T and frequencies of Y. There is no such thing as the correct number of groups. Associated with this is the fact that the model summarises a continuous distribution in a discrete number of groups. Whilst we have described the groups on the basis of 'forced' group assignment, it is important to remember that respondents are not actually in groups. Third, using observations per age year, as in our example, can be too crude. It is not possible to determine whether events actually happened at the same moment in time, or whether they just happened within the same year. Using more detailed data with smaller measurement intervals, such as months, would offer a neat solution to this problem.

A fourth limitation is the use of time-varying covariates. Because covariates can only explain deviations from the average trajectory, for respondents who follow roughly the same trajectory we do not know the extent to which the shape of the trajectory is influenced by the independent variable. It is possible, for example, that as a consequence of being unable to get a foothold in the employment market people turn to crime and become high frequency offenders. When looking at the effect of employment using a trajectory analysis we only see, for example, for the high frequency offenders how much additional variation within the high frequency group is accounted for by employment. It is likely that employment has a far larger effect, but a trajectory analysis will not highlight this. There is not really a solution to this problem, except to pay attention to the extent to which different life events occur within the different trajectory groups, as well as looking at the effect of these

Figure 7.11: Coefficients for the 5 group model including work as time-varying covariate

Model: Zero Inflated Poisson (ZIP)

Group	Parameter	Estimate	Standard Error	T for H0: Parameter=0	Prob > |T|
1	Intercept	-7.37355	1.12999	-6.525	0.0000
	Linear	6.62282	1.19582	5.538	0.0000
	Quadratic	-1.67015	0.30459	-5.483	0.0000
	employment_1	-0.73056	0.17544	-4.164	0.0000
2	Intercept	-6.92918	1.03789	-6.676	0.0000
	Linear	6.60814	1.02225	6.464	0.0000
	Quadratic	-1.42798	0.24070	-5.933	0.0000
	employment_1	-0.01326	0.13522	-0.098	0.9219
3	Intercept	-29.30276	9.35671	-3.132	0.0017
	Linear	38.76859	13.12147	2.955	0.0031
	Quadratic	-13.38823	4.56207	-2.935	0.0034
	employment_1	-16.04756	1637.14777	-0.010	0.9922
4	Intercept	-33.49564	10.18845	-3.288	0.0010
	Linear	42.00192	12.66314	3.317	0.0009
	Quadratic	-13.44249	3.94844	-3.405	0.0007
	employment_1	2.68087	0.56906	4.711	0.0000
5	Intercept	-12.75787	3.96397	-3.218	0.0013
	Linear	14.35255	4.18587	3.429	0.0006
	Quadratic	-4.17003	1.06508	-3.915	0.0001
	employment_1	2.16782	0.35367	6.129	0.0000
1	Alpha0	-2.48614	2.22103	-1.119	0.2630
2	Alpha0	-0.19031	0.16025	-1.188	0.2350
3	Alpha0	-15.76773	416.46395	-0.038	0.9698
4	Alpha0	-34.43815	.	-0.000	1.0000
5	Alpha0	-14.14073	454.02727	-0.031	0.9752

Group membership

Group		Estimate	Standard Error	T for H0: Parameter=0	Prob > |T|
1	(%)	34.12759	4.04324	8.441	0.0000
2	(%)	9.99788	1.92882	5.183	0.0000
3	(%)	48.86052	3.87775	12.600	0.0000
4	(%)	5.36636	2.18979	2.451	0.0143
5	(%)	1.64764	0.72974	2.258	0.0240

BIC= -3543.68 (N=6629) BIC= -3506.20 (N=500) AIC= -3445.09 L= -3416.09

different life events.This can be done by using the *maximum posterior probabilities of assignment* to 'force' group assignment.

Despite these limitations the *group-based trajectory model* has a number of advantages over the previously discussed methods. The most important of these is that the method provides a transparent way to summarise longitudinal data. This advantage is also apparent in the efficient way in which the continuous and often skewed development of behaviour, criminal or otherwise, is divided into a discrete number of groups. A second advantage is that the effects of time-varying covariates, such as being employed or married, can be estimated for each group independently. By estimating differential effects within homogeneous subgroups in this way, the covariate effect estimates are not distorted by selection effects.

7.9 Further reading

In this chapter we have used a number of concrete examples to introduce the trajectory model. In the *Handbook of Quantitative Criminology* Nagin (2010) provides a more detailed overview of the method. For details, background and further possibilities concerning this method we recommend *Group-Based Trajectory Modeling of Development* by Nagin (2005). We recommend Van der Geest, Bijleveld and Blokland (2011) for a criminological application of the method looking at the effect of employment on criminal behaviour and Blokland and Nieuwbeerta (2005) for the effect of marriage on criminal behaviour.

Finally, the method can be applied in areas other than individual development. For example, Weisburd, Bushway, Lum and Yang (2004) use the trajectory model to examine the development of crime within street sections. The model can of course be applied to fields other than criminology. For example, employment (Hynes and Clarkberg, 2005; Van der Geest et al., 2014), receipt of welfare (Hamil-Luker, 2005), substance use (Guo et al., 2002; Hamil-Luker et al., 2004), alcohol use (Hill et al., 2000) and depression (Stoolmiller et al., 2005), have all been examined using the trajectory model.

Chapter 8

Final remarks

In the preceding chapters we explored five data analysis techniques: propensity score matching, instrumental variables, the regression discontinuity design, fixed effects panel models, and trajectory models. All five provide solutions to the endogeneity bias problem associated with non-experimental data. As we discussed in the first chapter, the problem inherent in this kind of data is that we cannot be sure that differences on our outcome measure are the result of an intervention – and not of other individual characteristics associated with that intervention. We referred to this as observed or unobserved 'bias'.

Effects can be biased when allocation to receive an intervention is not carried out at random. Consequently, individuals in the experimental and the control groups are likely to differ on characteristics other than whether they received the intervention or not. As a result we do not know whether differences on the dependent variable can be ascribed, partly or entirely, to the intervention, or whether these differences are due to pre-existing observed or unobserved differences in background characteristics.

The way in which the five methods discussed are set up or the way in which they employ a particular technique can all help researchers make more confident conclusions as to the effect of an intervention. We emphasis the 'more confident conclusions' because of course none of the methods provides an absolute solution to the problem that the data is not the result of randomised research design. As we repeatedly pointed out, these solutions all have their limitations. In this final chapter we will briefly review the five methods and discuss their applicability and limitations.

With *propensity score matching* we have a experimental and control group of sorts. Part of the sample received the intervention and part did not. Using logistic regression analysis we try to predict who did and who did not receive the intervention as accurately as possible. As a result of the logistic regression each respondent is given a propensity score indicating how likely they are to receive the intervention on the basis of their observed characteristics. Having the same propensity score indicates that two people are just as likely to receive the intervention. The matching procedure is based on this score. The outcome measure scores for respondents with equal propensity scores but different scores on the treatment – matched respondents – can then be compared, in the knowledge that any distortions by observed background characteristics have been removed.

One of the big advantages of propensity score matching is that it is easy to understand, even for those with not a lot of methodological experience. The biggest disadvantage of the method is that it only controls for observed differences between respondents in the experimental (E) and the control (C) group; the logistic regression can only include in the prediction characteristics which have been measured. On top of this, in practice, it is often not possible to find a match for every respondent. Those with a very high or very low propensity score are often over-represented in the E group or the C group respectively and it is consequently difficult to find a match for them in the other group. This means that in practice our conclusions can only be applied with confidence to those with relatively average propensity scores. Even if we use alternative versions of the method, such as kernel matching where we basically include all respondents, the method generally performs best when the top or bottom end of the propensity score distribution is capped. Whether it is a problem or not that conclusions can only be related to those respondents with average propensity scores, those for whom receiving or not receiving an intervention hangs in the balance, is open to debate. In our example with sex offenders, those in the middle are precisely those for whom we want to know whether the intervention is effective or not. The choice of providing the intervention to those at high risk or those at low risk is more obvious. A final disadvantage of propensity score matching is that we lose respondents by matching them one to one, but if we reuse respondents we introduce dependence. The disadvantages are listed in Table 8.1.

With the *instrumental variables* approach we have an intervention, a dependent variable, and a third variable, the instrumental variable which correlates with the intervention, and is only related to the dependent variable via the intervention. The instrumental variable needs to fulfill two conditions: the instrumental variable must correlate with the intervention, i.e. it must be relevant, and can relate to the outcome measure via the intervention only, i.e. it must be exogenous. If the correlation with the intervention is not strong enough we have what is referred to as a weak instrument, and there is consequently little benefit to using the instrumental variables approach. Indeed, one of the consequences of using a weak instrument is larger standard errors and as a result less accurate estimates. A second consequence

Table 8.1: Overview of the methods discussed

technique	PSM	IV	RDD	FE	TRAJ
design	E & C group	E & C group	E & C group	longitudinal	longitudinal
control for	observed bias	(un)observed bias	(un)observed bias	not time-varying (un)observed bias	(un)observed bias
matching	E with C based on propensity score	E with C via IV	E with C around boundary value	individual with themselves	homogeneous groups
disadvantages	conclusions only for those in area of common support does not control for unobserved bias loss of research units if no reusing	limited application (dependent on available IV) exogeneity of IV not empirically testable not suitable if bias is large less accurate estimates	conclusions only for units falling around the threshold loss of research units, less power limited application (only with underlying continuum)	only for units which vary on at least one independent variable no controls for time-varying unobserved confounders less efficient (power)	correct number of groups does not exist and depends on N, T and frequencies of Y problems with causality in model with varying covariates units do not belong to groups

is that a weak instrument can lead to bias. Generally, if bias is high the instrumental variable method is not the best method to choose. The difficulty is of course that we do not know how much bias there is.

What this highlights is that everything depends on finding a good instrument, this is the essence of this method. If a good instrument is available this method can be extremely powerful. However, one weakness remains. Namely, that the exogeneity assumption cannot be tested. In practice therefore, the strength of any conclusions drawn is based on having plausible assumptions about the exogeneity of the instrument. Table 8.1 lists the disadvantages.

The *regression discontinuity design* can be used in situations where we have a continuous variable on which a given threshold determines whether respondents receive or do not receive an intervention. We can compare groups under the assumption that respondents scoring close to this threshold value, either just above or just below, do not differ from each other. Again, just as with propensity score matching, we are comparing respondents who fall within a given range; those who could as well have received the intervention as not received the intervention. We assume that the respondents have no control over whether their scores fall just above or just below the threshold. If they could influence this we could no longer assume that scoring just above and just below the threshold was exogenous. We can carry out a range of tests to examine whether this is the case, but from that we can only be sure that respondents just above and just below the threshold do not differ on observed characteristics. The possibility will always remain that there are unobserved differences between the two groups. If we examine respondents close enough to the threshold the assumption is that they are less likely to differ. But here again we are faced with the paradoxical situation that in order to have stable enough estimates of the regression lines we need to include respondents who fall into a range above and a range below the threshold. As the range increases the stability of the estimates increases, but at the same time the chance of bias also increases. Disadvantages of the regression discontinuity design are therefore, first, that we can only draw causal conclusions concerning scores on and around the threshold, and second, that we are likely to experience considerable loss of respondents. Furthermore, the regression discontinuity design can only be applied in particular circumstances in which an external criterion determines allocation to the intervention. Besides these limitations, the design is very powerful. See Table 8.1 for an overview.

Fixed effects and *trajectory* models both use longitudinal data. In terms of controlling for bias caused by time-invariant and unobserved heterogeneity, the strongest of the two methods is the fixed effects model. The model is conceptually easy to understand, even for those with not much methodological experience. The idea that respondents' scores at times when they are not exposed to an intervention are compared with their scores when they are exposed to an intervention is intuitively easy to follow. The method has strong internal validity, as unobserved as well as observed bias is removed. However, the price paid for this rigorous approach is considerable. Respondents who do not score differently over time on at least one independent variable are removed from the model. Consequently, the generalisability of the conclusions is limited and efficiency is lost through loss of power. Furthermore, the effect of the intervention is then likely to be underestimated, possibly severely so. Imagine that people who are always employed never commit criminal offences? This effect cannot be determined using a fixed effects model. This is a good reason to consider random effects models despite the fact they provide notably less effective control for bias. The final disadvantage worth mentioning is that the model can only control for observed and unobserved differences which do not vary over time, and not for unobserved time-varying differences. Table 8.1 lists these issues.

With the *trajectory model* respondents within a trajectory group who receive an intervention are compared to those within the same group who do not receive an intervention. The strong assumption with this method is that members of a trajectory group do not differ on relevant confounding factors. Given this assumption the analyses can provide useful information about the effect of an intervention. The method is exploratory and flexible, and it often results in interesting summaries and insights. Its exploratory nature can however be seen as its Achilles heel. The number of groups in a given population is not predetermined. Neither is it a given that respondents are definitely a member of one group rather than another, as for example is the case for whales: these can be categorized as definitely belonging to one species of whale and not another. In the trajectory model, by specifying the model slightly differently group membership can change. Furthermore, the number of groups varies depending on the number of respondents and on their activity levels on the dependent variable. One criticism of this method is that analysis of intervention effects based on these fuzzy group allocations can give the appearance of causality where none exists. This is a particular problem when examining effects which can be reciprocal. For example, take the effect of criminal behaviour on employment and vice versa: it is possible that employment plays a role in determining whether people follow a particular of criminal pathway, and therefore fall into certain trajectory groups. Whether this is true or not cannot be determined using this model. The model only indicates the effect of a given independent variable within homogeneous sub-groups (homogeneous in the sense that they display the same developmental pathway on the dependent variable). Again see Table 8.1 for an overview.

Given all that we have discussed the question remains: which method should be used in which situation? The first step is to consider the type of data to be analysed: is it cross sectional or longitudinal? If it is the latter fixed effects and trajectory models can be employed. From these two, the fixed effects model would be first choice if one wants to determine the effect of an intervention: observed and unobserved heterogeneity is controlled for and so internal validity is high. If there are strong indications that effects are differential then trajectory models would be a good choice, or alternatively fixed effects models including moderators.

If the data are cross-sectional, a regression discontinuity design can be employed provided there is an underlying continuum available, on which scoring above or below a threshold results in receiving or not receiving an intervention. There will, however, be many situations for which this is not the case, and so in practice this method is unlikely to be regularly used. Nevertheless we have included it in the book as of all the different cross-sectional methods this is the one which most resembles an actual experiment. The same could be said about instrumental variables. If there is a suitable, i.e. relevant and exogenous, instrumental variable available, then there are significant advantages to using this method. It corrects for observed and unobserved bias, i.e. heterogeneity, and therefore results in internally valid conclusions. The weakest candidate for examining cross-sectional data is propensity score matching. This method only controls for observed bias and consequently internal validity is compromised.

In this book we have provided a brief and condensed, but hopefully nonetheless appealing, overview of the different methods. For nearly all the techniques discussed here there are a number of books dedicated entirely to the given method and its different variations. Not all of this literature is accessible for the average social scientist, but we hope that here we have provided a clear and comprehensible introduction to these methods, which can form the basis for further exploration.

For the majority of situations in the social sciences the methods discussed in this book will be applicable. There are however other methods which can be used to deal with unusual datasets, for example datasets which contain time series data. We will very briefly mention three of these.

Robins, Hernán and Brumback (2000) developed the so-called *marginal structural models* to estimate the effect of a treatment which varies over time, and for which time varying confounding factors make estimating this effect difficult. Another kind of model is the *directed acyclic graphs*. These are essentially path models representing assumptions about causal, or at least probable, relationships between variables. These associations can be either causal, resultant or confounding. Pearl (1988) developed the precise specification of these models, as well as the mathematics that makes it possible to test the existence of relationships, and thereby effects, between the variables. The method does however have its critics. The *interrupted time series design* is less a method and more a design for data collection. In cases where only one group can be observed – the experimental group –

this design provides better protection against confounding factors such as maturation and test effects than the simple pretest-posttest design. Versions of this design alternate between providing and not providing respondents with a treatment. See Shadish et al. (2002) for more details.

Appendix A

Complete SPSS syntax

```
Comment ****************************************.
Comment Chapter 1.
Comment ****************************************.

*Define where data file is located.
define !data ()'C:\Data\' !enddefine.

* Opening data.
get file=!data+'VM-JSO.sav'.

Comment ****************************************.
Comment Chapter 3.
Comment ****************************************.

* Opening data.
GET FILE='C:\Data\VM-JSO.sav'.

* Crosstab  sexual recidivism and treatment.
```

```
CROSSTABS
   /TABLES=recidivism_sex BY treatment
   /FORMAT=AVALUE TABLES
   /STATISTICS=RISK
   /CELLS=COUNT COLUMN
   /COUNT ROUND CELL.

* Logistic regression to construct propensity scores.
* for treatment.

LOGISTIC REGRESSION VARIABLES treatment
   /METHOD=ENTER contact_peers
   psychopathology age_offence
   IQ neuroticism impulsivity ethnicity type_offender
   previous_sexoffence
   /CONTRAST (type_offender)=Indicator (1)
   /SAVE=PRED
   /CRITERIA=PIN(.05) POUT(.10) ITERATE(20) CUT(.5).

* Prior to the command below, one should first manually.
* make a caliper as described in the text.

TEMPORARY.
SELECT IF (CALIPER EQ 1).

* Crosstab  sexual recidivism and treatment.


CROSSTABS
   /TABLES=recidivism_sex BY treatment
   /FORMAT=AVALUE TABLES
   /STATISTICS=RISK
   /CELLS=COUNT COLUMN
   /COUNT ROUND CELL.

Comment ***************************************.
Comment Chapter 4.
Comment ***************************************.

* Frequency distribution of probation length.
```

```
FREQUENCIES probation.

* Descriptives of probation length..

DESCRIPTIVES probation.

* Logistic regression to predict recidivism from.
* probation length.

LOGISTIC REGRESSION VARIABLES recidivism_general
   /METHOD=ENTER probation
   /CRITERIA=PIN(.05) POUT(.10) ITERATE(20) CUT(.5).

* Average imposed probation length per type of offender.

MEANS TABLES=probation BY type_offender.

* Average imposed probation length per court.

MEANS TABLES=probation BY court.

* Recoding court in instrumental variable.
* from low to high.

RECODE court (3=1)(1=2) (8=3) (12=4) (17=5) (6=6)
   (5=7) (4=8) (18=9) (9=10) (7=11) (2=12) (14=13)
   (11=14) (16=15) (10=16) (15=17) (19=18)
   (13=19) INTO court_IV.

* Predict  probation length from court_IV.

REGRESSION
   /MISSING LISTWISE
   /STATISTICS COEFF OUTS R ANOVA
   /CRITERIA=PIN(.05) POUT(.10)
   /NOORIGIN
   /DEPENDENT probation
   /METHOD=ENTER court_IV
   /SAVE PRED.
```

```
* Predict recidivism from predicted scores.
* on probation length.

LOGISTIC REGRESSION VARIABLES recidivism_general
   /METHOD=ENTER PRE_1
   /CRITERIA=PIN(.05) POUT(.10) ITERATE(20) CUT(.5).

* 2SLS procedure for instrumental variable models.
* Note: the dependent variable is binary and therefore.
* strictly speaking not suitable for 2SLS.
* Note: example for illustrative purposes only.

2SLS recidivism_general WITH probation
   /INSTRUMENTS court_IV
   /CONSTANT.

Comment ****************************************.
Comment Chapter 5.
Comment ****************************************.

* T-tests for difference in arrests between treated.
* and untreated.

T-TEST GROUPS=treatment(0 1)
   /MISSING=ANALYSIS
   /VARIABLES=arrests
   /CRITERIA=CI(.95).

* Descriptives of JSOAP.

DESCRIPTIVES VARIABLES=JSOAP
   /STATISTICS=MEAN STDDEV MIN MAX.

* The command below produces Figure 5.10, the.
* scatterplot between JSOAP and arrests.
* In Figure 5.10 an exta line is drawn at a.
* JSOAP-score of 50 with the SPSS Chart Editor.
* This line will not be obtained with the command below.
```

```
GRAPH
   /SCATTERPLOT(BIVAR)=JSOAP WITH arrests
   /MISSING=LISTWISE.

* Select respondents around the treshold of 50.

USE ALL.
COMPUTE filter=(JSOAP >= 40 & JSOAP < 60).
FILTER BY filter.
EXECUTE.

* The command below produces Figure 5.11, the histogram.
* of JSOAP.
* The output obtained differs slightly from Figure 5.11.
* because Figure 5.11 was constructed with the  SPSS.
* Chart Builder in which the width of the bars can be edited.
* Because the syntax command of this Chart Builder is.
* not very clear, we show the simplified syntax.

GRAPH
   /HISTOGRAM=JSOAP.

* T-Tests for difference in background
* characteristics of groups around the treshold.

T-TEST GROUPS=treatment(0 1)
   /MISSING=ANALYSIS
   /VARIABLES=IQ neuroticism impulsivity
   contact_peers age_offence
   /CRITERIA=CI(.95).

* Chi-square tests for difference in background.
* characteristics of groups around the treshold.

CROSSTABS
   /TABLES=treatment BY ethnicity
   previous_sexoffence type_offender
   /FORMAT=AVALUE TABLES
   /STATISTICS=CHISQ
   /CELLS=COUNT
```

```
   /COUNT ROUND CELL.

* Centering JSOAP.

COMPUTE JSOAP_c=JSOAP-50.
EXECUTE.

* Splitting file into treated and untreated.

SORT CASES BY treatment.
SPLIT FILE SEPARATE BY treatment.

* Regression analysis to determine.
* the local treatment effect.

REGRESSION
   /MISSING LISTWISE
   /STATISTICS COEFF OUTS CI(95) R ANOVA
   /CRITERIA=PIN(.05) POUT(.10)
   /NOORIGIN
   /DEPENDENT arrests
   /METHOD=ENTER JSOAP_c.
SPLIT FILE OFF.

* Quick way to determine local treatment effect.
* Note: the file should still be filtered on the correct.
* bandwidth, but the split file command should be off.

REGRESSION
   /MISSING LISTWISE
   /STATISTICS COEFF OUTS R ANOVA
   /CRITERIA=PIN(.05) POUT(.10)
   /NOORIGIN
   /DEPENDENT arrests
   /METHOD=ENTER JSOAP treatment.

* Repeating analyses with different bandwidths.

USE ALL.
COMPUTE filter=(JSOAP >= 42 & JSOAP < 58).
```

```
FILTER BY filter.
EXECUTE.

REGRESSION
   /MISSING LISTWISE
   /STATISTICS COEFF OUTS R ANOVA
   /CRITERIA=PIN(.05) POUT(.10)
   /NOORIGIN
   /DEPENDENT arrests
   /METHOD=ENTER JSOAP treatment.

USE ALL.
COMPUTE filter=(JSOAP >= 45 & JSOAP < 55).
FILTER BY filter.
EXECUTE.

REGRESSION
   /MISSING LISTWISE
   /STATISTICS COEFF OUTS R ANOVA
   /CRITERIA=PIN(.05) POUT(.10)
   /NOORIGIN
   /DEPENDENT arrests
   /METHOD=ENTER JSOAP treatment.

USE ALL.
COMPUTE filter=(JSOAP >= 38 & JSOAP < 62).
FILTER BY filter.
EXECUTE.

REGRESSION
   /MISSING LISTWISE
   /STATISTICS COEFF OUTS R ANOVA
   /CRITERIA=PIN(.05) POUT(.10)
   /NOORIGIN
   /DEPENDENT arrests
   /METHOD=ENTER JSOAP treatment.

USE ALL.
COMPUTE filter=(JSOAP >= 35 & JSOAP < 65).
FILTER BY filter.
```

```
EXECUTE.


REGRESSION
   /MISSING LISTWISE
   /STATISTICS COEFF OUTS R ANOVA
   /CRITERIA=PIN(.05) POUT(.10)
   /NOORIGIN
   /DEPENDENT arrests
   /METHOD=ENTER JSOAP treatment.
```

Appendix B

Complete Stata syntax

```
*Chapter 1 Introduction

* Defining the location of datafile

global DATAMAP "C:\Data\"

* Opening data

use "${DATAMAP}VM-JSO.dta", clear

* Note that all Stata syntax should be on one line.
* Here we at times for readability divide syntax over
*  multiple lines.
* Hard returns must be deleted before running the syntax.


*Chapter 3 Propensity score matching

*Clearing possibly open data files

clear
clear matrix

* Opening data
```

```
use " C:\Data\VM-JSO.dta"

* Frequency distribution type_dader, and
* automatically computing dummy variables

tabulate type_offender, gen(type_offender)

* Downloading procedure pscore
* Choose the most recent Software update
* for pscore suite

findit pscore

* Constructing propensity scores

pscore treatment contact_peers
     psychopathology age_offence
     IQ neuroticism impulsivity ethnicity
     type_offender2 type_offender3
     previous_sexoffence, logit pscore(ps)

* Downloading the procedure psmatch2

ssc install psmatch2

* Entering a random starting value

set seed 123456789

* Caliper matching with a caliper of .05

psmatch2 treatment, pscore(ps) cal(.05)
     out(recidivism_sex) noreplace logit

* Caliper matching with a caliper of .01

psmatch2 treatment, pscore(ps) cal(.01)
     out(recidivism_sex) noreplace logit

* Kernel matching
```

```
psmatch2 treatment, pscore(ps) kernel
     out(recidivism_sex)
     logit kerneltype(epan)

* Kernel matching with trimming

psmatch2 treatment, pscore(ps) kernel
     out(recidivism_sex)
     logit kerneltype(epan) trim(22)


* Chapter 4 Instrumental variables

* Opening data

use " C:\Data\VM-JSO.dta"

* Constructing instrumental variable court_IV

recode court (3=1)(1=2) (8=3) (12=4) (17=5) (6=6)
     (5=7) (4=8) (18=9) (9=10) (7=11) (2=12) (14=13)
     (11=14) (16=15) (10=16) (15=17) (19=18)
     (13=19), generate (court_IV)

* Instrumental variable with probit regression

ivprobit recidivism_general (probation=court_IV),
     first

* Downloading procedure ivreg2

ssc install ivreg2

* Example instrumental variable with OLS regression
* Note: the dependent variable is binary and
* therefore not really suitable for ivreg2

ivreg2 recidivism_general (probation=court_IV),
     first
```

```
* Requesting Wu-Hausman F-test and Durbin-Wu-Hausman
* Chi-square test

ivendog


* Chapter 5 Regression discontinuity design

* Opening data

use " C:\Data\VM-JSO.dta"

* Selecting bandwidth

keep if JSOAP >= 40 & JSOAP < 60

* Regression discontinuity design in
* one regression analysis

regress arrests JSOAP treatment


* Chapter 6 Fixed effects panelmodels

* Opening data

use " C:\Data\VM-JSO.dta"

* idnummer is identification variable

reshape i idnumber

* year is time variable

reshape j year

* offence_ employment_ marriage_ and parent_ vary
* over persons and time
```

```
reshape xij offence_ employment_ marriage_ parent_
reshape long

* Frequency distribution of the dependent
* count-variable

tab offence_, mis

* Constructing the dichotomous dependent variable

gen offencedi=offence_>0 if offence_!=.

* Frequency distribution of the dichotomous
* dependent variable

tab offencedi, mis

* Define the panel structure of the data

xtset idnumber

* Deleting missings on employment, marriage,
* parenthood and offences

drop if employment_==.| marriage_==.| parent_==.|
     offencedi==.

* Logistic fixed effects panelmodel

xtlogit offencedi employment_ marriage_ parent_ , fe or

* Constructing period dummies

tab year, gen(year_)

* Two-way logistic fixed effects panelmodel

xtlogit offencedi employment_ marriage_ parent_
     year_2-year_15, fe or
```

```
* Constructing dummy variables for type of offender

tabulate type_offender, gen(type_offender)

* Logistic random effects panelmodel

xtlogit offencedi employment_ marriage_ parent_
     ethnicity contact_peers psychopathology
     age_offence IQ neuroticism impulsivity
     type_offender2 type_offender3
     previous_sexoffence, re or

* Save results logistic fixed effects panelmodel
* for Hausman-test

xtlogit offencedi employment_ marriage_
     parent_ , fe or

estimates store fixedlogit

* Estimate logistic random effects panelmodel
* and perform Hausman-test

xtlogit offencedi employment_ marriage_ parent_
     ethnicity contact_peers psychopathology
     age_offence IQ neuroticism impulsivity
     type_offender2 type_offender3
     previous_sexoffence, re or

hausman fixedlogit

* Linear fixed effects panelmodel
* Note: offence_ is not normally distributed and
* therefore not really suitable for xtreg

xtreg offence_ employment_ marriage_ parent_, fe

* Poisson fixed effects panelmodel
* Note: offence_ is not Poisson distributed and
* therefore not really suitable for xtpoisson
```

```
xtpoisson offence_ employment_ marriage_ parent_, fe


* Chapter 7 Trajectory models

* Opening data

use " C:\Data\VM-JSO.dta"

* Downloading add-on traj

net from http://www.andrew.cmu.edu/user/bjones/traj
net install traj, replace

* Constructing variables for 21 measurement points

* The command below should be on three separate lines

foreach val of numlist 1/21 {
gen t 'val'=('val'+11)/10
}

* Trajectory model and plot with one trajectory

traj, model(zip) var(offence_12-offence_32)
     indep(t1-t21) order(2) iorder(0)
trajplot, xtitle("age/10")
     ytitle("number of offences")

* Trajectory model and plot with two trajectories

traj, model(zip) var(offence_12-offence_32)
     indep(t1-t21) order(2 2) iorder(0 0)
trajplot, xtitle("age/10")
     ytitle("number of offences")

* Trajectory model and plot with three trajectories

traj, model(zip) var(offence_12-offence_32)
```

```
     indep(t1-t21) order(2 2 2) iorder(0 0 0)
trajplot, xtitle("age/10")
     ytitle("number of offences")

* Trajectory model and plot with four trajectories

traj, model(zip) var(offence_12-offence_32)
     indep(t1-t21) order(2 2 2 2) iorder(0 0 0 0)
trajplot, xtitle("age/10")
     ytitle("number of offences")

* Trajectory model and plot with five trajectories

traj, model(zip) var(offence_12-offence_32)
     indep(t1-t21) order(2 2 2 2 2) iorder(0 0 0 0 0)
trajplot, xtitle("Age/10") ytitle("N. of offences")

* Retrieving the average posterior probability

tab _traj_Group

* Retrieving the average posterior probability
* for each trajectory group

mean _traj_ProbG1 _traj_ProbG2 _traj_ProbG3
     _traj_ProbG4 _traj_ProbG5, over( _traj_Group)

* Save data in format that is compatible with SPSS

saveold "C:\Data\Filename"

* Trajectory model with five trajectories and
* IQ as covariate

traj, model(zip) var(offence_12-offence_32)
     indep(t1-t21) order(2 2 2 2 2) iorder(0 0 0 0 0)
     risk(IQ) refgroup(5)

* Entering starting values
```

```
matrix strt = (-6.25102, 6.00065, -1.29892, -2.54414,
     1.61781, -0.39010, -35.32780, 47.09330, -16.25538,
     -19.13713, 21.62181, -6.14158, -33.58398, 36.40549,
     -9.36645, -0.46451, -0.01163, -12.58304, -2.06361,
     -0.45340, 0, 0, 0, 0, 0, 0, 0, 0)

* Trajectory model with five trajectories and IQ as
     * covariate with starting values

traj, model(zip) var(offence_12-offence_32)
     indep(t1-t21) order(2 2 2 2 2) iorder(0 0 0 0 0)
     risk(IQ) refgroup(5) start (strt)

* Recoding missings on employment

recode employment_12 employment_13 employment_14
     employment_15 employment_16 employment_17
     (missing=0)

* Entering new startingvalues

matrix strt = (-6.25102, 6.00065, -1.29892, 0, -2.54414,
     1.61781, -0.39010, 0, -35.32780, 47.09330,
     -16.25538, 0, -19.13713, 21.62181, -6.14158,
     0, -33.58398, 36.40549, -9.36645, 0, -0.46451,
     -0.01163, -12.58304, -2.06361, -0.45340,
     0.076, 0.242, 0.494, 0.149, 0.05)

* Trajectory model with five trajectories and employment
* as time-varying covariate

traj, model(zip) var(offence_12-offence_32) indep(t1-t21)
     order(2 2 2 2 2) iorder(0 0 0 0 0)
     tcov(employment_12-employment_32) start (strt)
```

Bibliography

Aarten, P. G. M. (2014). *Suspended sentences: Public opinion, compliance and recidivism.* PhD thesis, Vrije Universiteit, Amsterdam.

Allison, P. D. and Waterman, R. (2002). Fixed-effects negative binomial regression models. *Sociological Methodology*, 32: 247–265.

Angrist, J. D. (2001). Estimation of limited dependent variable models with dummy endogenous regressors: Simple strategies for empirical practice. *Journal of Business & Economic Statistics*, 19: 2–16.

Angrist, J. D. (2006). Instrumental variables methods in experimental criminological research: What, why and how. *Journal of Experimental Criminology*, 2: 23–44.

Angrist, J. D. and Krueger, A. B. (2001). Instrumental variables and the search for identification: From supply and demand to natural experiments. *Journal of Economic Perspectives*, 15: 69–85.

Apel, R. e. a. (2008). Using state child labor laws to identify the causal effect of youth employment on deviant behavior and academic achievement. *Journal of Quantitative Criminology*, 24: 337–362.

Atkins, D. C. and Gallop, R. J. (2007). Rethinking how family researchers model infrequent outcomes: A tutorial on count regression and zero-inflated models. *Journal of Family Psychology*, 21: 726–735.

Austin, P. (2011). Optimal caliper widths for propensity-score matching when estimating differences in means and differences in proportions in observational studies. *Pharmaceutical Statistics*, 10: 150–161.

Austin, P. (2012). An introduction to propensity score methods for reducing the effects of confounding in observational studies. *Multivariate Behavioral Research*, 46: 399–424.

Averdijk, M. (2011). Reciprocal effects between victimization and routine activities. *Journal of Quantitative Criminology*, 27: 125–149.

Baltagi, B. H. (2005). *Econometric Analysis of Panel Data.* Wiley & Sons, Ltd., Chichester.

Berk, R. (2009). Recent perspectives on the regression discontinuity design. Technical report, www.crim.upenn.edu/faculty/papers/berk/RD.chapter.pdf; accessed 11 December 2012.

Berk, R., Barnes, G., Ahlmann, L., and Kurtz, E. (2010). When second best is good enough: A comparison between a true experiment and a regression discontinuity quasi-experiment. *Journal of Experimental Criminology*, 6: 191–208.

Berk, R. and MacDonald, J. (2007). Overdispersion and Poisson regression. Technical report, Universitity of Pennsylvania, http://www.udel.edu/soc/faculty/parker/SOCI836_S08_files/Berk%26MacDonald_JQCF.pdf; accessed 12 December 2014.

Berk, R. A. and de Leeuw, J. (1999). Evaluation of California's inmate classification system using a generalized discontinuity design. *Journal of the American Statistical Association*, 94: 1045–1052.

Bijleveld, C. C. J. H. (2015). *Methoden en Technieken van Onderzoek in de Criminologie. [Research Methods for Criminology]*. Boom Juridische uitgevers, Den Haag, 6th revised edition.

Bijleveld, C. C. J. H. and Commandeur, J. J. F. (2017). *Multivariate analyse. Een inleiding voor criminologen en andere sociale wetenschappers [Multivariate analysis. An introduction for criminologists and other social scientists]*. Boom Lemma Uitgevers, Den Haag, 4th revised edition.

Bijleveld, C. C. J. H., Hendriks, J., and van den Berg, C. A. M. (2010). Juvenile sex offenders in emerging adulthood: Offending, employment and intimate relations. Paper presented at the 10th Annual Conference of the European Society of Criminology, Liège.

Brüderl, J. (2005). Panel data analysis. Online paper, downloaded from www.sowi.uni-mannheim.de/lehrstuehle/lessm/veranst/Panelanalyse.pdf accessed January 9, 2013.

Bruinsma, G. J. N. and Luykx, F. (2003). De vuurwerkramp en de gevolgen daarvan op de criminaliteit in Enschede [The fireworks disaster and its impact on crime in Enschede]. *Tijdschrift voor Veiligheid en Veiligheidszorg*, 2: 3–24.

Bushway, S. and Apel, R. (2010). Instrumental variables in criminology and criminal justice. In Piquero, A. and Weisburd, D., editors, *Handbook of Quantitative Criminology*, pages 595–614. Springer, New York.

Cattaneo, M. D. and Escanciano, J. C. (2017). Regression discontinuity designs: Theory and applications. *Advances in Econometrics*, 38.

Cochran, W. G. (1968). The effectiveness of adjustment by subclassification in removing bias in observational studies. *Biometrics*, 24: 295–313.

Cook, T. D. (2008). 'Waiting for life to arrive'. A history of the regression discontinuity design in psychology, statistics and economics. *Journal of Econometrics*, 142: 636–654.

Cook, T. D. and Campbell, D. T. (1979). *Quasi–experimentation: Design and Analysis Issues for Field Settings*. Houghton Mifflin, Boston, MA.

Cullen, J. and Levitt, S. (1999). Crime, urban flight, and the consequences for cities. *The Review of Economics and Statistics*, 81: 159–169.

Cuong, C. N. (2013). Which covariates should be controlled for in propensity score matching? Evidence from a simulation study. *Statistica Neerlandica*, 67: 169–180.

De Vries, J. and De Graaf, P. M. (2008). Is the intergenerational transmission of high cultural activities biased by the retrospective measurement of parental high cultural activities? *Social Indicators Research*, 85: 311–327.

Dugan, L. (2010). Estimating effects over time for single and multiple units. In Piquero, A. R. and Weisburd, D., editors, *Handbook of Quantitative Criminology*, pages 741–763. Springer, New York.

Field, A. (2013). *Discovering statistics using IBM SPSS Statistics*. Sage, London, 4th edition.

Foster, E. M. (1997). Instrumental variables for logistic regression: An application of the generalized method of moments. *Social Science Research*, 26: 487–504.

Frölich, M. (2004). Finite-sample properties of propensity-score matching and weighting estimators. *The Review of Economics and Statistics*, 86: 77–90.

Gibson, C., Miller, J. M., Jennings, W. G., Swatt, M., and Gover, A. (2009). Using propensity score matching to understand the relationship between gang membership and violent victimization: A research note. *Justice Quarterly*, 26: 625–664.

Guo, J., Chung, I.-J., Hill, K. G., Hawkins, J. D., Catalano, R. F., and Abbott, R. D. (2002). Developmental relationships between adolescent substance use and risky sexual behavior in young adulthood. *Journal of Adolescent Health*, 31: 354–362.

Guo, S. and Fraser, M. W. (2015). *Propensity Score Analysis. Statistical Methods and Applications*. Sage, Thousand Oaks, CA, 2nd edition.

Halaby, C. N. (2004). Panel models in sociological research: Theory into practice. *Annual Review of Sociology*, 30: 507–544.

Hamil-Luker, J. (2005). Trajectories of public assistance receipt among female high school dropouts. *Population Research and Policy Review*, 24: 673–694.

Hamil-Luker, J., Land, K. C., and Blau, J. (2004). Diverse trajectories of cocaine use through early adulthood among rebellious and socially conforming youth. *Social Science Research*, 33: 300–321.

Hausman, J. A. (2001). Mismeasured variables in econometric analysis: Problems from the right and problems from the left. *Journal of Economic Perspectives*, 15: 57–67.

Hendriks, J. (2006). *Jeugdige zedendelinquenten: Een studie naar subtypen en recidive [Juvenile sex offenders: A study into subtypes and recidivism]*. PhD thesis, Vrije Universiteit, Amsterdam.

Hendriks, J. and Bijleveld, C. C. J. H. (1999). Jeugdige zedendelinquenten: Verschillen tussen groeps- en alleenplegers [Juvenile sex offenders: Differences between solo and group offenders]. *Delikt & Delinkwent*, 29: 722–736.

Hendriks, J., Bijleveld, C. C. J. H., and Muizer, M. (2002). Jeugdige zedendelinquenten: Misbruikers van leeftijdsgenoten gecontrasteerd met misbruikers van kinderen [Juvenile sex offenders: Peer abusers contrasted with child abusers]. *Delikt & Delinkwent*, 32: 489–506.

Hill, K. G., White, H. R., Chung, I.-J., Hawkins, J. D., and Catalano, R. F. (2000). Early adult outcomes of adolescent binge-drinking: Person- and variable-centered analyses of binge drinking trajectories. *Alcoholism: Clinical and Experimental Research*, 24: 892–901.

Hinkle, D. E., Wiersma, W., and Jurs, S. E. (2003). *Applied Statistics for the Behavioural Sciences*. Houghton Mifflin, Boston.

Hynes, K. and Clarkberg, M. (2005). Women's employment patterns during early parenthood: A group-based trajectory analysis. *Journal of Marriage and Family*, 67: 222–239.

Imbens, G. W. (2000). The role of the propensity score in estimating dose-response functions. *Biometrika*, 87: 706–710.

Imbens, G. W. and Lemieux, T. (2008). Regression discontinuity designs: A guide to practice. *Journal of Econometrics*, 14: 615–635.

Jacob, B. and Lefgren, L. (2003). Are idle hands the devil's workshop? Incapacitation, concentration and juvenile crime. *American Economic Review*, 93: 1560–1577.

Jones, A. S. and Gondolf, E. W. (2002). Assessing the effect of batterer program completion reassault: An instrumental variable analysis. *Journal of Quantitative Criminology*, 18: 71–98.

Jones, B. L., Nagin, D. S., and Roeder, K. (2001). A SAS procedure based on mixture models for estimating developmental trajectories. *Sociological Methods and Research*, 29: 374–393.

Keele, L. (2010). An overview of rbounds: An R package for Rosenbaum bounds sensitivity analysis with matched data. Technical report, Ohio State University, www.personal.psu.edu/ljk20/rbounds%20vignette.pdf; accessed 12 December 2014.

Kilmer, B. (2008). Does parolee drug testing influence employment and education outcomes? Evidence from a randomized experiment with non-compliance. *Journal of Quantitative Criminology*, 24: 83–123.

King, R., Massoglia, M., and MacMillan, R. (2007). The context of marriage and crime: Gender, the propensity to marry, and offending in early adulthood. *Criminology*, 45: 35–65.

Kleinbaum, D., Kupper, L., Nizam, A., and Rosenberg, E. (2014). *Applied Regression Analysis and Other Multivariable Methods*. Cengage Learning, Independence, KY, 5th edition.

Kling, J. R. (2006). Incarceration length, employment and earnings. *American Economic Review*, 96: 863–876.

Laub, J., Nagin, D. S., and Sampson, R. (1998). Trajectories of change in criminal offending: Good marriages and the desistance process. *American Sociological Review*, 63: 225–239.

Lazarsfeld, P. F. (1959). Problems in methodology. In Merton, R. K., Broom, L., and Cottrell Jr., L. S., editors, *Sociology today: Problems and prospects*, volume I, pages 39–72. Basic Books, New York.

Lederman, D., Loayza, N., and Menèndez, A. M. (2002). Violent crime: Does social capital matter? *Economic Development and Cultural Change*, 50: 509–539.

Lee, D. and Lemieux, T. (2015). Regression discontinuity designs in social sciences. In Best, H. and Wolf, C., editors, *The Sage Handbook of Regression Analysis and Causal Inference*, pages 301–326. Sage, London.

Levitt, S. D. (1996). The effect of prison population size on crime rates: Evidence from prison overcrowding litigation. *The Quarterly Journal of Economics*, 111: 319–351.

Lindgren, B. W. (1985). *Introduction to Probability and Statistics*. MacMillan, New York.

Listokin, Y. (2003). Does more crime mean more prisoners? An instrumental variables approach. *Journal of Law and Economics*, 46: 181–206.

McCaffrey, D. F., Ridgeway, G., and Morral, A. R. (2004). Propensity score estimation with boosted regression for evaluating causal effects in observational studies. *Psychological Methods*, 9: 403–425.

McCullagh, P. and Nelder, J. (1989). *Generalized Linear Models*. Chapman and Hall/CRC, Boca Raton, 2nd edition.

Mehlum, H., Miguel, E., and Torvik, R. (2006). Poverty and crime in 19th century Germany. *Journal of Urban Economics*, 59: 370–388.

Miguel, E., Satyanath, S., and Sergenti, E. (2004). Economic shocks and civil conflict: An instrumental variables approach. *Journal of Political Economy*, 112: 725–753.

Moffitt, T. E. (1993). Adolescence-limited and life-course-persistent antisocial behavior: A developmental taxonomy. *Psychological Review*, 100: 674–701.

Nagin, D. S. (1999). Analyzing developmental trajectories: A semi-parametric, group-based approach. *Psychological Methods*, 4: 139–177.

Nagin, D. S. (2005). *Group-Based Modeling of Development over the Life Course*. Harvard, Cambridge, MA.

Nagin, D. S., Farrington, D. P., and Moffitt, T. (1995). Life-course trajectories of different types of offenders. *Criminology*, 33: 111–140.

Nagin, D. S. and Land, K. C. (1993). Age, criminal careers, and population heterogeneity: Specific estimation of a nonparametric, mixed Poisson model. *Criminology*, 31: 327–362.

Nelder, J. and Wedderburn, R. (1972). Generalized linear models. *Journal of the Royal Statistical Society*, 135: 370–384.

Pearl, J. (1988). *Probabilistic Reasoning in Intelligent Systems*. Morgan and Kaufman, San Mateo.

Permutt, T. and Hebel, J. R. (1989). Simultaneous equation estimation in a clinical trial of the effect of smoking on birth weight. *Biometrics*, 45: 619–622.

Prentky, R. and Righthand, S. (2003). Juvenile sex offender assessment protocol-II (J-SOAP-II). Technical report, Office of Juvenile Justice and Delinquency Prevention, https://www.ncjrs.gov/pdffiles1/ojjdp/202316.pdf; accessed 12 May 2013.

Rabe-Hesketh, S. and Skrondal, A. (2008). *Multilevel and Longitudinal Modeling using Stata*. Stata Press, College Station, Texas, 2nd edition.

Raphael, S. and Winter-Ebmer, R. (2001). Identifying the effect of unemployment on crime. *Journal of Law and Economics*, 44: 259–283.

Rhodes, W. (2010). Estimating treatment effects and predicting recidivism for community supervision using survival analysis with instrumental variables. *Journal of Quantitative Criminology*, 26: 391–413.

Robins, J. M., Hernán, M. A., and Brumback, B. (2000). Marginal structural models and causal inference in epidemiology. *Epidemiology*, 11: 550–560.

Rosenbaum, P. R. (2002). *Observational studies*. Springer, New York.

Rosenbaum, P. R. and Rubin, D. B. (1983). The central role of the propensity score in observational studies for causal effects. *Biometrika*, 70: 41–55.

Rubin, D. B. (1986). Which ifs have causal answers? *Journal of the American Statistical Association*, 81: 961–962.

Scott Long, J. (2007). *Regression Models for Categorical and Limited Dependent Variables*. Sage, Thousand Oaks, CA.

Shadish, W. R., Cook, T. D., and Campbell, D. T. (2002). *Experimental and Quasi–Experimental Designs for Generalized Causal Inference*. Houghton Mifflin, Boston, MA.

Sherman, L. C., Gottfredson, D. C., MacKenzie, D. L., Eck, J., Reuter, P., and Bushway, S. D. (2007). Preventing crime: What works, what doesn't, what's promising. Technical report, National Institute of Justice, www.ncjrs.gov/pdffiles/171676.pdf, accessed 12 May 2013.

Snijders, T. and Bosker, R. (2012). *Multilevel Analysis: An Introduction to Basic and Advanced Multilevel Modeling*. Sage, London, 2nd edition.

Spreeuwenberg, M. D., Bartak, A., Croon, M. A., Hagenaars, J. A., van Busschbach, J. J., Andrea, H., Twisk, J., and Stijnen, T. (2010). The multiple propensity score as control for bias in the comparison of more than two treatment arms: An introduction from a case study in mental health. *Medical Care*, 48: 166–174.

Steering Committee of the Physician's Health Study Research Group (1989). Final report on the aspirin component of the ongoing Physicians' Health Study. *New England Journal of Medicine*, 321: 129–135.

Stock, J. H. and Trebbi, F. (2003). Retrospectives: Who invented instrumental variable regression? *Journal of Economic Perspectives*, 17: 177–194.

Stock, J. H. and Watson, M. (2010). *Introduction to Econometrics*. Addison-Wesley, Boston, 3rd edition.

Stoolmiller, M., Kim, H. K., and Capaldi, D. M. (2005). The course of depressive symptoms in men from early adolescence to young adulthood: Identifying latent trajectories and early predictors. *Journal of Abnormal Psychology*, 114: 331–345.

Stouthamer-Loeber, M. e. a. (2004). Desistance from persistent serious delinquency in the transition to adulthood. *Development and Psychopathology*, 16: 897–918.

Thistlethwaite, D. and Campbell, D. (1960). Regression-discontinuity analysis: An alternative to the ex-post facto experiment. *Journal of Educational Psychology*, 51: 309–317.

Thoemnes, F. (2011). Propensity score matching in SPSS. Technical report, University of Tübingen, arxiv.org/pdf/1201.6385.pdf; accessed 20 April 2014.

Tita, G. E., Petras, T. L., and Greenbaum, R. T. (2006). Crime and residential choice: A neighborhood level analysis of the impact of crime on housing prices. *Journal of Quantitative Criminology*, 22: 299–317.

Uggen, C. and Kruttschnitt, C. (1998). Crime in the breaking: Gender differences in desistance. *Law and Society Review*, 32: 339–366.

Uggen, C. and Wakefield, C. (2008). What have we learned from longitudinal studies of work and crime? In Liberman, A. M., editor, *The Long View of Crime: A Synthesis of Longitudinal Research*, pages 191–219. Springer, New York.

Van der Geest, V. R., Bijleveld, C. C. J. H., and Blokland, A. A. J. (2007). Ontwikkelingspaden van delinquent gedrag bij hoog-risicojongeren [Developmental pathways of delinquent behaviour in high-risk youth]. *Tijdschrift voor Criminologie*, 49: 351–369.

Van der Geest, V. R., Bijleveld, C. C. J. H., and Blokland, A. A. J. (2011). The effects of employment on longitudinal trajectories of offending: A follow up in high risk youth from ages 18 to 32. *Criminology*, 49: 1195–1234.

Van der Geest, V. R., Bijleveld, C. C. J. H., Blokland, A. A. J., and Nagin, D. (2014). The effects of incarceration on longitudinal trajectories of employment: A follow-up in high-risk youth from ages 23 to 32. *Crime & Delinquency*, 62: 107–140.

Van der Geest, V. R., Blokland, A. A. J., and Bijleveld, C. C. J. H. (2009). Delinquent development in a sample of high-risk youth: Shape, content and predictors of delinquent trajectories from age 12 to 32. *Journal of Research in Crime and Delinquency*, 46: 111–143.

Von Bortkiewicz, L. (1898). *Das Gesetz der Kleinen Zahlen*. Teubner, Leipzig.

Wang, J., Donnan, P. T., Steinke, D., and MacDonald, T. M. (2001). The multiple propensity score for analysis of dose-response relationships in drug safety studies. *Pharmacoepidemiology and Drug Safety*, 10: 105–111.

Weisburd, D., Bushway, S., Lum, C., and Yang, S.-M. (2004). Trajectories of crime at places: A longitudinal study of street segments in the city of Seattle. *Criminology*, 42: 283–322.

Wermink, H., Blokland, A., Nieuwbeerta, P., and Tollenaar, N. (2009). Recidive na werkstraffen en na gevangenisstraffen: Een gematchte vergelijking [Recidivism after a community service order and after imprisonment: A matched comparison]. *Tijdschrift voor Criminologie*, 51: 211–227.

Worrall, J. L. and Kovandzic, T. V. (2010). Police levels and crime rates: An instrumental variables approach. *Social Science Research*, 39: 506–516.

Wright, P. G. (1928). *The Tariff on Animal and Vegetable Oils*. MacMillan, New York.

Wright, S. G. (1921). Correlation and causation. *Journal of Agricultural Research*, 20: 557–585.

Wright, S. G. (1923). The theory of path coefficients: A reply to Niles' criticism. *Genetics*, 8: 239–255.

Zaalberg, A., Nijman, H., Bulten, E., Stroosma, L., and van der Staak, C. (2009). Effects of nutritional supplements on aggression, rule-breaking, and psychopathology among young adult prisoners. *Aggressive Behavior*, 35: 1–10.

Subject index